TECHNOLOGY AND ORGANIZATIONS

TECHNOLOGY AND ORGANIZATIONS

Paul S. Goodman
Lee S. Sproull
and Associates

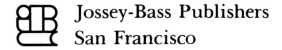

Jossey-Bass Publishers
San Francisco

TECHNOLOGY AND ORGANIZATIONS
by Paul S. Goodman, Lee S. Sproull, and Associates

Copyright © 1990 by: Jossey-Bass Inc., Publishers
350 Sansome Street
San Francisco, California 94104

Copyright under International, Pan American, and
Universal Copyright Conventions. All rights reserved.
No part of this book may be reproduced in any form—
except for brief quotation (not to exceed 1,000 words)
in a review or professional work—without permission
in writing from the publishers.

Library of Congress Cataloging-in-Publication Data

Goodman, Paul S.
  Technology and organizations / Paul S. Goodman,
Lee S. Sproull, and associates. — 1st ed.
    p. cm. —(The Jossey-Bass management series)
    Includes bibliographical references.
    ISBN 1-55542-209-8 (alk. paper)
    1. Technological innovations—Management. 2. Technology—
Management. 3. Organizational behavior. I. Sproull, Lee.
II. Title. III. Series.
HD45.G58 1990   89-26993
658.5′14—dc20   CIP

The paper used in this book is acid-free and meets the
State of California requirements for recycled paper
(50 percent recycled waste, including 10 percent
postconsumer waste), which are the strictest guidelines
for recycled paper currently in use in the United States.

JACKET DESIGN BY WILLI BAUM

FIRST EDITION

HB Printing   10 9 8 7 6 5 4 3 2

Code 9017

THE JOSSEY-BASS MANAGEMENT SERIES

Contents

Preface   xi

The Authors   xix

1. Technology as Equivoque: Sensemaking in
New Technologies   1
Karl E. Weick

2. Understanding Technology and the Individual
in an Organizational Context   45
*Paul S. Goodman, Terri L. Griffith,
Deborah B. Fenner*

3. Work Groups: Autonomy, Technology,
and Choice   87
Gerald I. Susman

4. Technology and Structure:
An Organizational-Level Perspective   109
W. Richard Scott

5. Technology, Management, and
    Competitive Advantage   144
    James G. March, Lee S. Sproull

6. Technology and Organizations:
    A Cross-National Analysis   174
    Leonard H. Lynn

7. Technology and Organizations:
    An Economic/Institutional Analysis   200
    David C. Mowery

8. A Technological Perspective on New Forms
    of Organizations   232
    Raj Reddy

9. Technology and Organizations:
    Integration and Opportunities   254
    Lee S. Sproull, Paul S. Goodman

    Index   267

Preface

⚒

This is an exciting time to study technology and organizations. Advances in computing and other forms of new technology have a pervasive effect on our organizational lives. It is difficult to find any form of organization or organizational process that has not been touched by advances in new technology. Manufacturing operations in the 1990s will look substantially different from operations in the 1980s. New technology in medical diagnosis and care has substantially changed how we organize and deliver health care. Advanced information systems and transaction processes are leading to the development of new financial markets and organizations. Wherever we look, new technology is pervasive in all organizational forms.

Technology is also a potent force. It serves as a force or power to extend human capability. The industrial revolution used technology to extend human physical capability. The computer or information revolution will extend our mental capability. Technology may change the basic way we think about organizational forms. Consider groups, which are a basic building block of most organizations. Most of the research and thinking about groups has focused on face-to-face groups. However, current forms of computer-mediated communication technology span both space and time. This creates the opportunity to think about groups in a fundamentally different way. The whole notion of work, as well as the boundaries of work, is being changed by new forms of technology.

Technology is dynamic and evolving. As forecasts suggest, computing developments have not run their course. The current pace of development will continue into the next century. This rapid development in new forms of technology makes it difficult to picture clearly what new forms of organizations will look like a decade from now.

The Purposes of This Book

Given this characterization of technology as pervasive and potent and as a dynamic force in our organizational lives, there is a clear imperative for better understanding technology's relationship to organizations, their design, and their functioning. Indeed, a major rationale for *Technology and Organizations* is to provide new ways to think about technology and its relationship to the organization.

Even apart from current and future developments, scholars and analysts have had an enduring fascination with technology. Technology serves as a mirror and metaphor: people as tool users and tool builders, people as artificers. These are the ways we have understood our evolution.

Another rationale for this book is that we use the subject of technology as an occasion for understanding human and organizational behavior. That is, our interest focuses not only on technology per se but also on using technology as a device to better understand organizational functioning. Technology becomes a laboratory for rethinking old concepts and developing and testing new concepts. What is an organization? This is a complicated question. A technology that spans space and time causes us to rethink what we mean by the terms *organizational boundaries* and *organization*. As we develop new technology to enhance search and other analytical processes, new insights into decision-making processes should evolve. As we apply such concepts as structuration and population ecology, which have been developed in other areas, to the study of technology, new understandings can be generated and the concepts themselves may be revised. Given the increased interest in and proliferation of technology in our everyday lives, we now have a unique opportunity to augment our understanding of some of the basic organizational and social processes in this context.

We have designed *Technology and Organizations* to change how people plan and do research about technology and organizations. Each of the chapters provides new perspectives on how we should think about and do research on technology and organizations. All of us who have contributed to this book hope it will stimulate new avenues of thinking. While researchers are the primary audience, we also want to influence the ways others (for example, senior line and staff managers) think about technology. Several of the chapters address the fundamental question about implementation: Why are technologies that are designed to enhance organizational functioning not used? This is a question central to both theory and practice. Our objective has been to generate new perspectives that will help increase our insights into that question and others related to technology and organizations.

Organization of This Book

We have organized this book around levels of analysis. We begin by trying to understand the concept of technology and then move on to the individual and technology, the group and technology, and so on. Levels of analysis is really a device to help us rethink our conceptual framework about technology and organizations. We acknowledge that the world is not neatly divided into different levels of analysis, but this provides a way to give a simpler presentation of a complicated phenomenon.

Once we adopted this form of organization, the key to the book was the expertise and excitement of the contributors. We were fortunate to bring together people who have been deeply involved in thinking about technology. The quality of the book rests in the scholarship, imagination, and experience of these contributors.

Once we had identified the organizational form and the contributors, each chapter unfolded on the basis of the interests of the writer. We felt this freedom would lead to more creative chapters than we would have obtained by spelling out certain content topics. Our strategy, then, was not to cover a list of topics; for example, many topics (technological forecasting, technological assessment, regulation of technology, human factors, and so on) are not covered. Our strategy was to select the best possible contributors and create an environment for their new perspectives on technology and organizations to develop.

Overview of the Contents

In Chapter One, Karl E. Weick explores the meaning of technology. He first examines some prevailing thoughts about technology and then discusses properties of new technologies, as well as four conceptual shifts that can enhance our understanding of the relationship between technology and organizations.

Paul S. Goodman, Terri L. Griffith, and Deborah B. Fenner, in Chapter Two, explore the relationship between technology and the individual in the organization. A major focus of their work is presenting a conceptualization of the individual's model of technology, of how that model leads to changes in technology, and of a set of processes that modify the individual's model of technology. Two cases of new technological change are presented to illustrate the dynamic interplay between technology and organizations.

Gerald I. Susman, in Chapter Three, examines the relationship between advanced manufacturing and groups. A major issue concerns the compatibility of this type of technology with work-group autonomy, a form of work groups considered to enhance productivity and quality of working life. Susman attacks the issue of compatibility by examining the role of managerial choice on the impact of advanced manufacturing technology on work-group autonomy.

W. Richard Scott, in Chapter Four, focuses on technology and the organizational level of analysis. He begins with a careful examination of the dominant contingency paradigm and some revisions of this theoretical framework. He then moves on to a reconceptualization of the technology-structure relationships. He provides some provocative ideas by demonstrating how more macro levels of analysis (for example, population studies and organizational community studies) can inform our understanding of the technology-structure relationship.

James G. March and Lee S. Sproull, in Chapter Five, address the broad issues of technological change, competition among technologies, and the survival of some technologies. A major focus of the chapter is on a technological failure— the failure of senior managers to use computer-based technologies. A stimulating analysis is presented to explain this technological failure. The authors move from this specific case to broader theory of competition and survival of technologies. A critical question is why historical processes do not move reliably to better technology and why poorer technologies survive.

Leonard H. Lynn, in Chapter Six, presents a cross-national approach to understanding technology and organizations. Why do some societies excel or lag in using new technology? Lynn is particularly interested in the interaction between cultural and noncultural (political, economic) factors with respect to how technology is used by organizations in different countries.

In Chapter Seven, David C. Mowery takes us to a very different level of analysis—the economic/institutional perspective. His basic approach is to use economic theory and empirical economic research to examine the interaction between technological change and institutions of economic life—factories, laboratories, and corporations.

In Chapter Eight, Raj Reddy examines the relationship between technology and organizations from a technologist's perspective. This chapter takes a different form in that it focuses on technologies that will be part of our organizational future and on the implications of these technologies for organizational structure, process, and decision making.

In Chapter Nine, Lee S. Sproull and Paul S. Goodman address a set of critical themes that cut across all of the preceding chapters. Efforts are made to identify commonalities and divergences among these themes. Attention is also given to identifying the implications of these themes for theoretical and empirical work on technology and organizations.

Genesis of the Book

Technology and Organizations was created from a dynamic set of activities. It began with discussions between us about our own research interests in technology and organizations. Our next step was to draw on some of the unique aspects of Carnegie Mellon University, clearly an institution on the frontier in many new technological areas. It is also a university with a group of social scientists dedicated to understanding the relationship between technology and people in organizations. Thus, we brought together a series of groups of people in engineering, computer science, social science, and management to discuss critical issues about new technology and organizations. The meetings were exciting and provocative and led to a list of issues and to the design of this book.

The unique feature of *Technology and Organizations* is the caliber of the principal contributors. Leonard H. Lynn, James G. March, David C. Mowery, Raj Reddy, W. Richard Scott, Gerald I. Susman, and Karl E. Weick have produced significant contributions to the field. We contracted with each author or team of authors for an original chapter—one that would extend our thinking about technology and organizations. Initial drafts were circulated to all the participants. Then we met at Carnegie Mellon for two and a half days of intensive discussion to generate new ideas on each chapter. We were in a workshop mode to improve the chapters, not in a conference format. Tapes of the discussions, plus editorial comments from all the contributors, were given to each author to revise the individual chapters.

The effectiveness of the workshop format in generating new ideas was stimulated by a group of Carnegie Mellon faculty members who served as provocateurs for the discussion of the chapters. The group included Linda Argote, Alison Davis-Blake, Carol Kulik, Daniel Levinthal, and Jerry Ross.

The major support for this endeavor came from the Center for the Management of Technology. This center is an applied research unit in the Graduate School of Industrial Administration and is designed to conduct research on new technology that will affect theory and practice.

Pittsburgh, Pennsylvania   Paul S. Goodman
January 1990   Lee S. Sproull

The Authors

※

Paul S. Goodman is a professor of industrial administration and psychology at the Graduate School of Industrial Administration, Carnegie Mellon University. Previously he was on the faculty of the Graduate School of Business at the University of Chicago and was a visiting professor at Cornell University. He was educated at Trinity College (Hartford, Connecticut), where he received a B.A. degree in economics in 1959. His master's work was done at the Amos Tuck School of Dartmouth College in 1961, and he received his Ph.D. degree in organizational psychology from Cornell University in 1966.

Goodman's main professional interests are in research on work motivation and attitudes, organizational design and change, productivity, and organizational effectiveness. His research has been published in many professional journals, including the *Journal of Applied Psychology, Organizational Behavior and Human Performance,* and *Human Relations.* He is author of *Assessing Organizational Change* (1979) and coauthor of *Change in Organizations: New Perspectives on Theory, Research, and Practice* (1982), *Absenteeism: New Approaches to Understanding, Measuring, and Managing Employee Absence* (1984), and *Designing Effective Work Groups* (1986).

He is currently director of the Center for the Management of Technology at Carnegie Mellon University. The center sponsors joint research with industry on the management of technology.

Lee S. Sproull is associate professor of social sciences in the Department of Social and Decision Sciences, Carnegie Mellon University. She received a B.A. degree (1967) in English from Wellesley College, an M.A. degree (1975) in sociology from Stanford University, and a Ph.D. degree (1977) in sociology of education, also from Stanford University.

Sproull's main professional interest is in research on information behavior in organizations. Her research has been published in many professional journals, including *Organization Science, Administrative Science Quarterly, Management Science,* and *Academy of Management Journal.* Recent books include *Computing and Change on Campus* (1987 with Sara B. Kiesler) and *Connections: New Ways of Working in the Networked Organization* (forthcoming, with Sara B. Kiesler).

Deborah B. Fenner is a doctoral student in the Graduate School of Industrial Administration, Carnegie Mellon University.

Terri L. Griffith is assistant professor in the department of management and policy, University of Arizona.

Leonard H. Lynn is associate professor of management policy in the Weatherhead School of Management, Case Western Reserve University.

James G. March is Fred H. Merrill Professor of Management in the Stanford Graduate School of Business, Stanford University.

David C. Mowery is associate professor in the School of Business, University of California, Berkeley.

Raj Reddy is university professor and director of robotics in the Robotics Institute, Carnegie Mellon University.

W. Richard Scott is professor in the Department of Sociology at Stanford University.

Gerald I. Susman is Robert and Judith Klein Professor of Management at Pennsylvania State University.

Karl E. Weick is Rensis Likert Collegiate Professor of Organizational Behavior and Psychology in the School of Business Administration, University of Michigan.

1

※

Technology as Equivoque: Sensemaking in New Technologies

Karl E. Weick

New technologies, such as complex production systems that use computers (Ettlie, 1988; Majchrzak, 1988; Susman and Chase, 1986; Zuboff, 1988), create unusual problems in sensemaking for managers and operators. For example, people now face the novel problem of how to recover from incomprehensible failures in production systems and computer systems. To solve this problem, people must assume the role of failure managers who are heavily dependent on their mental models of what might have happened, although they can never be sure because so much is concealed. Not only does failure take on new forms, but there is also continuous intervention, improvement, and redesign, which means that the implementation state of development never stops (Berniker and Wacker, 1988, p. 2).

Problems like these affect organizational structure in ways not previously discussed by organizational scholars. To understand new technologies and their impacts, we need to

I acknowledge with gratitude the valuable comments of George Huber, Dan Denison, Chet Miller, and especially Eli Berniker on earlier drafts of this chapter.

supplement existing concepts. Thus, the purpose of this chapter is to describe features of new technologies that necessitate a revision in the concepts we use to understand their place in organized life and then to suggest what some of those revised concepts might be.

The central idea is captured by the phrase *technology as equivoque*. An *equivoque* is something that admits of several possible or plausible interpretations and therefore can be esoteric, subject to misunderstandings, uncertain, complex, and recondite. New technologies mean many things because they are simultaneously the source of stochastic events, continuous events, and abstract events. Complex systems composed of these three classes of events make both limited sense and many different kinds of sense. They make limited sense because so little is visible and so much is transient, and they make many different kinds of sense because the dense interactions that occur within them can be modeled in so many different ways. Because new technologies are equivocal, they require ongoing structuring and sensemaking if they are to be managed.

The effects of these equivocal properties on organizations can be grasped more readily if analysts talk about structuration rather than structure, affect rather than analysis, dynamic interactive complexity rather than static interactive complexity, and premise control rather than behavioral control.

To flesh out this analysis, we will briefly examine prevailing thought about technology, after which we will discuss properties of new technologies and then four conceptual shifts that help us understand the organizational implications of these properties. We will conclude by reframing the main argument.

Definitions of Technology

Three definitions of technology provide a context that illustrates strengths and weaknesses of prevailing thought about technology:

1. "We define technology as the physical combined with the intellectual or knowledge processes by which materials in some form are transformed into outputs used by another organization or subsystem within the same organization" (Hulin and Roznowski, 1985, p. 47).
2. Technology is "a family of methods for associating and channeling other entities and forces, both human and nonhuman. It is a method, one method, for the conduct of heterogeneous engineering, for the construction of a relatively stable system of related bits and pieces with emergent properties in a hostile or indifferent environment" (Law, 1987, p. 115).
3. "Technology refers to a body of knowledge about the means by which we work on the world, our arts and our methods. Essentially, it is knowledge about the cause and effect relations of our actions. . . . Technology is knowledge that can be studied, codified, and taught to others" (Berniker, 1987, p. 10).

Definition 1 is representative in the sense that it includes the components of skills, equipment, and knowledge mentioned by most scholars of technology. In contrast to many other definitions, however, explicit mention is made of raw materials and a transformation process, items that are often implicit in other definitions. Also novel to this definition is the mention that output might be used within the same organization. Inclusion of this contingency makes it possible to talk about multiple, diverse technologies within the same organization. Finally, this definition is noteworthy because of its emphasis on processes rather than on static knowledge, skills, and equipment. By equating technology with process, the authors alert us to the importance of changes over time and sequence.

Definition 2 is rather unusual. The definition highlights the contentious, adversarial environment of multiple constituencies that have a stake in the design and operation of technology (for example, see Perrow's [1984] discussion of production pressures for one source of contention). The definition captures better than most the fact that, both in its design and in its operation, technology is a partially fortuitous emergent outcome of a relatively stable network of relations among quite diverse elements. The definition counterbalances those definitions of technology that depict the process as deliberate, rationalized, homogeneous, planned, systematized, and controlled by prospective rationality. The design and operation of technology do share some of those qualities, but they do not exhaust the character of the process when it unfolds in politicized organizations, and Law's (1987) definition allows us to describe technology in a way more compatible with this quality of organizations.

Definition 3 becomes most sensible when it is supplemented by the author's definition of a technical system as "a specific combination of machines, equipment, and methods used to produce some valued outcome. . . . Every technical system embodies a technology. It derives from a large body of knowledge which provides the basis for design decisions" (Berniker, 1987, p. 10).

By differentiating between the opportunities provided by knowledge ("technology") and the choice of one combination from this larger set as "the" technical system, Berniker makes the design of technology a more explicit, more public process that need not be left to engineers. Definitions such as definition 1 fold together knowledge, design, and a specific manifestation of technology, with the result that technology becomes a given, rather than a variable. As we will see shortly, the very complexity and incomprehensibility of new technologies may warrant a reexamination of our knowledge of cause-effect relations in human actions and the choice of a different combination of machines, equipment, and methods to produce the outcomes for which new technologies are instrumental.

Berniker's portrait, however, is not without problems, since technology often follows rather than precedes a technical system. Especially with new technologies, a specific technical system is often the vehicle to discover cause-effect linkages in human action that we had not seen before, but which can now be used in subsequent designs. Thus, technology is both an a posteriori product of lessons learned while implementing a specific technical system and an a priori source of options that can be realized in a specific technical system.

While we will try in our subsequent discussion to distinguish between technology as knowledge and a technical system as a specific subset of that knowledge, this will often be difficult, precisely because new technologies have considerable overlap between their technology and their technical systems. Given their short history and novel engines, the size of the understanding is not much larger than the size of any one technical system. This in no way cuts down the number of combinations that are possible in technical systems involving new technology, but it does mean that these combinations are informed by hunches rather than by well-developed knowledge, that considerable improvisation is involved, and that design and operation have a strong core of experimentation and unjustified trial and error. The very fact that new technologies have technologies and technical systems that are roughly similar in size recommends their description as equivoques.

Definitions of technology similar to those just reviewed have been translated into survey items intended to capture variations in skills, equipment, and technique. Scott (1987) and Hancock, Macy, and Peterson (1983) provide helpful summaries of the measurement that has been attempted.

One of the more influential frameworks to capture variations in technology is Perrow's (1967) attempt to differentiate technologies on the basis of the number of exceptions that performers encounter and the extent to which the exceptions they do encounter are analyzable. Lynch (1974) and Withey, Daft, and Cooper (1983) have developed instruments that assess these two dimensions. Perrow (1986, p. 143) has suggested that the essence of his notion can be tapped informally with this interview question: "Ask people about the frequency with which they come across problems for which there is no ready solution at hand, and about which no one else is likely

to know much." While this line of questioning may elicit
reactions to such accompaniments of technology as uncertainty, unpredictability, and variability, it obscures important
details of this variability. For example, the item assumes that
people know when they come across problems, and yet many
of the newer technologies, such as nuclear power generation,
have as one of their distinguishing properties the fact that
operators often do not even realize that problems exist for
which they need solutions. Thus, to ask people about exceptions and analyzability misses key aspects of newer technologies characterized by interactive complexity (Perrow, 1984).
The Perrow items also bury other organizational information
that becomes important in the context of newer technologies.
When a person reports that there is no ready solution at hand,
that may reflect the technology but it also may reflect aspects
of the respondent, such as trained incapacity, specialization
in some other technology, limited experience, low self-esteem,
low cognitive complexity, and so on. The report of no ready
solution at hand may also reflect organizational dimensions.
For example, one of the many streams found in organized
anarchies is a steady stream of solutions in search of problems. If people report that solutions are not at hand, this
could mean that existing access structures are funneling solutions away from the respondent or funneling novel problems
toward that person.

When respondents report not only that they do not
know of solutions but also that no one else is likely to know
either, that may say something about the technology but it
also may mean that people have no network, or that they
have a network but it has no weak ties, or that they are reluctant to ask for help, or that they are not reluctant but instead
assume that no one has the answer, a prophecy that becomes
fulfilled when they seek out no one and remain without an
answer.

As technologies become more automated, abstract, continuous, flexible, and complex, they may become less analyzable and encounter more exceptions. These changes in
analyzability and exceptions should be patterned, but the

question is whether our concepts and instruments are sufficiently sensitive to capture these patterns and to differentiate degrees of routineness (Perrow, 1986) and degrees of analyzability. The answer seems to be no.

Properties of New Technologies

The purpose of this section is to single out three qualities of newer technologies—stochastic events, continuous events, and abstract events—that, while present in older technologies, seem now to be more prominent and to have distinctive organizational implications. Furthermore, these three properties seem not to be reflected in existing measures of technology, which means they are not yet important independent variables in organizational explanations. All three properties also underscore why it is now more crucial than ever to articulate the micro side of technology and to link it with macro concepts.

Stochastic Events. Davis and Taylor (1976) suggest that previous industrial-era technologies were deterministic, with clear cause-effect relationships among what was to be done, how it was to be done, and when it was to be done. Newer automated technologies no longer are dominated by determinism. Instead, "people operate in an environment whose 'important events' are randomly occurring and unpredictable" (Davis and Taylor, 1976, p. 388).

For example, Buchanan and Bessant (1985) describe the difficulties people had replacing batch production of pigments with computerized process controls, because their understanding of the mechanisms of pigment chemistry was weak. Neither the speed of the reactions nor the nature of the side effects was well understood, which meant that manufacturing was closer to alchemy than anything else. A world of alchemy is a world of stochastic events. Berniker (1987) describes technical systems built around poorly understood processes and notes as an example the lingering uncertainty involved in smelting aluminum from bauxite and in bonding metal parts in aircraft. Technical systems that involve dense interaction (such as military command and control systems) are continually vulnerable to unexpected interruptions from staff who request explanations, justifications, revisions, or attention to the fact that they exist (Roberts, forthcoming; Metcalf, 1986).

While technologies have always had stochastic events—for example, steam boilers did blow up (Burke, 1972)—the unique twist in new technologies is that the uncertainties are permanent rather than transient. All technologies surprise operators at first, but as learning develops, surprises recede. That normal development, however, occurs less often with new technologies, because of their poorly understood processes and raw material, continuous revision of the design of the process, and the fact that implementation often is the means by which the technology itself is designed. Furthermore, with increased dependence on computers, there is the dual problem that computers often do not give a complete and accurate picture of the state of the process and, when they do, "operator state identification and control activities gradually become decoupled from actual process state as a function of execution problems or the unexpected" (Woods, O'Brien, and Hanes, 1987, p. 1741).

Existing concepts in organizational theory are generally insensitive to sources and consequences of stochastic events, referring instead simply to variable inputs and outcomes, to unanalyzable exceptions (Perrow, 1967), or to unclear cause-effect relations that require the decision strategy of judgment (Thompson and Tuden, 1959). The problem is not that these concepts are wrong but rather that they lump together diverse crucial properties of new technologies that have diverse consequences. For example, Berniker (private communication) has suggested that stochastic events can occur in one of four forms. They can either be understood or not be understood, and they can occur either once or recurrently. Stochastic events that occur once and are understood are the most common and are not especially arousing. Single events that are not understood are outside the organization's experience and are much more stressful. If puzzling events occur repeatedly, then there is some chance for learning, but only if the organization operates in an experimental mode, which can be dangerous with some technologies (Weick, 1988a). While all four forms have unclear cause-effect relations, the implications for adaptation, learning, and structuring are quite different among them.

If new technologies have a larger stochastic component, this suggests several things. Concepts need to be tuned more finely, to differentiate among forms that stochastic events can take. Campbell's (1988) elaboration of forms of task complexity is a move in this direction. Dornbusch and Scott's (1975) concept of the active task incorporates distinctions that are relevant to understanding stochastic events. They argue that tasks vary in predictability of resistance ("Can I predict the problems to be encountered?"), efficacy ("Can I handle the problems I predict?"), and clarity ("Are the goals to be realized by my performance clear?"). (See Dornbusch and Scott, 1975, p. 106, for items to measure these dimensions.) The attractiveness of their dimensions is the separation of diagnosis, action and such organizational constraints as performance pressure. As we will see, new technologies are hard to diagnose because of the substantial mental demands they make on operators and the many ways in which surprises can occur; but new technologies are also hard to control because of interactive complexity, and they are hard to measure because people disagree about what constitutes effective performance.

The skill requirements of a stochastic environment are unique. A large repertoire of skills must be maintained, even though they are used infrequently; people are usually on standby, giving special attention to startup and to anticipating faults that may lead to downtime; the distinction between operations and maintenance is blurred; skills in monitoring and diagnostics are crucial; people must be committed to do what is necessary on their own initiative and have the autonomy to do so; and people have now assumed the role of "variance absorber, dealing with and counteracting the unexpected" (Davis and Taylor, 1976, pp. 388–389).

As we noted earlier, stochastic environments represent a moving target for learning because they can change faster than people can accumulate knowledge about them. When recurrence is scarce, so is learning, which is why stochastic events have become a permanent fixture of new technologies.

The preceding descriptions, with their emphasis on chronic surprise, suggest the possibility that operators and managers alike should be tense during much of the time they interact with these technologies. That suggestion will be amplified throughout this chapter, but here we simply note that a stochastic environment can be an arousing environment. Furthermore, since new technologies typically represent a division of labor in which routine tasks are automated and nonroutine tasks are left for human judgment, humans face a complex task composed of an unbroken string of tough decisions. Evidence shows that performance of complex tasks is more vulnerable to disruption from excessive arousal than is performance of simple tasks. Those disruptions that do occur (for example, perception narrows, and dominant responses dominate) tend to reduce learning and induce error.

Continuous Events. An expanded version of Woodward's (1965) continuous process technology provides a prototype that captures additional properties of new technologies. Traditionally, process production has been illustrated by batch production of chemicals, by continuous-flow production of gases, liquids, and solids, and by description of the outputs as dimensional products measured by width, capacity, or volume, rather than as integral products that can be counted (Scott, 1981). Continuous process production tends to be more heavily automated than the mechanized process of mass production (Mintzberg, 1983), which means that some of the issues discussed as stochastic events still apply when we emphasize continuity rather than unpredictability. While continuity and stochastic events covary, we intend to pry them apart as much as possible because they represent distinct issues in new technologies.

Continuous processes impose their own imperative—the reliability imperative—and this sets them apart from stochastic events. This shift from efficiency to reliability may constitute the single most important change associated with new technologies. Reliability is salient in continuous processing because the overriding requirement is to keep the process doing what it is supposed to do. This means there is a premium on maintaining the continuity and integrity of the process. "Responsibility for assuring operations continuity is more important than responsibility for effort" (Adler, 1986, p. 20).

Reliability has recently been highlighted as an issue of safety in the context of dangerous technologies (for example, nuclear power plants), but the issue of reliability is larger than the question of safety. Most of the technologies associated with safety issues are part of a larger group of technologies, all of which involve continuous processes. The problems posed by continuous processing are more visible and consequential in such technologies as nuclear reactors, but the problems are indigenous to all members of this class. Thus, the current concern with issues of reliability is not just a reaction to an increase in the number of dangerous technologies; it is symptomatic of a larger set of unique issues associated with postindustrial technology in general. While efficiency was the hallmark of deterministic industrial-era technology, reliability is the hallmark of stochastic, continuous technology associated with the postindustrial era.

There are numerous examples of an upswing in continuous processing. Bank tellers now deal with a level of automation that is qualitatively higher than that of continuous-flow chemical refineries (Adler, 1986). When transaction entries are made, adjustments are made instantaneously to all relevant bank accounts. Since the data base is on line for entry and access, any error means that the bank uses inaccurate data for all subsequent operations and calculations. Air traffic control in heavily loaded sectors requires continuous processing (Finkelman and Kirschner, 1980). Activities that normally look like mass production, such as the production of soap operas (Intintoli, 1984), in fact turn out to resemble continuous production more closely.

Transaction processing in general has become more continuous, as is evident in automatic teller machines, computerized reservation systems, toll-free phone numbers that can be switched from one answering location to another according to the time of day, and point-of-sale debit machines that can support continuous transaction processing in direct sales. Unlike previous continuous process technologies, which were confined to one location (such as a factory or refinery), newer technologies use communication technology and construct organization without location. New technologies knit separate actors, transactions, and locations together into a continuous process.

One of the most interesting examples of continuous processing is flexible, automated manufacturing. The fascinating quality of this technology is that it allows continuous processing of customized products. Less standardized low-volume unique products, usually made in a job shop, can now be made by a quasi-continuous process (Adler, 1988). This capability lends new significance to the similarities that Woodward (1965) observed between unit production systems and process production systems. She found that both systems employed more organic structures than did mass production. As Miles states, "Both appear to be organized into small production groups or teams, with more general role responsibilities and greater informality and autonomy in task-related interactions. Elaborate controls and sanctions are not feasible in the highly routine unit-production system, and they are not needed in the process technologies because they are built into the throughput system itself" (Miles, 1980, p. 59).

A technology that combines craft and continuous processing (a combination that is possible, given some of the similarities observed by Woodward) may provide a core image to understand newer technologies. Denison (personal communication) has suggested that reliability assurance becomes the craft. As the supervisor of continuous processing pays more attention to the process and the product than to people, he or she may often become the most skilled worker, or someone very much like a person involved in unit production (Davis and Taylor, 1976).

People confronted with problems of continuity and reliability need a different set of sensitivities and skills than do people confronted with problems of discreteness and efficiency. It is important, for example, for them to visualize and think in terms of processes rather than products. Burack (cited in Davis and Taylor, 1976) has suggested that such aptitudes as high attention to work processes, rapid response to emergencies, ability to stay calm in tense environments, and early detection of malfunctions are crucial. Adler (1986) argues that newer technologies, which put a premium on continuous processing, require that people assume higher task responsibility, deal comfortably with higher levels of abstraction, and develop a deeper appreciation for the qualitatively higher levels of interdependence involved in their work.

Perrow's (1984) diagnosis that the coincidence of tight coupling and technological complexity has created conditions of interactive complexity and a new family of failures (called "normal accidents") may be an early recognition that continuous processing in general presents unique problems that require unique structures. Classical examples of continuous processing technologies, such as chemical plants, are described by Perrow (1984, p. 97) as "interactively complex," although he describes other process technologies, such as drug and bread production, as "linear, tight." As we will argue shortly, a linear, tight system is vulnerable because if members lose some comprehension of cause and effect, the system becomes more interactively complex and more prone to failure. All agree that continuous processes, by definition, have no buffers, which compounds the problems created by more frequent stochastic events and higher mental workloads.

The coexistence of stochastic events and continuous events creates several problems of analysis. For example, it could be argued that stochastic events—which have been around as long as technology itself—are no more common in new technologies than they were before but simply seem that way because they stand out more vividly against the background of more continuous processing. The argument throughout this chapter is that the combination of increased cognitive demands, increased electronic complexity, and dense interdependence over larger areas increases the incidence of unexpected outcomes that ramify in unexpected ways. These unexpected ramifications need not be synonymous with failure because they may also be occasions for innovation and learning. The point is that we assume there are more stochastic events with new technologies, rather than more salience for relatively the same number of stochastic events as were associated with older technologies; but we could be wrong.

Abstract Events. More and more of the work associated with new technologies has disappeared into machines, which means that managers and operators experience increased cognitive demands for inference, imagination, integration, problem solving, and mental maps to monitor and understand what is going on out of sight. Buchanan and Bessant (1985, p. 303) argue that people who work with new technologies have to have a complex understanding of at least four components: "1. the process—its layout, sequence of events and interdependencies; 2. the product—its key characteristics, properties and variability of raw materials; 3. the equipment—their functions, capabilities and limitations; 4. the controls—their functions, capabilities and limitations, and the effects of control actions on performance." These four understandings are crucial because the technology is partially self-controlled, and people have to handle the unexpected and provide backup control when automatic control systems fail. People need sufficient understanding of abstract events so that they can intervene at any time and pick up the process or assemble a recovery.

The unique and sizable cognitive demands imposed by new technologies suggest that the concept of operator error is misleading and should be replaced. Part of the argument for replacement is that operators are often blamed for errors that lie with designers and systems (Perrow, 1984). In Berniker's (private communication) colorful language, "Operator error is the fig leaf of scoundrels promoting complex systems." Thus, at the minimum, we should talk about operating error rather than operator error.

Aside from that issue, I want to argue that new technologies foster operator *mistakes* rather than operator errors. The difference is not trivial. An error occurs when a person strays from a guide or a prescribed course of action through inadvertence and is blameworthy, whereas a mistake occurs when there is a misconception, a misidentification, or a misunderstanding. Some problems in new technologies do occur when operators stray from rote procedures and err in executing an intention, but a more frequent and more serious source of problems develops when people form their intentions in the first place.

Mistakes that arise during the formation of intentions have many sources, but one of the most crucial is the control philosophy of "one measurement–one indicator" (Woods, O'Brien, and Hanes, 1987, p. 1728). When implemented, this philosophy means that each dial and meter in a control room registers the output of one sensor out in the plant. Information is provided to the operator at the lowest level of detail, which means that integration, pattern recognition, and diagnosis are wholly dependent on human processing and on whatever models and experience the operator brings to the monitoring task. Inadequate sampling of displayed information, inattention to information on the periphery, and distractions during the building of a representation of a problem all can affect the formation of an intention.

The problem of distractions, in particular, deserves closer attention because of its subtlety and its tendency to amplify, and because it is a prototype of the issues that arise because of the tight association between new technologies and computer controls. Integration of single indicators into a recognizable pattern is easier when data are presented simultaneously rather than serially. Operators who are able to sweep visually across an array of dials can create and execute novel search sequences with relatively little effort. They can see immediately the rate at which indicators are changing, as well as relative rates of change among dials, and they can test hypotheses by rapid inspection. They can also stumble onto odd readings that they were not looking for. This pattern of visual search changes sharply when indicators are displayed on separate screens of video display terminals. To access indicators in a novel sequence, operators must consciously execute a novel set of commands, which can be distracting, and they must remember what the earlier screens have registered and hope that the readings have not changed while subsequent screens were being accessed. Serendipitous diagnosis based on accidental discovery of an anomalous reading is less likely, and the skill required to transform a serial data presentation into a parallel presentation is not trivial (the transformation resembles that required for an air traffic controller to mentally transform a two-dimensional display on a flat radar screen into a three-dimensional picture of airplanes converging from different altitudes).

Mistakes in the formation of an intention tend to be surprisingly resistant to change, as was evident at Three Mile Island (Perrow, 1984); at Tenerife, when the pilot of KLM flight 4805 persisted in his hypothesis that the cloud-shrouded runway was clear for takeoff (Weick, 1988b); and in several studies of operator performance (Woods, O'Brien, and Hanes, 1987). These mistakes usually are not corrected until a "fresh viewpoint enters the situation" (Woods, O'Brien, and Hanes, 1987, p. 1745).

While we could cite numerous other examples of the ways in which new technologies have become more abstract, with a corresponding higher mental workload, we need instead to highlight the significance of this change. New technologies are basically dual rather than singular. They involve the self-contained, invisible material process that is actually unfolding, as well as the equally self-contained, equally invisible imagined process that is mentally unfolding in the mind of an individual or a team. There are relatively few points at which the mental representation can be checked against and corrected by the actual process. True, there are hundreds of discrete sensors that track fluctuations, but those readings do not convey a direct picture of relationships, be they cause-effect, goals-means, or physical relationships. Relational information is the most crucial information when the object being monitored is a continuous process.

Thus, unlike any other technologies that have been used previously as predictors by organizational theorists, the new technologies exist as much in the head of the operator as they do on the plant floor. This is not to argue that one technology is more important than another, but it is to argue that cognition and micro-level processes are keys to understanding the organizational impact of new technologies.

An operator's representation of a process technology, and the resulting formation of intentions and choice of control activities, can gradually become decoupled from the actual process state, so that the operator's control intervention literally creates a new technical system that is understood neither by the operator nor by the devices for self-control originally designed into the material technology. The human construction is itself an intact and plausible view. The decoupling is gradual. The immediate consequences of decoupling are invisible except for dial fluctuations that could be errors, separate independent deviations of separate sensors, or a single problem with multiple symptoms. Therefore, it is not surprising that so-called mistakes persist.

New technologies are parallel technologies involving a technology in the head and a technology on the floor. Each is self-contained. Each is coordinated with the other intermittently rather than continuously. Each corrects the other discontinuously. Each can have a sizable effect on the other, and the parallel technologies have a constant amount of mystery that is due to the invisibility of the processes each contains.

Conceptualizing New Technologies

Such concepts as structure, analysis, complexity, and behavior control have been prominent in previous discussions of deterministic, mechanized, physical technologies that impose their imperatives on organizational functioning. As technologies become more stochastic, continuous, and abstract, those same concepts no longer explain as much as they used to. In their place, we now need to talk more about structuration, affect, dynamic interactive complexity, and premise control. The following discussion shows why.

From Structure to Structuration. Deterministic, stable technology is compatible with deterministic organizational structure, but the shift toward stochastic, automated technology requires that we pay more attention to structuration and structuring. Structuration is defined as "the production and reproduction of a social system through members' use of rules and resources in interaction" (Poole, n.d., p. 6). The important ideas in that statement are that systems are built from interactions and rules; that such resources as action are the tools people use to enact their organizations; and, most important, that structures are both the medium and the outcome of interaction. People create structural constraints, which then constrain them (Turner, 1987). Structuration pays equal attention to both sides of that structuring process (constraining and being constrained), whereas earlier notions emphasized one side and neglected the other.

The idea that structure constrains action (Khandwalla, 1974) dominated earlier discussions of mechanized technology, but this emphasis was flawed because it treated structure as a given and underestimated the degree to which human action can alter it. The opposite emphasis, represented by the idea that structure is an emergent property of ongoing action (Weick, 1969), made the opposite error. It suggested that ongoing action unfolds free of any preconceptions, and it underestimated the degree to which institutional patterns impose prior constraints on the action from which structures emerge.

The concept of structuration is exemplified by Goffman's marvelous observation that "in everyday life actors are simultaneously the marks as well as the shills of social order" (cited in Barley, 1986, p. 79): the same person is both the shill who constructs the game and the mark who is drawn in by the game that has been constructed; victimizer becomes victim through frameworks laid down during prior interaction.

An illustration of how technology affects structuration has been supplied by Barley's (1986) analysis of two radiology departments that adopted CAT scanners. In one department, initial expertise was lodged in the technicians (Suburban Hospital); in the other, expertise was lodged in radiologists (Urban Hospital). The new technology introduced in both settings was identical—a Technicare 2060 whole-body computed topography scanner. This technology is stochastic (for example, bone artifacts sometimes appear unpredictably in pictures of the basal brain area, which makes interpretation difficult) and continuous (for example, the timing of injections of dye to highlight portions of the body affects the conclusions that may be drawn), and the mental workload is substantial because the system uses novel diagnostic signs. The technology is hypothesized to affect structuration in the following manner. At first the technology is exogenous. When translated into a technical system, it either confirms ingrained interaction patterns or disturbs and reformulates them. These patterns are carried by scripts—"standard plots of types of encounters whose repetition constitutes the setting's interaction order" (Barley, 1986, p. 83)—which create reciprocal links between structure and action. Thus, the technology ratifies or alters scripts that have grown up as a result of previous structuring. When the new body-imaging technologies were introduced to both departments, radiologists and technicians alike drew on traditional, institutionalized patterns of signification, legitimation, and domination (see Riley, 1983) to construct roles to deal with this technology and to interpret the strange products that it produced. However, the traditional pattern of technicians' deference to professional radiologists proved inadequate, especially at Suburban, because radiologists had only modest understanding of the technology. The puzzling technology introduced slippage between the idealized patterns of dominance and legitimation built up from past practice and the immediate problem of trying to discover what the novel diagnostic signs meant. Given this slippage, new patterns of action emerged and were incorporated into scripts that made a lasting change in institutional structure.

To understand how structures were both created and altered by interactions between radiologists and technicians, we need to look more closely at the scripts that emerged from actions involving the new technology. Some of these scripts, such as direction giving, countermands, usurping the controls, direction seeking, and expected criticisms, ratified traditional institutional forms. Other scripts, such as preference stating, clandestine teaching, role reversal, and mutual execution, modified these traditional forms. Each script was built from actions evoked by the technology, but the influence of the technology on structure occurred through the ratio of ratification scripts to modification scripts, not through some more static vehicle, such as workflow rigidity. For example, the ratio of preference stating (a modification script) to direction giving (a ratification script) was lower at Suburban (1:1.7) than at Urban (1:4.7), which meant that the same technology produced more structural change at Suburban than at Urban and did so because it led to the construction of a different social order. Direction giving is a straightforward enactment of the prevailing institutionalized dominance of radiologists over technologists; direction giving is a pure expression of existing structure. But as the frequency of this pure enactment is moderated by scripts that place greater emphasis on collegiality, the traditional form is changed. Ongoing affirmations and modifications such as these are the means by which technology both shapes structure and is itself shaped by structure when different techniques are built and used to run it.

The relationships between structuration and technology can be diagrammed into the deviation-amplifying system shown in Figure 1.1. The linkage from C to D represents action as a constraint on structure. The linkage from E to B represents institutional constraints on action. Scripts are found at steps B and C, and either ratification or modification

Figure 1.1. Structuration and Technology.

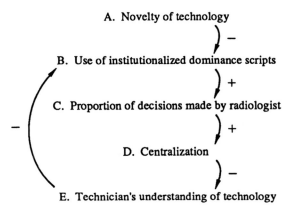

A. Novelty of technology

) −

B. Use of institutionalized dominance scripts

) +

C. Proportion of decisions made by radiologist

) +

D. Centralization

) −

E. Technician's understanding of technology

can occur at each of those two stages. Notice that when we depict the structural effects of technology in this way, once technology provides the initial "kick" to the process, its effects are then dependent on how it becomes woven into the process of action. This embedding is a mixture of action, scripts, and institutional forms, but the technology itself becomes something different, according to how these three components interact. That is the central point of the structuration hypothesis, and it is an important point to maintain as technologies become more fluid and more difficult to comprehend, with less transparent effects on shifting organizational structures.

There are several ways to enlarge Barley's (1986) analysis and bring in additional dimensions of technology. The point at which technology is introduced is the point at which it is most susceptible to influence (Winner, 1986), and Barley's analysis shows why. When conceptualized in the context of structure, technologies are treated as self-evident artifacts to which people accommodate, rather than as open-ended artifacts that accommodate to interactions. Structuration sensitizes the observer to look for an ongoing redefinition among structure, action, and technology. Beginnings are of special importance for structuration because they constrain what is learned about the technology and how fast it is learned (for example, Urban Hospital technicians learned less and learned more slowly, even though it was assumed that they understood the technology).

Barley's (1986) description could be parsed with concepts other than structuration, partly because uncertainty is such a prominent part of the events and varies between the two settings. Uncertainty seemed to be higher at Suburban Hospital than at Urban Hospital because Suburban added the uncertainty of a new social order, in which technicians had more expertise than medical professionals did, to the uncertainty of a novel technology, which was shared with Urban.

Contingency theories of power (Hickson and others, 1971) are relevant to Barley's analysis because the radiologists at Urban and the technologists at Suburban both were in a position to resolve important uncertainties. This powerful position was consistent with a division of labor traditional at Urban but not at Suburban. While these power differentials are evident, contingency theory does not spell out explicit mechanisms by which these differences will affect interaction, technology definition, and structure, which is why structuration is a useful complementary perspective.

The uncertainty connected with a CAT scanner might also be viewed as a stimulus for the development of new coordinating mechanisms, such as mutual adjustment, lateral communication, and meetings (Van de Ven, Delbecq, and Koenig, 1976), and more of these should be developed at Suburban than at Urban. This prediction is consistent with the data, although the process implied is not sufficiently sensitive to history and institutional mechanisms to predict how coordination was built and what the implications were for performance.

While there are other ways than structuration to understand Barley's data, none of them preserve quite so succinctly the point that technology is both a cause and a consequence of structure. This dual role of technology occurs because structuring is an ongoing process that shapes the meaning of artifacts through scripts, interaction, and tradition and is itself shaped by those meanings. The ability to treat structure in this manner is an important conceptual change that we need for understanding the effects of new technologies.

From Analysis to Affect. Throughout the preceding discussion, we have implied that new technologies trigger strong feelings. These feelings have a substantial effect on the operation of the technologies. Thus, we need to understand not only how operators solve problems within the bounds of their mental maps but also how they do so under pressure. Problem solving under pressure means coping both with interruptions and with excessive arousal. We review these two issues in that order.

When a continuous process begins to fail, in an environment where excessive deviation in one measurement–one indication is signaled by one alarm, operators are hit with an "avalanche" of alarms (Woods, O'Brien, and Hanes, 1987, p. 1735). In the first few minutes after a sudden change in a parameter, two hundred alarm points may be active. Since the alarms are hardwired and not conditioned by multivariable patterns, the operator gets no help in pattern recognition from the alarms themselves. Furthermore, the search for patterns is carried out amidst considerable distraction.

The theorizing about emotion done by Berscheid (1983) and Mandler (1984) suggests that interruptions, similar to those that alarms create, are a sufficient and possibly necessary condition for arousal and emotional experience. Since interruption is a chronic threat to continuous processing, and since stochastic events are a chronic source of interruptions, we may expect that strong emotions are coexistent with new technologies.

This conjunction of strong emotions and new technologies can be understood if we look more closely at the relationship between arousal and interruption. A necessary condition for emotion is arousal, or discharge in the autonomic nervous system. Arousal has physiological significance because it prepares people for fight-or-flight reactions. Of even more importance is the fact that arousal also has psy-

chological significance. The perception of arousal provides a
warning that there is some stimulus to which attention must
be paid in order to initiate appropriate action. This signal
suggests that one's well-being may be at stake.

An important property of arousal, often neglected by
those who do research on stress, is that it develops slowly.
Arousal occurs roughly two to three seconds after a stimulus
has occurred, and this delay gives time for a more appropriate
direct action to occur. Thus, the autonomic nervous system
is a secondary, backup, support system, which is activated
largely when direct action fails. When heightened arousal is
perceived it is appraised, and some link between the present
situation and relevant prior situations is established to impose
meaning on the present. Arousal leads people to search for an
answer to the question "What's up?" Answers differ according
to socialization.

The variables of arousal and cognitive appraisal are
found in many formulations dealing with emotion, but the
unique quality of Mandler's (1984) and Berscheid's (1983)
research is their emphasis on the interruption of action
sequences as the occasion for emotion. Organized action sequences in organizations are illustrated by standard operating
procedures (SOPs), continuous processing, scripts, and roles.
All of these tend to become more tightly organized the more
frequently they are executed. The interruption of an ongoing
SOP or plan is a sufficient and possibly necessary condition
for arousal of the autonomic nervous system.

Interruption is a signal that important changes have
occurred in the environment; thus, a key event for emotion is
the interruption of an expectation. It makes good evolutionary sense to construct an organism that reacts significantly
when the world is no longer the way it was.

Emotion is what happens between the time that an
organized sequence is interrupted and the time at which the
interrupting stimulus is removed or a substitute response is
found that allows the sequence to be completed. Until either
event occurs, autonomic arousal increases. When interruption
first occurs, there is redoubled effort to complete the original

interrupted sequence, which means that both redoubled effort and subjective emotional experience may occur at the same time. The more tightly organized an interrupted action sequence is, the greater the arousal. If there are many different ways in which an interrupted sequence can be completed, then arousal is not likely to build very much. This suggests that people who are able to improvise should show less emotional behavior and less extreme emotions. They can create more substitute behaviors, and so their arousal should not build to the same high levels that are experienced by people who have fewer substitute behaviors. Finally, the interruption of higher-order and more pervasive plans should be more arousing than the disruption of lower-order plans.

If we apply these propositions to new technologies, we start by asking, "What is the distribution of interruption in technology? Where are interruptions most likely to occur, and how organized are the actions and plans that are likely to be interrupted?" If we can describe this, then we can predict where emotional experiences are most likely to occur and how intense they will be. For example, systems with newer, less well organized response sequences, settings with fewer standard operating procedures, and settings that are more loosely coupled should be settings in which there is less emotion because interruptions are less disruptive. Settings in which there are few developed plans should be less interruptible and therefore should elicit less emotion.

So far, we have talked only about the frequency of emotion, not about the kind of emotion that occurs. Negative emotions are likely to occur when an organized behavioral sequence is interrupted unexpectedly and the interruption is interpreted as harmful or detrimental. If there is no means to remove or circumvent the interruption, the negative emotion should become more intense the longer the interruption lasts.

To summarize the key points, "emotion is essentially a non-response activity, occurring between the awareness of the interrupting event and an action alternative that will maintain or promote the individual's well-being in the face of an event" (Berscheid, Gangestad, and Kulakowski, forthcoming, p. 396). When people perform an organized action sequence and are interrupted, they search for an explanation and a remedy. The longer they search, the higher the arousal and the stronger the emotion. If people find that the interruption has slowed the accomplishment of a sequence, they are likely to experience anger. If they find that the interruption has accelerated accomplishment, then they are likely to experience pleasure. If they find that the interruption can be circumvented, then they experience relief. If they find that the interruption has thwarted a higher-level plan, then the anger is likely to turn into rage, and if they find that the interruption has thwarted a minor behavioral sequence, then they are likely to feel disappointment or minor irritation. All of these emotional experiences are accompanied by redoubled effort to complete the original sequence that was interrupted.

Other than redoubled effort, what other behavioral consequences of emotion might we expect in new technologies? To ask this question is to confront the venerable issue of whether emotion disrupts adaptive functioning or energizes it. Given the staying power of this controversy, we must assume that both views are partially correct and that we must specify when emotion disorganizes and when it energizes. To do so, we make the controversial assumption that the relation between emotion and performance follows the inverted U curve associated with the Yerkes-Dodson law (Broadhurst, 1957). While Neiss's (1988) recent review raises important questions about the notion of global arousal and reminds us that motor performance is overdetermined, we retain the concept of arousal throughout this chapter as shorthand for the idea that uncertainty about something important (McGrath, 1976) affects performance in a manner analogous to the Yerkes-Dodson law. Since uncertainty about something important seems to be an apt description of what people face when they operate stochastic, continuous, abstract new technologies, we find it useful to retain the concept of arousal and the inverted U hypothesis as an orderly starting point to think about these issues.

This starting point consists of the basic idea that an increase in emotional intensity from some zero point produces an increase in the quality of performance up to some point, beyond which performance deteriorates and finally is disorganized. "The optimal point is reached sooner, that is to say, at lower intensities, the less well-learned or more complex is the performance; increase in emotional intensity supposedly affects finer skills, finer discriminations, complex reasoning tasks, and recently acquired skills more readily than routine activities" (Frijda, 1986, p. 113).

Thus, the question of whether emotion energizes or disorganizes depends on whether one is ascending (energizes) or descending (disorganizes) the inverted U. To move beyond the coarse grain of the inverted U toward a more specific understanding of the relationship between emotion and performance, we must ask additional questions.

1. Are the unlearned, better-practiced, dominant responses that become salient in an emotional situation task-relevant (emotion improves performance) or task-irrelevant (emotion degrades performance)?

2. Does emotion reduce attentional capacity (Weltman, Smith, and Egstrom, 1971) only moderately, so that peripheral cues for performance are ignored but central cues continue to be noticed (emotion improves performance), or does it reduce attentional capacity significantly, so that both peripheral and some central cues are ignored (emotion degrades performance)?

3. Does emotion induce a regression toward a more primitive, simpler, overlearned way of behaving, with corresponding abandonment of newer, more complex, less fully learned responses (Eysenck, 1982)? Darwin called emotions states of functional decortication, by which he meant that lower centers overrule higher ones. Frijda (1986) notes that stubbornly persisting in behavior one is used to can be considered a regressive response mode. It will be recalled that perseveration in simple diagnoses is a persistent problem in control-room diagnoses.

The key point for technology is that the breadth of attention varies in response to fluctuations in emotion (Weltman, Smith, and Egstrom, 1971; Berkun, 1964; Wachtel, 1967). This variation could affect both task conceptions and performance. Assuming that people try to make sense of whatever they notice, as the breadth of their attention varies, so should their descriptions of what they are doing. Thus, task conceptions themselves, not just task performance, should change as arousal changes. Unreliable performance may persist because the operator is performing a different task than observers realize. The point is that this discrepancy in conception may be due to differences in pressure rather than to differences in authority and position.

There is a clear example of this possibility in Barley's (1986) data. Technicians at Urban Hospital were the object of a steady stream of directives, imperative speech, puzzling countermands, sarcasm, and usurped control generated by radiologists. These could easily have raised the level of threat and arousal experienced by technicians, which in turn could have narrowed their attention, made complex learning more difficult, and actually altered their conception of what kind of task CAT-scanner technology posed for them. These effects could have slowed their learning, which should then have intensified the pressure that radiologists imposed, making further learning even more difficult.

This scenario of obstructed learning produced by heightened arousal places less emphasis on differences in position, authority, and structure and more emphasis on the disruptive effects of emotions, such as threat and fear, when they occur under conditions of high arousal and complex technology. Since ongoing learning is so much a part of new technologies, anything that obstructs learning, such as arousal, is of considerable importance.

Since new technologies make greater demands for abstract mental work, we must pay as much attention to the fact that there is an increase in demands as to the fact that those demands are mental. To cope with mental workload is an arousing, emotional experience, which means that mental processes will be modified by affect. New technologies have properties that seem likely to intensify affect. If that intensification occurs, then affect can shape the technology because it attenuates the attention directed at it. As attention varies, so do conceptions of the technology and the effectiveness and reliability of performance. To change how people cope with this technology requires an understanding of these fluctuations in attention. As we have suggested, these fluctuations are driven by uncertainties that seem to affect people in a manner analogous to those postulated for the concept of global arousal.

From Static to Dynamic Interacive Complexity. The fact that stochastic, continuous processing occurs under conditions of high arousal has implications beyond the individual level of analysis. This can be illustrated by an extension of Perrow's (1984) concept of interactive complexity. Figure 1.2 contains the essential ideas. From top to bottom, Perrow (1984) categorizes organizations on the basis of complexity (linear, complex) and coupling (loose, tight); interactive complexity occurs in cell B, where aircraft, nuclear power reactors, and chemical processing plants are assigned. In the middle of Figure 1.2 is the classical inverted U curve relating performance and arousal. The numbers spaced along this curve represent four different stages of arousal (1 = lowest, 4 = highest), and these numbers retain this same meaning in the set of four diagrams at the bottom of Figure 1.2. The four diagrams at the bottom show what may happen to diverse systems when people in them experience increasing levels of stress. For example, diagram 2 asserts that when stress increases from point 1 on the curve to point 2, loosely coupled systems become more tightly coupled. Diagram 3 asserts that as stress increases even more, linear systems become complex. And diagram 4 asserts that when stress intensifies still more, complex interactive systems fall apart into complex arrangements of loosely coupled parts.

Figure 1.2. Interactive Complexity.

	Linear	Complex
Tight	A. Power grid	B. Aircraft
Loose	C. Post office	D. Universities

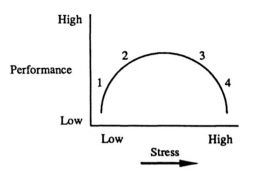

1.

A	B
C	D

2. A C | B D

3. | A C
       | B D

4. | A C
           | B D

The processes responsible for these organizational and technological changes are those observed to accompany changes in arousal. When arousal increases from step 1 to step 2, there is a tendency for groups to become more centralized (Hermann, 1963), and there is a tendency for individuals to ignore peripheral cues in task performance and to focus on central cues (Easterbrook, 1959). As people become more task-oriented, performance improves and interdependences become tightened. Loosely coupled relations become tighter, but there is no change in technical complexity because all cues that are crucial for task performance are still being monitored.

When pressure increases still more, as in diagram 3, then people, operators and managers alike, begin to ignore cues that are central to task performance. They lose sight of some information they need to know, which means that everything becomes more complex and less comprehensible than it normally is. When people ignore information that is central to performance, existing interactions between variables are ignored or misperceived, and through their interventions new interventions may be triggered inadvertently. The situation becomes both more complex and more tightly coupled, which means that all organizations, not just those that start with interactive complexity, experience this condition. Perrow's analysis implies that once an organization is assigned to one of his four cells, it remains there. That implication overlooks the important effects that arousal can have on task conceptions. The combination of centralization, perceptual narrowing, and regression produced by increased arousal can alter perceptions of tasks and structures, thereby altering combinations of coupling and complexity.

By making the assignment of an organization to one of Perrow's four categories more fluid, as a result of arousal, we can extend his analysis. Organizations that routinely function as tightly coupled complex systems (cell B) should know more about that condition and be better able to cope with it than organizations that routinely function in the other three cells. Organizations in cell C (loose/linear) know the least about interactive complexity (tight/complex), which means that when they become tighter and more complex, they should be the most unsettled by this experience and cope with it least adequately. Organizations in cells A and D should cope with interactive complexity equally well—better than C, but worse than B.

One index of inability to cope with interactive complexity might be the speed with which organizations disintegrate and move from cell B to cell D. If we assume that those with less experience with interactive complexity deteriorate more quickly, then loose linear organizations should exit from cell B first, followed by loose/complex and tight/linear organizations. Organizations that are accustomed to interactive complexity will fold eventually in the face of continuing extreme arousal, but they should survive longer, making better decisions than any other form of organization.

Whether increases in arousal come from resource scarcity (Lawrence and Dyer, 1983), demands on attention (March and Olsen, 1986), or from "contradictory information, unexpected and mysterious interactions, and the need to follow rigid procedures that are written by the experts and that may be inappropriate in a particular instance" (Perrow, 1984, p. 151), these increases are likely to be more frequent, more intense, and more disruptive when they occur in conjunction with continuous processing, stochastic events, and a higher mental workload.

Interactive complexity is not a fixed commodity tied to specific technologies, such as nuclear reactors. Since arousal tends to increase when control and prediction become problematic, and since newer technologies alter many of the processes of control and prediction that people are accustomed to, arousal is likely to accompany many of the newer technologies much of the time. What makes this so serious is that virtually all of the effects of arousal on the already complex newer technology are in the direction of making it even more complex. Stochastic events become even more so when the few patterns that are still visible in them vanish in the face of perceptual narrowing.

When we argue that interactive complexity is dynamic

rather than static, this does not give researchers license to study perception and ignore material artifacts and structure. Material artifacts set sensemaking processes in motion; sensemaking is constrained by actions, which themselves are constrained by artifacts; and sensemaking attempts to diagnose symptoms emitted by the technology. What we are trying to emphasize in recasting the concept of interactive complexity is that the increased mental workload created by new technologies forces people to impose more of their own interpretations to understand what is occurring. These interpretations are necessarily incomplete, which means that a greater number of material events interact longer, with potentially more severe consequences—out of sight but, more seriously, out of mind. When people use fallible models to cope with stochastic, continuous, abstract events under conditions of excessive arousal, interactive complexity is one consequence.

The gradual decoupling of a mental model of a process from the actual steps that occur in that process allows events to unfold that ramify in their consequences and grow increasingly incomprehensible. These outcomes potentially occur whenever excessive arousal contracts attention and allows events to interact unnoticed and unmonitored, so that a new technical system and a new set of interactions are created, without any person intending it. It is in this sense that humans can transform a simple linear system into one that is interactively complex, and it is in this sense that interactive complexity and new technologies are closely associated.

The point of all this is not to lay one more shortcoming at the door of the human operator; quite the opposite. What we are suggesting is that the design of technical systems often fails to moderate arousal levels, make complex judgment tasks simpler, distribute responsibilities among team members, reduce distractions, provide incentives for early reporting of error and problem solving, reduce production pressure, heighten perceptions of control, and add slack capacity to attention.

Considering what they face, it is remarkable that operators do as well as they do. If, after three years, teams of professional analysts still were not completely certain of what had happened at Three Mile Island, then we can hardly fault a handful of operators who had thirteen seconds to decide what had happened. As Frijda (1986, pp. 476–477) observes, "A human being cannot have been made to stand and withstand all contingencies life presents. What can you expect from a system that only takes nine months to produce and merely weighs about 70 kilograms? . . . One may assume that humans have been fitted out with provisions to deal effectively with a number of important contingencies. There is necessarily a cost to this. Several emotion provisions, for instance, are emergency provisions. They produce response fast, and upon a minimum of information processing. If the system can do that, one should not complain that its information processing on these occasions is truncated, or that response is being made when finer meaning analysis might have shown it to be unnecessary."

From Behavior and Output Control to Premise Control. As new technologies increasingly take on the form of abstract working knowledge, they move deeper inside the operator's head, which means that effective control over these technologies will be exerted by cognitive variables and unobtrusive controls. Obtrusive controls, such as orders, rules, regulations, specialization, or hierarchy (Perrow, 1977), require more observables than are ordinarily present with new technologies. For example, behavior control (Ouchi and McGuire, 1975) is more difficult in new technologies because visible behaviors comprise a smaller portion of the actual inputs. Thus, behavior is a less meaningful object of control: there is less behavior to monitor, the effects of observed behaviors are mystified by interactive complexity, and the same behaviors may be mediated by private diagnoses that vary widely in their accuracy. All of these complications mean that observed behaviors are less diagnostic of how well the process is progressing.

Output control is also difficult, for many of the same reasons. Visible outputs are less meaningful because so many unobservable determinants other than operators' actions can affect them. While an operator can be held accountable for the output, that accountability is empty if neither the operator nor the monitor understand what is occurring or why.

Obtrusive managerial controls, such as direct surveillance and standardization, are relatively ineffective ways to influence the operation of new technologies because less obtrudes to be monitored or standardized. This does not mean that obtrusive controls have disappeared in organizations with new technologies, but it does mean that unobtrusive controls in the form of decision premises (for example, managerial psychosocial assumptions incorporated into work arrangements) should have more impact. Decision premises have become more crucial now that more of the organization is carried in the head and less of it is carried by visible, sensible, transparent artifacts. Cognition is an increasingly important determinant of organizational outcomes because, with fewer visible artifacts, more of the organization has to be imagined, visualized, and filled in from cryptic cues. All of this fleshing out is cognitive and is affected by decision premises.

When premises underlying action are controlled, according to Perrow (1986, p. 129), "the subordinate *voluntarily* restricts the range of stimuli that will be attended to ('Those sorts of things are irrelevant' or 'What has that got to do with the matter?') and the range of alternatives that would be considered ('It would never occur to me to do that')." Premise controls are important when work is nonroutine, which is why we have highlighted them in the context of stochastic technologies.

Premise controls are often created when managerial psychosocial assumptions are incorporated into technological and organizational designs. As Dornbusch and Scott (1975, p. 89) note, work arrangements, which consist of such components as allocation of responsibility, procedures for the evaluation of performance, and rules governing task performance, usually "are messages concerning the nature of the tasks from those who control to those who perform." At the center of these messages is either a delegation premise (that performers can make nontrivial decisions regarding a course of action) or a directive premise (that they cannot). These premises may be unconsidered choices by managers, but that does not make them any less potent.

Much of the potency of managerial assumptions derives from the fact that they act like self-fulfilling prophecies. Davis and Taylor (1976, p. 412) provide the example of "when assumptions are held that a system is comprised [sic] of reliable technical elements and unreliable social elements, then in order to provide total system reliability, the technical design must call for parts of people as replaceable machine elements to be regulated by the technical system or by a superstructure of personal control. On the other hand, if the system designers' assumptions are that the social elements are reliable, learning, self-organizing, and committed elements, then the technical system will require whole, unique people performing the regulatory activities. Experience has shown that in the latter case such a technical system design produces effects markedly different than [in] the former."

It becomes more plausible to link technology with determination by self-fulfilling prophecies when a sizable portion of the technology exists in the form of decision premises. Self-fulfilling prophecies are themselves decision premises, which become realized when they are treated as if they were true.

An interesting current puzzle in technology may be the result of a self-fulfilling prophecy incorporated into managerial assumptions. American implementation of flexible manufacturing systems differs dramatically from Japanese implementation of the same systems. Thurow (1987) observes that the average American system makes ten parts while the average Japanese system makes ninety-three different parts. Adler (1988) cites data showing that American systems produce eight parts, on average, whereas those in Japan produce an average of thirty parts and those in Germany as many as eighty-five parts. In other words, flexible manufacturing systems in the United States show a remarkable lack of flexibility. Although flexible manufacturing is more like batch or continuous processing, managers may still assume it is a long-linked assembly line and embed the system in a mechanistic structure, which fulfills the prophecy that it is simply an electronic assembly line. Again, the imposed premises define, flesh out, and actualize a portion of the technology.

It does not matter that the operators are more sensitive to nonroutine qualities of the technology that the manager overlooks. Managerial assumptions typically dominate, and this is especially serious when managers underestimate the skills required for operation of new systems (Adler, 1986). This underestimation is not trivial, since it is backed up with directives rather than with delegation. These directives either squeeze out the flexibility that was designed into the technology or, more seriously, restrict perception and make it harder for people to operate the technology in a reliable manner.

Our point is that managers and designers are able to exert substantial influence over the form of new technologies because key parts of these technologies exist in the form of decision premises, which makes these forms more vulnerable to the premises imposed by managers.

If those premises are imposed by managers who feel threatened by the potential loss of their authority (Davis and Taylor, 1976) or by designers who want to centralize decisions, promulgate rules, and differentiate tasks (Scott, 1981), then technologies will be run with less judgment than is necessary to manage and comprehend their complexity. As a result, these technologies will become more interactively complex because directives will make it harder for operators to monitor, learn about, and respond to the full range of states that a machine can assume. The artificial restriction of perception and action by directives does not stop elements of the technology from interacting, but it does curtail comprehension of these interactions, which means the technology becomes more complex and more puzzling.

Thus, interactive complexity can be a social construction, as well as an indigenous feature of new technologies. This is why, throughout this chapter, it is assumed that interactive complexity is more common, more easily created, and more pervasive as an accompaniment of newer technologies than has previously been recognized. Furthermore, decision premises are an important source of interactive complexity. Designers whose assumptions issue in directives create more interactive complexity than do designers whose assumptions issue in delegations.

Conclusions

The preceding analysis suggests that an important pathway by which new technology affects organizations is variation in the ability of people to reason about the deep structure of new systems. Reasoning of some sort is mandatory because the systems are equivocal. The adequacy of reasoning depends on the extent to which the mental models used by people who work with new technologies are equivalent to the processes they model. These models represent an imagined technology that people assume parallels the actual technology, which they can see only through its punctate sensors.

Reasoning about new technologies can have a consequential effect on the way those technologies function. Our recurrent theme has been that technical systems and organizational constraints can reduce meaning, control, and predictability, which raises arousal, which affects the material interactions that are set in motion, which affects the outcome, which then feeds back and has a further effect on meaning, control, and predictability. The cycle can be broken, reversed, or dampened at any one of these points. Part of what we have tried to articulate is ways in which people can gain some control over the increasingly private, increasingly equivocal new technologies, which often test the limits of human comprehension.

This rephrasing of the main argument is an attempt to articulate the implications for individuals, as well as for organizations, of a set of technological qualities that we have not seen together before in quite this combination. Just as the novel combination of complex structures and tight coupling has produced interactive complexity and normal accidents at the organizational level, so has the novel combination of stochastic events and continuous processes produced cognitive-emotional complexity and operator mistakes at the individual level. More important, normal accidents and operator mistakes derive from analogous assumptions and mechanisms, the one set emphasizing macro material determinants and the other emphasizing micro perceptual determinants.

New technologies are fascinating because, in their complex equivocality, they force us to grapple with a key issue in technology—namely, how to apply perceptual perspectives to a material world. In the preceding discussion, I have tried to blend the material and the perceptual, the micro and the macro. In the process, the picture that has emerged is one in which fallible people prove to be more resourceful and more adaptable than any control system yet fabricated. At the same time, these people are also so skilled at sensemaking that it is hard for them to detect when a mental model is becoming decoupled from the process they are trying to model and control. The model that is gradually becoming decoupled remains sufficiently plausible that the prospect of a mismatch between it and the actual process seems remote. Ironically, that very remoteness may be so reassuring to people that they remain only moderately aroused; their attention may range more widely, and they may then notice the incipient decoupling and correct it. Such are the oddities associated with new technologies: they may become least comprehensible when people worry most about comprehending them.

New technologies are paradoxical, as well as equivocal. These descriptions are not intended merely as clever phrases. Instead, they speak to the core issues we need to resolve if we want to understand technologies in which mental representation plays a central role in operation.

New technologies introduce a set of issues in technology that organizational theorists have yet to grapple with. Unless they do, the power of technology as a predictor of organizational functioning will diminish. That has been the message of this chapter.

References

Adler, P. "New Technologies, New Skills." *California Management Review*, 1986, *29*, 9–28.

Adler, P. S. "Managing Flexible Automation." *California Management Review*, 1988, *30*, 34–56.

Barley, S. R. "Technology as an Occasion for Structuring: Evidence from Observations of CT Scanners and the Social Order of Radiology Departments." *Administrative Science Quarterly*, 1986, *31*, 78–108.

Berkun, N. M. "Performance Decrement Under Psychological Stress." *Human Factors*, 1964, *6*, 21–30.

Berniker, E. "Understanding Technical Systems." Paper presented at Symposium on Management Training Programs: Implications of New Technologies, Geneva, Switzerland, Nov. 1987.

Berniker, E., and Wacker, G. "Advanced Manufacturing Systems." Unpublished manuscript, 1988.

Berscheid, E. "Emotion." In H. H. Kelley and others (eds.), *Close Relationships*. New York: W. H. Freeman, 1983.

Berscheid, E., Gangestad, S. W., and Kulakowski, D. "Emotion in Close Relationship: Implications for Relationship Counseling." In *Handbook of Counseling Psychology*. New York: Wiley, forthcoming.

Broadhurst, P. L. "Emotionality and the Yerkes-Dodson Law." *Journal of Experimental Psychology*, 1957, *54*, 345–352.

Buchanan, D. A., and Bessant, J. "Failure, Uncertainty, and Control: The Role of Operators in a Computer-Integrated Production System." *Journal of Management Studies*, 1985, *22*, 292–308.

Burke, J. G. "Bursting Boilers and the Federal Power." In M. Kranzberg and W. H. Davenport (eds.), *Technology and Culture: An Anthology*. New York: Schocken, 1972.

Campbell, D. J. "Task Complexity: A Review and Analysis." *Academy of Management Review*, 1988, *13*, 40–52.

Davis, L. E., and Taylor, J. C. "Technology, Organization, and Job Structure." In R. Dubin (ed.), *Handbook of Work, Organization, and Society*. Skokie, Ill.: Rand-McNally, 1976.

Dornbusch, S. M., and Scott, W. R. *Evaluation and the Exercise of Authority.* San Francisco: Jossey-Bass, 1975.

Easterbrook, J. A. "The Effect of Emotion on Cue Utilization and the Organization of Behavior." *Psychological Review,* 1959, *66,* 183–201.

Ettlie, J. E. *Taking Charge of Manufacturing: How Companies Are Combining Technological and Organizational Innovations to Compete Successfully.* San Francisco: Jossey-Bass, 1988.

Eysenck, M. W. *Attention and Arousal.* New York: Springer-Verlag, 1982.

Finkelman, J. M., and Kirschner, C. "An Information-Processing Interpretation of Air Traffic Control Stress." *Human Factors,* 1980, *22,* 561–567.

Frijda, N. F. *The Emotions.* New York: Cambridge University Press, 1986.

Hancock, W. M., Macy, B. A., and Peterson, S. "Assessment of Technologies and Their Utilization." In S. E. Seashore, E. E. Lawler III, P. H. Mirvis, and C. Cammann (eds.), *Assessing Organizational Change.* New York: Wiley, 1983.

Hermann, C. F. "Some Consequences of Crisis Which Limit the Viability of Organizations." *Administrative Science Quarterly,* 1963, *8,* 61–82.

Hickson, D. J., and others. "A Strategic-Contingencies Theory of Intraorganizational Power." *Administrative Science Quarterly,* 1971, *16,* 216–229.

Hulin, C. L., and Roznowski, M. "Organizational Technologies: Effects on Organizations' Characteristics and Individuals' Responses." In L. L. Cummins and B. M. Staw (eds.), *Research in Organizational Behavior.* Vol. 7. Greenwich, Conn.: JAI Press, 1985.

Intintoli, M. J. *Taking Soaps Seriously: The World of "Guiding Light."* New York: Praeger, 1984.

Khandwalla, P. N. "Mass-Output Orientation of Operations Technology and Organizational Structure." *Administrative Science Quarterly,* 1974, *19,* 74–97.

Law, J. "Technology and Heterogeneous Engineering: The Case of Portuguese Expansion." In W. E. Bijker, T. P.

Hughes, and T. J. Pinch (eds.), *The Social Construction of Technological Systems.* Cambridge, Mass.: MIT Press, 1987.

Lawrence, P. R., and Dyer, D. *Renewing American Industry.* New York: Free Press, 1983.

Lynch, B. P. "An Empirical Assessment of Perrow's Technology Construct." *Administrative Science Quarterly,* 1974, *19,* 338-356.

McGrath, J. E. "Stress and Behavior in Organizations." In M. D. Dunnette (ed.), *Handbook of Industrial and Organizational Psychology.* Skokie, Ill.: Rand-McNally, 1976.

Majchrzak, A. *The Human Side of Factory Automation: Managerial and Human Resource Strategies for Making Automation Succeed.* San Francisco: Jossey-Bass, 1988.

Mandler, G. *Mind and Body: Psychology of Emotion and Stress.* New York: Norton, 1984.

March, J. G., and Olsen, J. P. "Garbage Can Models of Decision Making in Organizations." In J. G. March and R. Weissinger-Baylon (eds.), *Ambiguity and Command.* Marshfield, Mass.: Pitman, 1986.

Metcalf, J., III. "Decision Making and the Grenada Rescue Operation." In J. G. March and R. Weissinger-Baylon (eds.), *Ambiguity and Command.* Marshfield, Mass.: Pitman, 1986.

Miles, R. H. *Macro Organizational Behavior.* Santa Monica, Calif.: Goodyear, 1980.

Mintzberg, H. *Structure in Fives.* Englewood Cliffs, N.J.: Prentice-Hall, 1983.

Neiss, R. "Reconceptualizing Arousal: Psychobiological States in Motor Performance." *Psychological Bulletin,* 1988, *103,* 345-366.

Ouchi, W. G., and McGuire, M. A. "Organizational Control: Two Functions." *Administrative Science Quarterly,* 1975, *20,* 559-569.

Perrow, C. "A Framework for the Comparative Analysis of Organizations." *American Sociological Review,* 1967, *32,* 194-208.

Perrow, C. "The Bureaucratic Paradox: The Efficient Organization Centralizes in Order to Decentralize." *Organizational Dynamics,* Spring 1977, pp. 3-14.

Perrow, C. *Normal Accidents: Living with High-Risk Technologies.* New York: Basic Books, 1984.

Perrow, C. *Complex Organizations.* (3rd ed.) New York: Random House, 1986.

Poole, M. S. "Communication and the Structuring of Organizations." Unpublished manuscript, n.d.

Riley, P. "A Structurationist Account of Political Culture." *Administrative Science Quarterly,* 1983, *28,* 414-437.

Roberts, K. H. "Bishop Rock Dead Ahead: The Grounding of U.S.S. *Enterprise." Naval Institute Proceedings,* forthcoming.

Scott, W. R. *Organizations: Rational, Natural, and Open Systems.* Englewood Cliffs, N.J.: Prentice-Hall, 1981.

Scott, W. R. *Organizations: Rational, Natural, and Open Systems.* (2nd ed.) Englewood Cliffs, N.J.: Prentice-Hall, 1987.

Susman, G. I., and Chase, R. B. "A Sociotechnical Analysis of the Integrated Factory." *Journal of Applied Behavioral Science,* 1986, *22,* 257-270.

Thompson, J. D., and Tuden, A. "Strategies, Structures, and Processes of Organization Decision." In J. D. Thompson (ed.), *Comparative Studies in Administration.* Pittsburgh, Pa.: University of Pittsburgh Press, 1959.

Thurow, L. C. "A Weakness in Process Technology." *Science,* 1987, *238,* 1659-1663.

Turner, J. H. "Analytical Theorizing." In A. Giddens and J. H. Turner (eds.), *Social Theory Today.* Stanford, Calif.: Stanford University Press, 1987.

Van de Ven, A. H., Delbecq, A. L., and Koenig, R. "Determinants of Coordination Modes Within Organizations." *American Sociological Review,* 1976, *41,* 322-338.

Wachtel, P. L. "Conceptions of Broad and Narrow Attention." *Psychological Bulletin,* 1967, *68,* 417-429.

Weick, K. E. *The Social Psychology of Organizing.* Reading, Mass.: Addison-Wesley, 1969.

Weick, K. E. "Enacting Sensemaking in Crisis Situations." *Journal of Management Studies,* 1988a, *25,* 305-317.

Weick, K. E. "We Are at Takeoff: Lessons from Tenerife." Paper presented at Stanford University, Nov. 1988b.

Weltman, G., Smith, J. E., and Egstrom, G. H. "Perceptual Narrowing During Simulated Pressure-Chamber Exposure." *Human Factors,* 1971, *13,* 99–107.

Winner, L. *The Whale and the Reactor.* Chicago: University of Chicago Press, 1986.

Withey, M., Daft, R. L., and Cooper, W. H. "Measures of Perrow's Work-Unit Technology: An Empirical Assessment and a New Scale." *Academy of Management Journal,* 1983, *26,* 45–63.

Woods, D. P., O'Brien, J. F., and Hanes, L. F. "Human Factors Challenges in Process Control: The Case of Nuclear Power Plants." In G. Salvendy (ed.), *Handbook of Human Factors.* New York: Wiley, 1987.

Woodward, J. *Industrial Organization: Theory and Practice.* London: Oxford University Press, 1965.

Zuboff, S. *In the Age of the Smart Machine: The Future of Work and Power.* New York: Basic Books, 1988.

2
⚜

Understanding Technology and the Individual in an Organizational Context

Paul S. Goodman
Terri L. Griffith
Deborah B. Fenner

The goal of this chapter is to expand our knowledge of the relationship between new technology and the individual in the organizational context. We explore both the impact of technology on the individual and the impact of the individual on technology. Our key products will be a set of intellectual tools that should enhance research in this area.

The proliferation of new technology permeates our everyday lives. Both inside and outside work, technology plays a role in our daily activities. The decreasing costs and increasing power of our computing environment create a host of opportunities, both positive and negative, for each of us.

As the rate of technological change increases, so do our images of technology in regard to the individual. Images of job loss, deskilling, enhancements to decision making, and so on, are pervasive. Applications of technology are not neutral. Given the pervasiveness of technology and its potential impacts, it is our responsibility as organizational researchers to understand its relationship to the individual.

Our focus is on delineating a set of intellectual tools in the form of concepts and critical processes. This loosely coupled set of tools helps focus attention on critical issues underlying the relationship between technology and the individual. Real understanding happens when the tools are applied to a specific technology in a specific setting. This fine-grained understanding of the intersections among the individual, technology, and the organization represents the key to generating and subsequently testing propositions about the individual–technology relationship. These tools are obviously designed for the researcher who wants to shed light on such issues as deskilling, stress, and decision making in the context of new technology, but they are also designed for the manager or policymaker concerned with introducing technological change or with the impact of this change on the individual.

Current Status of the Literature

Our analysis of the literature on the impact of technology on the individual indicates the need for more refined theoretical concepts and methods. The empirical literature seems primarily organized by outcomes (for example, deskilling, job loss, worker attitudes, stress) or by technology (for example, electronic mail, electronic monitoring, teleconferencing). While it is not within the scope of this chapter to review this literature (compare Kling, 1980), we can characterize the empirical literature as having a lot of conflicting findings and not a well-defined cumulative body of knowledge. For example, in the deskilling literature, there is evidence for and against deskilling (Attewell and Rule, 1984). Some studies (Cyert and Mowery, 1987) report that technology will increase job loss; others do not. Research on the impacts of technology on attitudes and stress shows both positive and negative effects. A review by Edwards (1989) reports that the introduction of the same technology in the same job could lead to different results, in terms of work attitudes.

One problem with the empirical research on the impact of technology on the individual is methodological in nature. Some of the studies use incomplete data sets. For example, studies on deskilling need information on both intraoccupational and interoccupational changes. Many of the designs do not permit tracing the impact of technological changes on changes in skill requirements within and between occupations. The absence of many longitudinal studies precludes understanding of the dynamic relationship between technology and the individual. These methodological problems account in part for the conflicting findings and lack of a cumulative set of knowledge.

The other major problem is the lack of well-developed theories—that is, there are not well-developed concepts that would help explain and predict the interrelationship between technology and the individual. Over the last eight to ten years, there has been some interesting theoretical work on typologies relevant to the impact of technology on the individual (Hirscheim, 1986; Kling and Scacchi, 1982; Markus and Robey, 1988). The typologies describe the implicit theory in most of the empirical research in this area. The implicit theory contains assumptions about causality (or the nature of impacts), appropriate scientific methods, theories of organizations, and values about technology. The typologist's role is to make explicit these implicit theories and the associated dimensions that drive research on technology and the individual.

These typologies are useful in identifying key issues (for example, whether technology is an objective or socially constructed entity) and organizing the literature, but they do not generate new research paradigms or new predictions. To move ahead, we need to identify the critical concepts and processes that drive the relationship between technology and the individual.

Basic Concepts, Assumptions, and Implications

The following section presents our basic conceptual apparatus. We begin by defining technology, identifying some

assumptions about technology, and examining the meaning
of the words *impact of technology*. Next, we present the basic
framework—the individual model of technology and the critical processes. Whenever possible, we try to provide some
empirical illustrations and to draw out the implications of
our conceptualization.

Our goal is to demonstrate that these concepts provide
new insights into understanding the individual–technology
relationship. Strategically, we hope researchers will apply this
set of loosely connected concepts to studying specific technological configurations in specific organizational settings.
Over time, we would expect these concepts to generate a set
of recurrent findings that have implications for theory and
practice.

Technology: Definition and Assumptions. Technology
is a system of components involved in acting on and/or
changing an object from one state to another (Goodman,
1986). The object can be a living being, a symbol, or an
inanimate object. *Changing*, in this context, means transforming inputs into outputs. *Acting on* means affecting an object
without changing its basic state. In an automated warehouse,
technology acts on an object by moving it in space; electronic
mail moves information from one space to another.

The technological system is composed of four components: equipment, materials, physical environment, and
programs. *Equipment* may refer to a simple tool or to complicated, programmable equipment (including hardware and
software). *Materials* represent the object being worked on, or
animate and inanimate objects necessary to transform the
object in question. The *physical environment* refers to the
physical context in which the transformation takes place. *Programs* are rules, procedures, or design heuristics used in the
transformation process. Some of the programs are organized
into tasks; others link tasks and production processes.

Our view of technology is broad rather than narrow.
Technology is found throughout the organization, in the core
and buffer parts of the production system and in the nonpro-

duction parts of the organization (such as personnel or marketing). While we draw our examples from such forms of new technology as computer-aided design (CAD), computer-integrated manufacturing (CIM), robotics, and electronic monitoring, the basic elements of our conceptual apparatus should apply to all kinds of technology.

Assumptions and Implications. 1. The same technology can be configured in a variety of different ways to produce the same results. There are several implications of this observation. First, it is probably not useful to analyze the impacts of robotics or CIM per se. Each of these systems can be configured in a variety of different ways in different organizational settings. Therefore, to understand the impacts, one must know the specific configuration. Second, while different configurations may lead to the same results, the process of any change may be quite different. Therefore, to understand impacts, one must know the specific configurations and processes.

2. Changes in any component or in multiple components of the technological system can affect multiple activities, interactions, and work-related outcomes. The literature has a tendency to focus on single outcomes, such as skill or stress. This is a much too simplified position. One needs to examine multiple outcomes over time, both positive and negative. Technological changes in a particular job may also affect activities, interactions, and outcomes in other jobs, and so it is important to trace the impacts of a technology on a system of jobs, not simply the immediate target.

3. Technology is a heterogeneous rather than a homogeneous concept in any given organizational context. There is a tendency in much of the organizational research on technology to treat technology as homogeneous; indeed, many of the operational strategies measure the firm's technology in terms of general labels, such as *predictability* or *uncertainty* (see the review by Goodman, 1986). Implicit in this measurement procedure is the assumption that technology is homogeneous, at least in that organizational context. Our view is

that one should start with the assumption of heterogeneity and then look for homogeneity. For example, in an automotive assembly plant, the general transformation process is involved in putting materials together to produce a vehicle. However, the technological components of a paint shop are very different from those of a body shop in the same organization. The implications of the heterogeneity assumption are that within any organization, group, or task there may be different types of technology that can be configured in different ways. Therefore, the focus should be on examining a specific homogeneous configuration of a specific technology at a particular level of analysis.

4. Technological changes evoke organizational changes; the opposite may also be true. Organizational changes include new forms of training, pay recognition, support services, and so on. The issue is that organizational and technological changes will simultaneously affect the individual. It is also likely that the individual will view technological and organizational changes as part of a totality. The implications are to chart out the organizational and technological changes, acknowledge the link between the two types of changes, recognize that multiple outcomes will flow from the technological and organizational changes, and determine how people assign meaning to these multiple outcomes.

Meanings of Impacts. Implicit in our analysis is the assumption that technology can have an impact on the individual and the individual can have an impact on a technology. *To have an impact* means to change or to effect a change. In this section, we explore the issue of causal structures.

The rationale for this exploration is quite straightforward: our view of the causal structure drives how we think and conduct research. In much of the literature, the assumption is that there is a fairly direct and traceable link between changes in technology and changes in the individual; the causal flow is from technology to the individual. In this section, we question that assumption.

One way to introduce this idea is to briefly describe a

study on the introduction of a roboticized machine cell in a manufacturing plant. The setting of the study (Argote, Goodman, and Schkade, 1983) was a nonunion manufacturing plant with one thousand employees, involved in the production of turbine blades. The cell was introduced into a department primarily involved in milling and grinding operations.

The robot was placed in the department at the beginning of the workflow, in a horseshoe configuration. The primary function of the robot was to load and unload two milling operations. One person operated the robot each shift. In the past, two people had performed this operation.

Table 2.1 describes the task program for work activities before and after the technological change. The major changes should be very clear. The introduction of the equipment changed the physical environment and the character of the task activities. In terms of task activities, there was a shift from manual activities to a greater reliance on monitoring and new programming activities; that is, there was a shift from manual to more perceptual, conceptual, and problem-solving activities.

What can we learn from this brief description? First, the introduction of the robot changed the environment, as well as a set of core task programs, and the changes in the programs initiated changes in job and pay evaluation.

Second, there was nothing inherent in the equipment that could have predicted the form of the task programs or

Table 2.1. Major Task Activities.

Before Robot	After Robot
1. Set up machines	1. Program robot
2. Lift bar stock	2. Start robot
3. Place stock on drilling machine A	3. Monitor cycle
4. Clamp stock to machine	
5. Initiate machine operation	
6. Monitor cycle	
7. Stop machine operation	
8. Unclamp bar	
9. Move bar to milling machine B	
10. Repeat cycle on milling machine B	

subsequent organizational changes; that is, the programming activity might or might not have been allocated to the operator, and the organizational changes (in terms of job evaluation and pay changes) might or might not have occurred. The point is that the causal structure is loosely constructed. The dilemma is that we can trace through the effects of the robotic installation, but only ex post facto. There was no way that we could have inferred before, from the robot's general characteristics, what chain of events would follow; there were many possible chains. A corollary point is that although we know that the introduction of the robot led to a new configuration of task activities, which affected what the individual did, there was nothing inherent in the robot that would have permitted predicting specific individual responses.

Third, the introduction of the robot caused changes in physical and social reality for the individual. Physical reality reflects observable phenomena that can be validated by objective means, such as measurement. Objects in social reality derive their meaning from the opinions of others. In the context of new technology, physical reality may include size, the speed of the machine, the length of the work cycle, reliability, and so on. Social reality may include fairness of pay, difficulty of a job, and so on. This social construction of the meaning of the technology partly determines how people use and react to the technology. The process of ascribing social meaning is a way the individual can modify the technology. For example, if the employees attribute favorable, humanlike qualities to the robot, their acceptance of and behavior toward the robot will be more positive than if they attribute negative, machinelike qualities. The basic point is that the construction and evolution of this socially constructed model of the technology creates reciprocal causation between the technology and the individual.

Fourth, social constructions of the technology are the result of three variables: the technology itself, the organizational context and history, and the implementation process. We think the process of implementation is an important variable, which is omitted in many analyses of the impact of technology on the individual. The basic idea is quite simple. The process of introducing technological change is independent of the technology, and yet the process is the major way people learn and, hence, construct an image of the technology. At one level, the formal implementation process attempts to create a specific, socially constructed image of the technology. Nevertheless, there are many informal processes filtering and reinventing the image of the technology. A final point: the inclusion of the implementation process further confounds the causal structure between technology and the individual. The nature of the implementation process can mitigate any impact of the technology on the individual, or the implementation process can increase the variance in socially constructed views of the technology, which would confound any link between the technology and the individual.

The Individual's Model of Technology. The individual's representation or model of a technology is a critical concept in our kit of intellectual tools. The model directs the assignment of meaning of the technology and the use of the technology by the individual. It is the model of this technology that permits the individual to modify the technology, an important link in the individual–technology relationship. In this section, we identify the function, structure, and development of this model.

The model of technology functions to simplify a complex technological and organizational environment. It is a system of categories that helps people interpret and assign meaning to objects. In this context, the objects are technological in nature. The specific functions in assigning meaning include selecting information from the environment, retaining information in memory, and making inferences about the environment.

The structure of the individual's model is composed of a set of schemata. A schema is a knowledge system that contains attributes of a concept and relationships among the attributes. The information in a schema is in an abstract form: a generalization from specific, concrete instances of an object (Fiske and Taylor, 1984). Thus, a schema concerning robots would include abstract attributes of the robot, as well as relationships among the attributes.

There are different types of schemata. They can be abstract systems about physical objects. A schema concerning robots would be an example of this type. We would expect this system to include descriptors, functions, and consequences of robots. Schemata can also be about events. This type of schema may be a standard sequence of events evoked by a particular stimulus. For example, a standard operating procedure for dealing with a "down" robot may be an event schema. Finally, a schema may be concerned with roles. These would be normative behaviors assigned to specific organizational positions. In terms of the robot example, there would be different roles (for example, engineering, maintenance) involved in the operation of the robot. The functions of all three of these schemata are the same: to select information, to retain information, and to permit inferences about missing information. All these different types of schemata reside in the individual's model of technology.

Another way to characterize the structure of this model is in terms of three types of orientation: cognitive, affective, and evaluative. Some of the components of the individual's model of technology are primarily cognitive in nature. A schema about robots that is composed of abstractions about description (for example, mechanical arm) and functionality (for example, lifts and loads) is primarily cognitive in nature. Over time, some of the components will have cognitive and affective orientations. For example, abstractions about consequences contain cognitive elements ("Robots eliminate obnoxious aspects of my job"), which can lead to positive affective orientations ("I like to work with the robot"). Finally, some components can have cognitive, affective, and evaluative orientations. Evaluative orientations include norms about the technology ("All the members of our work group should apply appropriate maintenance procedures to ensure effective operation of the robots") and values ("Others ought to adopt robots").

In summary, we can draw the following implications from our description of the structure of the individual's model of technology. First, the model is composed of different types of schemata (for example, object, event, role). Second, over time, we would expect these schema to reflect cognitive, affective, and evaluative orientations. Initially, we would expect primarily cognitive orientations, as the individual develops some basic knowledge structures about the technology. Over time, the individual's direct task experiences with the technology should lead to positive and/or negative reinforcement, which should facilitate the development of affective orientations. Others' experiences should also shape the affective orientations. If there is consistency in the development of cognitive and affective orientations, evaluative orientation should follow (Breer and Locke, 1965). If we could trace the individual's model over time, we would see order among the orientations, with cognitive orientation preceding the affective, which in turn precedes the evaluative (Goodman and Dean, 1982).

The development of a schema in the model follows a particular pattern (Fiske and Taylor, 1984). The individual faces concrete instances of a particular phenomenon (for example, robots). If there is some commonality across these instances, some generalization and more abstract representation of the phenomenon should occur; that is, similarities among information from task experiences and others should evoke a generalization process. As the schema matures and becomes more abstract, there is some indication that it also becomes more complex and exhibits more organization among the attributes. Fiske and Taylor (1984) also indicate that mature schemata demonstrate a perseverance effect; that is, they resist change, even in the light of contrary information. The implication of this developmental account is that we trace models over time and should see greater evidence of abstraction, more categories, more organization of categories, and greater resistance to change.

We now turn to the critical processes that shape the individual's model of technology and his or her behavior with respect to the technology. Five critical processes underlie the relationship between technology and the individual. The processes are not unique to any particular type of technology, and they are not proposed as an integrated theory; rather, the five processes are loosely associated, as is the relationship between technology and the individual. Their function is to help explain how the individual's model of technology develops, how changes occur in individual behavior with respect to the technology, and how the technology evolves over time. The five processes are socialization, commitment, reward allocation, sensing and redesigning, and diffusion.

Socialization. Socialization refers to the processes by which individuals acquire knowledge and skills and affective and evaluative orientations. In our context, the processes focus on the acquisition of those dimensions (for example, knowledge) relevant to some technology. There are a number of assumptions underlying this conceptualization of socialization (Van Maanen and Schein, 1979). First, the introduction of new technology, or the transition into a job with new technology, produces anxiety. Research by Sproull, Kiesler, and Zubrow (1987) shows how computers can be an alien culture for novices, and this state induces anxiety and tension. One of the functions of socialization is to impart information that will reduce anxiety. Second, there are many sources of socialization. In a work context, trainers, peers, vendors, and subordinates are all potential sources of socialization. Third, there are many forms of socialization. Formal classroom training, hands-on experience, trial and error, and coaching from a peer are all different forms of training. Fourth, socialization is a continuous (versus "one shot") process because the individual and technology are continually evolving, which leads to conditions where the anticipated events and actual events are discrepant. These discrepancies or surprises (Louis, 1980) induce tension and motivate the individual to resolve the discrepancies. In the process of resolving the discrepancies through cognitive or behavioral acts, the individual will acquire new forms of information. This acquisition of information is a form of socialization, which will be continuous as long as discrepancies or surprises occur.

We can specify some of the content of socialization. In the context of the individual and technology, skill acquisition is important. Manual skills, perceptual skills, conceptual problem-solving skills, and interpersonal skills are classes of skills relevant to technology (Majchrzak, 1988). Other major content areas include affective and evaluative orientations (for example, norms and values). In some of our own research (Goodman and Miller, 1988) on new technology, we find most of the focus is on skill acquisition versus affective or evaluative orientations.

While all three content areas appear in the socialization of any new work role, there are characteristics of new technology that require a different emphasis in the socialization process. First, most new technologies (for example, CAD and CIM) require computer and software literacy. In new production facilities, we sometimes find (Goodman and Miller, 1988) that the level of literacy required is significantly higher than the level initially found in the work population. Second, the technology is more complex and is provided by different vendors. Knowledge about any one system must come from different areas of expertise and different organizations. The socialization dilemma is to integrate these different sources of knowledge about skills so that the total technological system will function. Third, the new technological systems tend to be more highly integrated, which requires greater coordination. Moreover, boundaries between work areas tend to be blurred. The socialization challenge is to develop multiskilled individuals who work across boundaries. The focus changes from acquisition of knowledge in a single role to knowledge across different roles. The demand for greater coordination places demands on interpersonal skills. Finally, since the new technology requires high capital investments and is highly integrated, there is a greater premium on reducing downtime. This fact requires greater emphasis on fast and effective maintenance monitoring and on problem-solving skills, as well as on conceptual understanding of the technological system.

There are many forms or mechanisms (Van Maanen and Schein, 1979) of socialization. Two dimensions seem important in our analysis of the new technological environment. First, the mechanism can be formal or informal. Formal mechanisms are initiated by the firm and typically focus on groups of employees. Informal mechanisms are initiated by the individual employee and usually focus on the individual. Second, the mechanisms can be more or less structured; that is, there can be variation in the degree to which socialization activities are planned in a sequence and occur over a fixed period. Table 2.2 shows four classes of socialization mechanisms and examples. In the first cell—classroom training—a group of individuals are segregated by the firm from the regular work force and exposed to knowledge in some structured manner. In cell 2, workers are sent (again by the firm) to work several weeks in the vendor's factory, to assemble and debug equipment. This experience, which is not as structured as the classroom, is an important learning mechanism. However, much of the key learning we have observed is not formally initiated. In one instance, we talked with a skilled tradesperson who learned to manage the new technology by working out a relationship with the resident expert. They jointly (and informally) worked out a structured way to learn about the new technology (cell 3). A lot of other learning seems to occur in an informal, relatively unstructured context. Simply talking to co-workers or experimenting with the new equipment represents an important way for people to learn (cell 4).

Table 2.2. Forms of Socialization.

	Formal	Informal
Structured	1 Classroom training	3 Working with resident expert
Less structured	2 Working at vendor's plant	4 Observing others; talking with co-workers

What are some of the implications of these four classes of socialization mechanisms? All four types of socialization are important. One may be exposed to different combinations of these socialization mechanisms. The mechanisms differ in terms of their functionality. If the general goal is to impart a new base of knowledge and have common understandings of activities, then classroom training would be more appropriate. If the goal is to understand complex problem solving in maintenance, then a more apprentice-type training program, where the expert and the trainee solve actual problems in a structured way (cell 3), is an appropriate mechanism when coupled with classroom training. The rationale is that apprenticeship work in real problem-solving activities will facilitate the acquisition of problem-solving skills. If the goal is to make sense of surprises (discrepancies between anticipated and actual events), the mechanisms in cell 4 may be more appropriate. Surprises are random and are tied to an individual's experiences. Cell 4 deals with informal and unstructured socialization activities relevant to a specific individual. The concluding point is that there are many forms of socialization, with different functionalities.

The basic issue in understanding the impact of the socialization process is relating the different content areas (cognitive, affective, and evaluative)—in light of the differences in demands of new technology (interpreting diverse knowledge areas, levels of complexity, and interdependence)—to different classes of socialization (formal, informal, structured, and less structured).

Commitment. A second process that affects the individual–technology relationship is commitment. *Commitment* refers to the binding of the individual to certain behavioral acts relevant to technology. The level of commitment depends on the explicitness, revocability, volition, and publicity of an act (Salancik, 1977). The greater the explicitness, irrevocability, volition, and publicness of an act, the greater the commitment.

What is the role of the commitment process for the individual–technology relationship? First, within the individual's model of technology, the greater the commitment, the greater the consistency among retrospective accounts of behavior, other cognitions, attitudes, and values. Earlier, we introduced the concept of surprises, which referred to the discrepancies between expectations and actual experiences with technology. Surprises are a natural occurrence in the evolution of technology. We said individuals attempt to reconcile the discrepancies through sensemaking activities. Given our earlier conceptualization about commitment, individuals highly committed to certain acts relevant to technology should avoid information inconsistent with these acts and should reconcile any discrepancies in a way consistent with these acts. A second implication is that there should be greater consistency among behavioral acts over time, given high levels of commitment. A third point is that higher levels of commitment are associated with greater levels of resistance to change. Thus, a person highly committed to one form of technology may be more resistant to adopting other forms of technology. This point indicates that high levels of commitment may be functional or dysfunctional for the individual or the organization. Much of the organization literature assumes high commitment is functional.

How does one change levels of commitment? To increase commitment, the process should facilitate the free choice of acts that are public, explicit, and irrevocable. This can be accomplished in a number of ways. The individuals can be involved in the design of the technology. This would provide an opportunity for individual discretion. In this context, individuals can better align their own skills and needs with the inherent characteristics of the technology. If the individuals were not involved in design decisions, it would be important to determine whether the technology in question was primarily discretionary or nondiscretionary. In discretionary technology, the individual has the choice to use or not use the technology; nonuse does not stop or prevent the total production system from operation. In a CIM plant, information systems on workflow would be discretionary. The automated scheduling system in a CIM plant would be nondiscretionary; without that system, the production system stops. Discretionary technology facilitates commitment, since it provides a choice.

Involvement in other decisions—such as operational decisions (who runs the technology and when, where, and how) and implementation decisions (how to introduce the technology)—should also increase levels of commitment. The design decision, however, is probably the most powerful form of involvement. It provides the greatest choice opportunities.

Reducing levels of commitment is more complicated. Salancik (1977, p. 47) suggests that one can remove a highly committed individual from his position or "you try to unwind his behavior by providing the resister justification for his behavior which explains the behavior independent of his own volition." Another option is to reduce opportunities for recommitment over time.

Reward Allocation. Reward allocation, the third process, refers to the distribution of different types of rewards. The frequency and type of reward distribution has several implications for the individual–technology relationship. Behavior, with respect to the utilization of technology, will be affected by the process of reward allocation. The form of the individual's model of technology will also be determined by reward allocation. For example, the affective orientations toward technology should be related directly to the types and frequency of allocated rewards.

While we cannot propose a set of propositions about the process of reward allocation, there is a set of issues the researcher should consider when tracing out the effect of reward-allocation decisions on the individual–technology relationship. This is consistent with the general goal of this chapter: providing tools or concepts to better understand the individual–technology relationship.

First, there is the paradox of values (Sproull and Hofmeister, 1986). In any implementation (for example, of technology), there will be a tendency to emphasize the positive values of the object. The greater the emphasis on the positive attributes, the greater the negative surprises when actual values are less than the expected positive values. Negative surprises lead to a more negative evaluation of the new object. The dilemma is that not emphasizing the positive values during implementation reduces the likelihood that people will utilize the new technology. The implications of the paradox of values are that the emphasis on positive outcomes of implementing a new technology can lead to negative evaluations of these outcomes over time. A readjustment of the emphasis of positive and negative outcomes seems desirable. For example, emphasizing more of the negative outcomes during implementation may reduce some of the negative surprises.

Second, there are important manifest and latent rewards associated with new technology. As we have said, there is a tendency from the designers or implementers to focus on the manifest beneficial outcomes. However, it is also important to identify some of the latent positive and negative outcomes. In one of our studies on robotics (Argote, Goodman, and Schkade, 1983), the benefits of learning new skills and of less fatiguing work were emphasized in the introduction. However, there were latent benefits, such as increased recognition, and latent costs, such as greater stress. The point is that the distinction between manifest and latent benefits helps us enumerate the total set of rewards and costs, which is necessary in analyzing the individual–technology relationship.

Third, it is important to consider different sources of rewards in the context of the technological life cycle and multiple roles. Rewards (or costs) can be found in the technology itself, in the formal organizational reward system, and in informal reward systems. These sources of rewards can appear at different points in the technological life cycle. The life cycle begins with a design phase and moves to a building phase, to an implementation phase, and, eventually, to some steady state (Goodman and Miller, 1988). The different sources of rewards may affect different roles or actors at different points in the life cycle. For example, the reward system for the designer, the implementer, and user are likely to be different. Our argument is that most research on the impact of technology and the individual focuses on rewards for the user. This is too limited. We need to trace the effects of different sources of rewards at different points in the cycle for different actors. For example, the functionality of the technology has important consequences for the utilization of that technology (Goodman and Griffith, 1989), but do we know how the reward systems of the designer and the implementer affect the functionality of the technology?

Sensing and Redesigning. The terms *sensing* and *redesigning* refer to the process by which data are collected on the performance of a piece of technology and by which the technology is redesigned. The data stimulate redesign by pointing to problems in performance or to new opportunities for enhancing performance. The basic assumption underlying this process is that technology is constantly evolving. Changes in products, processes, or people require modifications in the technology. The goal of the sensing and redesigning process is the reconfiguration of the technology. This process is important because it focuses on invention. Much of the literature on technological change in organizations focuses on utilization. While there is not a lot of research on the sensing and redesigning process, several dimensions should be examined. First, to what extent is the process formalized? We need to determine whether this process is formally recognized in some role description or in group activities. For example, data could be collected by the operator and fed back to the design engineer for redesign. In addition, there may be specifications about when to collect data and what types of data to collect. Formalization, in this context, focuses more attention on the importance of invention, and this should stimulate the evolution of the technology. Second, the operationality of information or any standards should facilitate the sensing and redesigning process. The character of the information collected can determine whether the redesigning process will be initiated. If the information or the standards about acceptable performance are ambiguous, then it is less likely that the redesigning process will be initiated. It is clear that any technology can be built from functional specifications, and one can compare the specifications to the technology. That is not the focus here. We are interested in how information about the operation of a technology stimulates invention.

Diffusion. Diffusion, the fifth process, refers to the process by which the technology is extended to other parts of the organization. This process is different from the others discussed here, since it focuses on organizational-level phenomena versus individual-level phenomena. The role of diffusion is to create the opportunity for the development of normative and value consensus, two dimensions in the individual's model of technology. As diffusion occurs, an infrastructure to support the technology develops. In addition, it creates the opportunity for multiple others to use the technology and to be aware that others are using the technology. These conditions create the necessary environment for the formation of normative and value consensus about the new technology. Normative consensus and value consensus are the basic ingredients for institutionalization of the technology. In the study on robotics (Argote, Goodman, and Schkade, 1983), we examined a factory where there was only one robotic installation in one job area in one department. This installation was an island in a nonrobotic environment. While the technology was successfully introduced, it was very fragile. There was no form of normative or value structure to support its existence. Our selection of diffusion as the last process is based on the belief that it creates opportunities for normative and value consensus, which, in turn, can help institutionalize the technology in the social environment.

Some Illustrations

Our basic argument is that we need some new tools to work through the relationship between technology and the individual. Here, we illustrate these concepts in two settings employing new technology.

Case A: Vision System. We have been working in three high-technology automotive assembly plants. The plants are new and have state-of-the-art CIM technology. All three produce the same product. A vision system is a laser computer-based system that measures dimensional quality. In these plants, the vision system is located in the body shop and measures the dimensional quality of different production lines. For example, do the dimensional specifications of the door match the dimensions measured by the vision system? Physically, the vision system is composed of a series of cameras, a video display terminal, and a computer system. Measurements of the vehicle parts are observable on the terminal. Various statistical packages permit the user to obtain different measures of different parts, as well as to calculate means, trends, and so on.

The vision system presents data on every vehicle. Prior to the installation of the vision system, one would physically take two or three parts (for example, doors or a completed body) off the line per shift and measure the dimensions with a fixture and gauges. Given a line rate of sixty to seventy vehicles per hour, the old system would collect data only on a few parts per shift. If problems were discovered, one would have a very small sample from which to infer trends, and if there was a problem, more than five hundred vehicles would have passed through the body shop prior to detection. Thus, the vision system provides a proactive way to deal with quality. Indeed, in our initial interviews, before the system went on line, the operators believed the vision system would provide the opportunity for proactive monitoring, problem identification, problem analysis, and corrective action.

We have followed this system for two years. Formal and informal interviews and formal and informal observations have been the primary means of collecting data. A good description of this system and the individuals involved is well beyond the scope of this chapter. Our interest here is to show how our conceptual tools focus attention on the critical aspects of the relationship.

What happened? Did the vision system increase opportunities for proactive monitoring and problem solution? Initially, during the plant startup, there was little actual use of the vision system. New plant startups are very demanding and complicated events. The goal was to get the production and assembly lines going. While the vision systems were physically in place, some were not operational, and others were not calibrated. The end of the plant acceleration (one year) is a good time to provide a "snapshot." What we saw was that about 10 percent of the operator's time was spent interacting with the vision machine. The use was primarily involved in monitoring, verifying whether a signaled problem was an actual problem or a problem with the vision system itself, and working on problems with the vision system. Most of the monitoring activity was reactive. There was little problem analysis. One aspect of the employees' models of the system after one year was that the vision system had great potential for improving dimensional quality, but problems of system downtime, difficulties with cameras, and measurement unreliability hurt the credibility of the system.

Given the seemingly straightforward advantages of the vision system, how can our concepts help us understand what happened? First, the *socialization process* was critical. Initially, there was some classroom training (formal and structured) on how to operate the system. However, there were other key behaviors, such as trouble-shooting and problem analysis, that were critical. Teaching someone to operate a vision system (that is, to generate data) is different from training in trouble-shooting the system or doing analysis on data generated from the system. None of this training was available. It could be argued that trouble-shooting and problem analysis are better learned in a more informal, tutorial, less structured mode. We think this is probably true, but it did not happen. Therefore, it is not surprising that knowledge and performance of trouble-shooting and problem analysis were not observed. The inability to trouble-shoot the system aggravated beliefs about the credibility of the system.

There were no formal means to elicit a *commitment* to the vision system; that is, the system was put in place without any involvement in the design, operational form, or implementation of this technology. The great demands of the initial plant startup focused attention away from the vision system. Many operators were working six to seven days a week to get the production system up. These sets of pressures precluded attention and commitment to the vision system.

In terms of *reward allocation*, there were inherent problems in this new vision system that diminished its expected functionality; that is, there were important discrepancies between promised functionality and actual functionality (the paradox of value). Most important were problems with maintaining the quality of the data. These were caused by problems with cameras, measurement procedures, and so on. In addition, there was not a good infrastructure to resolve these problems quickly. Moreover, when problems were found with dimensions of the vehicle (when measurement was good), the typical reason was bad metal, a problem originating outside the plant. The basic idea is that the expected and actual benefits were different, both at the point of introduction and one year later. This example focuses on rewards derived from the functionality of the new technology. It was also clear that there were not contingent rewards in the formal or informal system to encourage greater utilization of the vision system.

The vision system was limited to five lines in the body shop. One year into the program, no other systems were in operation. The lack of *diffusion* hindered the development of an infrastructure and social legitimation to support the system. There was no evidence of normative or value consensus developing to support the vision system.

There were no formal internal mechanisms for *sensing and redesigning;* that is, there was no mechanism within the vision system, from the operators, or from the body shop that fed back data on the actual use of the system and compared it to the intended use. Some inventions did occur. In one plant, an alarm system was put in to improve on-line monitoring. The alarm (a buzzer) went off whenever a part was reported out of tolerance. Other changes included developing a statistical system to translate the data into trends. Some of the plants are trying new measurement procedures to improve the credibility of the data. Others are reorganizing to get more clear responsibility for the operation and maintenance of the system. These changes are not yet in place. The source of these inventions is less clear. The research team's feedback, a change in management, meetings among users in the three plants, and selling by the vendor all contributed to the inventions, but it is fair to say that these emerged over a long period and not in any particular order. A view of change that characterizes the invention process is chaotic and disorderly.

The individual's model of the technology reflected many of the above dynamics. In our interview, in the beginning of the first year, most of the operators had general cognitions about the description and functionality of the vision system. Since the system was not yet operational, most of these cognitions were influenced by the formal training class and by discussion with others. Cognitions about benefits were primarily positive. The most salient discrepancy concerned the benefits of the system and the perception that the data from the vision system might not be reliable. This discrepancy was maintained (not resolved) in the initial use of the system because initial problems with data can be expected in a new system. A year later, our interviews captured a more complex view of the vision system, but the level of positive affect, or optimism, had declined. Experiences over the year with continued measurement problems and lack of development of normative consensus led to more negative views of the system and primarily reactive use. This is only a brief picture of what is a complicated emerging relationship, occurring over a long period of time. The impact of the vision system on the individuals and of the individuals on the vision system is still unfolding in a relatively unpredictable way. We have proposed some concepts to provide some structure to this emerging picture. In this illustration, socialization and reward allocation (specifically, actual experiences with the functionality of the technology) are the most robust in clarifying the picture.

Case B: Roboticized Machine Cell. The thesis of this chapter is that the concepts we present can help us organize the complicated relationship between technology and the individual. In this example, we focus more on elements of the individual's model of technology. In the prior illustration, we focused more on processes. Our position on the individual's model of technology is that it is composed of schemata about objects, roles, or events, which may be characterized by cognitive, affective, and evaluative components. Over time, these components may become more abstract, differentiated, or organized.

The setting for this illustration is the introduction of a roboticized machine cell into a department performing milling and grinding operations (see Table 2.1). The operator's job was changed from primarily doing an operation to monitoring the operation of the machine cell.

We collected interview and observational material two and a half months prior to the installation of the machine cell and two and a half months after the introduction of the cell. The socialization process included an open house, in which the operation of the robot was demonstrated; talks by the plant managers about the machine cell; discussions between employees and first-line supervisors; meetings and audiovisual presentations; readings; and so on.

The cognitive component of the individual's model should be the first to form. One part of that component was the individual's picture of the robot. In response to a question ("How would you describe the robot to a friend?"), the primary descriptors initially used included "mechanical man," "preprogrammed machine," "TV image," "better productivity," and "loads machine." These images, reported after the introduction but before the actual installation, can be organized in terms of *description* (mechanical man), *function* (loads machine), and *consequences* (better productivity). Where did the initial images come from? Respondents reported that movies and television were important socializing sources in addition to the plant sources. Indeed, the humanlike robots in the media probably contributed to the workers' naming the robot and endowing it with human qualities. These early beliefs about the robot, particularly the attribution of human qualities, represent the individual's redefinition (change) of the technology and create an early initial context for further development of the individual's model—that is, a positive, humanlike attribution about the robot should facilitate development of positive affects and use of the robot.

When we repeated this question after the machine had been in operation for two and a half months, the same types of images occurred, but each individual reported more images. This is consistent with the proposition about greater differentiation over time. While this discussion about our research focused primarily on object schemata (the robot), there were data in the interviews indicating development of schemata about roles and events relevant to the robot.

We were particularly interested in beliefs about the consequences of the technology, since it should evoke affective orientations, and so we asked questions about eight possible consequences (for example, productivity, downtime, and skill requirements). Prior to the introduction, there was a fairly optimistic view that the roboticized cell would increase productivity, lower costs, lower accidents, improve quality, and so on. These beliefs seemed closely tied to the public position taken by management during the introduction of the new technology. As workers gained more experience within the machine cell, their beliefs became more pessimistic. Respondents said during the second set of interviews that there were greater chances for accidents, increases in costs, and decreases in quality. This change within the individual's model represents an adaptation to experienced reality or communicated reality. Our data were collected during the startup period, when setup costs would be high. This reality appeared discrepant with management's statements that the roboticized cell would reduce costs. The salience of the initial startup costs probably led to the belief that costs would increase. Beliefs about increasing accidents and decreasing quality probably grew out of the communicated reality among the employees; that is, the perceived decrease in quality was a social construction that was passed around. However, there were no objective data to support the perceived decrease in quality.

The prior discussion focused on beliefs about organizational consequences. Let us turn to the immediate consequences of the technology for the worker, as displayed in the components of beliefs, behavior, and attitudes at the time of the second set of interviews. The new cell did change work activities (see Table 2.1). The operator performed fewer manual activities and more monitoring, conceptual, and problem-solving activities.

How are these activities related to the cognitive and affective components, and how did they develop? Operators reported beliefs about the following topics:

1. *Less fatiguing work:* This belief grew out of initial communications about benefits of the technology and the objective fact that the robot did the lifting. Positive feelings were attached to this consequence.
2. *Greater recognition:* This unintended consequence can be attributed to the fact that management increased contact with the operators to see how things were going. This contributed to positive feelings but also contributed to increased stress.
3. *Greater skill:* The operators' acquisition of programming skills probably accounted for this belief. Since the operators voluntarily requested these jobs, in part to learn new skills, it is not surprising to find positive affect assigned to this skill.
4. *Greater responsibility:* The operators were managing three rather than two machines. The feelings of responsibility generated both positive feelings and feelings of stress.
5. *Less social interaction:* The second-interview data were collected during the learning period of this new installation, and so there had been limited time for social interaction, an unintended consequence. This enumeration of consequences also indicates the need to track manifest and latent consequences. The increased recognition and stress were latent consequences.

Some of the processes played a role in the development of these cognitive and affective components. The initial *socialization* processes contributed to positive beliefs about the technology, such as greater skill and less fatigue. Since the operators voluntarily and publicly accepted the job *(commitment)*, it is likely that they would look for positive beliefs and feelings about the job. The reinforcements that grew out of that actual task experience can explain the positive feelings about less fatiguing work, as well as the increased feelings of stress.

Unfortunately, we were not able to collect a third set of measures. Changes in the individual's model of the technology would have continued to unfold. It is likely that some of the beliefs about recognition would have declined as the technology became less novel. Some of the feelings of stress might have adjusted as attention from management declined and as the operators moved to the equilibrium point of the learning curve. Whether there would have been norms and values developed about this technology is questionable. There were no plans to diffuse the technology within the department or the plant. It is also unlikely that there would have been major changes in the cell. This was a stand-alone system, without any formal mechanisms for sensing and redesigning.

Critical Issues

In this section, we look at some new issues relevant to doing work on technology and the individual. Their primary utility is to focus attention on strategies for theory, method, and practice.

Theory Issues

Problem Framing. It should be clear from this analysis that how the problem is framed bears heavily on the methods, results, and conclusions. A problem framed around deskilling is a good case in point. It implicitly assumes an answer and greatly simplifies the relationship between technology and skill. As another example, one might want to see how technology affects stress. Even if one adopted a neutral stance (that is, technology may or may not increase stress), the framing greatly simplifies the array of outcomes stimulated externally (by the technology) and internally. In studying technology, we need to acknowledge that each individual entertains multiple outcomes, that there are multiple individuals with multiple outcomes, and that the system of outcomes is in a constant state of flux. Focusing on a single outcome is an unfortunate form of ultrasimplification. Another tack is to frame a problem in terms of a technology—say, an investigation of the effects of robotics. We have argued that there is too much surplus meaning in the word *robotics;* that is, there are many different forms of robotics, the technology is not homogeneous, and the organizational configurations associated with any robotic installation can vary. Thus, framing research about a general class of technology is not informative and is unlikely to generate valuable research.

The proposed strategy is to frame the problem in terms of the basic processes and the individual's model of technology and then apply the concepts to a specific technological and organizational configuration. The real issue is to understand and explain the evolution of the relationship between the technology and the individual.

Levels of Theory. There are not well-developed theories about the relationship between technology and the individual. We do not think that well-specified models will be developed in the future. We have argued that one should operate at two different levels. The most general level is characterized by the five processes and the components of the individual's model of technology. These are a set of loosely coupled concepts to map the complicated system of reciprocal relationships between technology and the individual. The second level of theorizing is primarily inductive. When the concepts are used to map the relationship between technology and the individual, specific facts will emerge. Each fact is unique to a specific situation and time. Other, similar, facts should emerge over time, creating a stylized fact about a particular relationship. The emerging facts probably will be about things that have happened rather than traditional propositions (for example, variation in X leads to variation in Y). An example from a different field comes from the literature on quality of work life (QWL). If one looked at all of the studies about QWL organizational innovations that decentralized control and power to the work force, a recurring theme would appear: that problems and stress are experienced by first-line and middle managers. Whatever the design or population, that fact seems to occur. It is a recurring event, which is both theoretically and practically important.

Idiographic Approach Versus Generalizability. The theme in this chapter of learning from the specific setting raises questions about generalizability. Basically, one could argue that we will be learning about results of particular configurations of technology in particular settings at particular times. The results may not be generalizable to particular kinds of technology (for example, to robotics). Over time, we also would expect the emergence of new types of technology. This apparent idiographic approach may not help us learn about these emerging new forms of technology.

Our response is twofold. First, the five processes are generalizable to any type of technology existing now or in the future. They are an exhaustive set of processes to explain the evolution of the relationship between technology and the individual. While their importance may vary by situation, we believe that all of the processes play a role in explaining this relationship, and this assertion could be subjected to some form of confirmability. Second, we also see the process of inducing stylized facts as addressing the concept of generalizability. Over time, we see the emergence of facts (such as the QWL finding about problems experienced by first-line supervisors) as speaking to the issue of generalizability; that is, the appearance of a common phenomenon over time and across situations speaks to generalizability.

Substantive Issues

In addition to issues of problem formulation and theory construction, there are many other substantive issues to be solved under the individual–technology heading. We list a few. The structure of the individual's model of technology is relatively unexplored. We have tried to add to knowledge in this area by suggesting some of the components of this model and their interrelationships, but this concept is still not well delineated. The individual's model of technology is a function of both objective and social reality, but we know little about the intersection of these two types of reality. How do different socialization mechanisms change the components of an individual's model of technology? In our illustrations, we pointed out that the cognitive and affective components change over time. We know something about the different forms of socialization, but we really do not know how, in any refined way, these processes work. How do inconsistencies among the components get resolved? Do individuals use any combinatory rules to sum across different types of outcomes? We indicated that most technologies generate multiple outcomes at the individual level. Our own experience is that these cognitive or affective components may remain relatively independent and may not be combined. Individuals in the same job and organizational setting develop different models of the same technology. Why does this occur?

Another interesting problem concerns the utilization of new technologies designed to enhance decision making. A clear characteristic of some forms of new technology is the generation of new and better kinds of information for problem solving. Rather than substituting machines for individuals, the technology enables or enhances individuals' work (Zuboff, 1988). There are many interesting issues in this area. We will comment on two. First, why do people decide to use or not to use the enabling technology? In our work, we have seen systems (for example, the vision system) that provide new information and that, in some objective sense, are better than existing alternatives, but these information systems are not used. A second issue concerns the characteristics of problem-solving work. Many of these systems are designed to enhance problem detection, analysis, and action. In our work, we have seen examples of problem detection but little activity in the area of problem diagnosis. Why is there so little activity in problem diagnosis—attempting to get at root causes of production or quality problems? One reason is that the organizational reward system focuses attention on day-to-day events (for example, problem detection) and not on problem diagnosis, which requires longer periods. However, while the reward system is clearly important, if we refocused attention on problem diagnosis, it probably would not happen successfully. What is probably missing is some explicit model of the process one wants to diagnose. When we, as researchers, analyze data, we have a model of the phenomena we want to test. When an employee, working with the vision system or with statistical process control, is given data, there also needs to be a model of the process. In our field work, in general, we do not see people with these types of models. Interesting questions, given the focus of current technology on proactive problem solving, are how important these models of the production system are, what their form is, how they are learned, and how the complexity of current forms of technology facilitates or inhibits this learning.

Another problem area concerns the influence of the individual on technology. For the most part, the literature on technology and the individual focuses on how technology affects the individual. We have tried to make clear that it is a reciprocal process. The concept of the individual's model of technology is the mechanism we used to show how the individual modifies the technology. In the case of the vision system, decreasing credibility about the information in this system affected behaviors toward the system, as well as external attempts to redesign the system. Thus, the model can lead to behaviors that facilitate or inhibit the system, filter information about the system, and so on. The issue is that we need to know more about this process (Kiesler and Sproull, 1987). One fascinating area concerns invention. We have argued that throughout the life cycle of the individual–technology relationship the technology continually evolves. In the vision system, some inventions were initiated. Why did these occur? What is the process that initiates internal inventions? A formal sensing and redesigning system would make a difference, but what other factors are important?

Methodological Issues

Sampling. Several issues that concern sampling bear on research about technology and the individual. One issue is that many of the studies have focused on single occupational groups. For example, research in the factory has focused on the operator, and research in the office has focused on the clerical worker. Our theoretical orientation points to sampling *systems* of users. Thus, if the initial analysis is of the blue-collar operator, one must enlarge the sample frame to reflect the appropriate role system (for example, maintenance, supervision, quality, production, control, and so on). A second point is that much of the literature on technological impacts has focused on organizations producing goods or services. It would be interesting to examine the individual--technology relationships in other types of organizations (for example, religious and problem-solving organizations).

Design. There are many possible designs for studying the individual–technology relationship. What is critical is that the research be theory driven (that is, using the five processes), fine-grained, appropriate in its sampling frame, and longitudinal. The case study is one of the most frequently used designs in this research area. In terms of our theoretical emphasis on developing fine-grained descriptions of the evolutionary relationship between technology and the individual, the case seems an appropriate choice. The critics of case studies point out limitations, in terms of confirmability and generalizability. One reaction to the confirmability issue is to design cases in a different way. Instead of private data collection and interpretation of data, the process becomes public. The initial researchers systematically collect data via qualitative and quantitative methods on characteristics of the organization, the technology, the individual, the five processes, and the individual's model of the organization. Another set of researchers are given the same set of data (for example, field data), without knowledge of the interpretations by the initial researchers. The task is to use the concepts in this chapter to generate regularities from the data. If independent raters identify the same regularities, there is some movement toward convergent validity. It would also be possible to have another researcher gather selective data, to give an indication of the reliability of the initial data. The issue of generalizability could be addressed by building multiple case studies among similar kinds of technology and in similar settings.

Other designs, of a more experimental nature, may be utilized to demonstrate or explore certain attributes of the individual-technology relationship. An organizational simulation may be the forum to demonstrate certain phenomena (Griffith, 1988). In the simulation, the experimenter sets up an organization and hires employees to perform certain tasks. In the context of these activities, certain work conditions are created that may contribute to the presence or absence of a particular phenomenon. Goodman (1987) has argued that it may be advisable to make these organizations semipermanent rather than temporary in nature, as is typically found in the literature. These organizations could be sponsored by existing organizations that want to learn more about technological design decisions. They gain relevant information about the design decisions without the costs of changing their organization.

The laboratory can also serve as a useful design option. Here, the laboratory would be used to explore relationships, rather than to test causal relationships. In the previous section, we posed a variety of researchable areas. For example, learning about the process of change in the individual's model of technology seems quite an appropriate problem in this experimental context.

Measurement. Given our theoretical position on the complexity of the evolving relationship between the individual and technology, it is probably useful to think about alternative ways to collect data. One of the most obvious ways is to use the technology itself. In studies (for example, Griffith, 1988) on electronic monitoring, it is possible via software to keep very detailed records of actual use of personal computers. If one were studying electronic mail, similar measurement procedures would be available within the technology. The key point is that measurement by the technology itself produces continuous data. Another point concerns the relative advantage of doing more observation. In our research on the vision system, we have found the traditional survey instrument less useful for tapping the complexities of workers' interactions. Assigning observers to specific production lines develops rich data logs on complete work activities.

The issues of measurement are not solely ones of method. There are also content issues. What should be measured? One of our visions is the development of a language of technology. The language would be a set of categories used to describe technology.

Why is there the need for such a language? There are at least two reasons. First, one of the problems in most organizational research about technology is that the researchers do not describe the technology to the reader (see Goodman, 1986). How can we understand technology unless it is well described? The attention typically is on outcomes. A common language would help, just as the common language we use when writing up a method section for an experiment helps. A good writeup tells us what the experimenter has done. The second reason for a language system is on a grander scale. There is an interesting data source called the Human Relations Area Files. It was created before and during World War II to provide knowledge about societies, in existence and no longer in existence, in the Pacific Ocean area. The findings contain detailed accounts by ethnographers of different societies, sorted by a common category scheme. Thus, if one wanted to look at the concept of time in different societies, one could look at a category such as "calendar." The idea for us is to build a file of case studies contributed by different researchers on the individual-technology relationship. In order to build a common data set, we need a common language to organize the data set. The data set would permit us to look at relationships over a variety of settings and categories.

How can such a common language be built? Our initial conceptualization of technology was that it is a system of components, including equipment, physical space, material, and programs; a good case could be made for such categories as "capacity," "reliability," "speed of work cycle," "level of intelligence," and so on, to describe the nature of the equipment. Programs can be divided into those that provide core support and those that have a linking function (Goodman, 1986), and skills associated with different classes of programs can be sorted into those that are manual, perceptual, conceptual, related to problem solving, and interpersonal (Majchrzak, 1988). This strategy begins with the initial four components of technology and then builds a category system. A similar classification system would be needed for the organization and the individual. If researchers used this classification system, there would be a common data set, which would provide a more robust way of studying relationships between technology and the individual.

Practice Issues

Managing New Technology. Managers and consultants are continually involved in finding new ways to successfully introduce and manage technology. There are many examples in the literature of unsuccessful attempts to manage technology, and so finding new approaches would seem to be a valuable contribution to practice. In this chapter, the five processes can be a useful way to focus attention on improving this practice; that is, these concepts can provide direction in the process of change. For example, the socialization process is obviously critical in change, and most managers would acknowledge this. However, in our experience, their primary

interpretation of socialization is in terms of the formal training (in the classroom) done initially in the change process.
We have tried to point out that there are multiple sources of
socialization, both formal and informal. We have also tried
to point out that the informal kinds of training are often the
most critical. For example, a key way to learn some of the
subtleties of the vision system is to work on the assembly line
with one of the resident experts. The other issue emphasized
in our discussion is the long period of time for the individual-technology relationship to evolve. This means that the
socialization process needs to be thought out over a longer
time than is typically the case.

Employment Contracts. The form of new technologies
may have some practical implications for designing "employment contracts" (March and Simon, 1958). While we clearly
have said that any type of technology can be configured in a
variety of ways, we also stated that there are qualitative differences with new forms of technology. Some of the differences
include the shift from manual work to observational activities. One of the characteristics of manual activities is that
inputs and outputs are visible; this is less true of observational
or monitoring activities. Another difference with new forms
of technology is that the greater "intelligence" of new technology can permit machines themselves to do monitoring
and correction. This loosens the connection between the individual and the machine; that is, constant monitoring may
not be necessary, and the individual is freed from staying in
a particular space at a particular time. New technology also
permits one to work outside the traditional boundaries of
work. This means that there will be changes in the visibility
of the individual's contribution, in terms of space and time.
To some extent, these changes challenge aspects of the traditional employment contract, whereby someone comes to work
at a specific time in a specific place and contributes to the
organization's work in a visible way.

In terms of the new technology, actual work activities
are less visible, and boundaries concerning space and time

become fuzzy. This makes assessing the contribution side of
the contribution–inducement relationship (see March and
Simon, 1958) more difficult. From the inducement side, there
are interesting problems. Consider a monitoring task. How
should we reward that activity? Should we reward the input
side (that is, the amount of time the individual looks at the
screen)? Looking at a screen and working may be very different. We could look at the output of the job, such as the ratio
of good pieces produced to defective pieces, but this output is
not really within the control of the employee doing the monitoring. We could identify the ratio of corrected problems to
total problems available, but this ratio may be confounded by
the actual number of problems, which is outside the operator's control. If we switch the frame of reference to the operator's point of view (versus the organization's), we can ask
what, given the increase in monitoring activities, the focus
of the reward system will be and whether the worker finds
rewards valuable? The basic issue is that the contribution-
inducement contract has a long historical tradition, and it is
based on visible work in space and time. As those dimensions
change, we need to think about changing the basic form of
the contract.

   *Integrating Technology and Quality of Work Life
(QWL).* Two major movements in current organizational life
are the evolution of new technology and organizational
change to enhance QWL. An interesting issue is whether these
two movements are complementary or in conflict. Our position is that they are in conflict, although this is not a function
of some inherent characteristic of the technology. We want to
focus attention on this conflict and cause the reader to think
about this dilemma, although a detailed analysis or set of solutions are not within the scope of this discussion.

   QWL, at one level, refers to shifting more control and
responsibilities to the worker; providing opportunities for
participation; providing more information about the organization and its environment; and creating dignity, security,
and opportunities for development in work. At another level,
the concepts of QWL are manifested in self-designing teams,

quality circles, job redesign, pay for knowledge systems, labor-management cooperation teams, and so on.

The conflict between new technology and QWL-related changes occurs when the technology is designed and installed without workers' involvement; variety and challenge are removed from jobs; control is transferred outside the work area to technical experts; and work teams no longer can be involved in scheduling or planning work, assigning who does what, or performing administrative activities (for example, controlling inventory) because of technological changes.

The degree to which this conflict actually exists is difficult to determine. One can look in the literature and find examples of choices about technology that are antagonistic to QWL changes. In our own experience, we have been in manufacturing plants that had elaborate investments in QWL activities and at the same time introduced technologies counter to the values and programs of QWL. What was interesting is that these apparent contradictions existed in the organization but were never acknowledged. Our position is that these contradictions are dysfunctional for the organization.

Any resolution of this dilemma will come first through explicit statement of the values underlying both types of change. Earlier, we said that the form of technology depends on choices made by people. Thus, choices can be made to be consistent or inconsistent with the organization's value systems.

After the value issue is clarified, the next problem is how to integrate changes in technology and QWL. If an organization values employees' involvement, then the place to start is in the adoption and design decisions. If self-designing teams are the basis of the organizational structure, then the technology needs to be designed in a manner that reflects that decision. The key issue for the practitioner is to make explicit the values underlying both QWL and technological change efforts and to develop strategies to integrate these two forces.

Conclusions

The relationship between technology and the individual is very complex. The causal structure is a set of reciprocal paths that are continually in flux. In many respects, the current literature has painted a much simpler version of this relationship. Our goal here has been to generate some concepts for tracing the complicated relationships among technology, the individual, and the organization; there are many exciting and challenging problems ahead.

References

Argote, L., Goodman, P. S., and Schkade, D. "The Human Side of Robotics: How Workers React to a Robot." *Sloan Management Review*, 1983, *24* (3), 31-41.

Attewell, P., and Rule, J. "Computing and Organizations: What We Know and What We Don't Know." *Communications of the ACM*, 1984, 27 (12), 1184-1192.

Breer, P., and Locke, E. *Task Experience as a Source of Attitudes*. Homewood, Ill.: Dorsey Press, 1965.

Cyert, R. M., and Mowery, D. C. (eds.). *Technology and Employment: Innovation and Growth in the U.S. Economy*. Report of the Panel on Technology and Employment. Washington, D.C.: National Academy Press, 1987.

Edwards, J. R. "Computer Manufacturing and Worker Well-Being: A Review of Research." *Behavior and Information Technology*, 1989, *8*, 157-174.

Fiske, S., and Taylor, S. E. *Social Cognition: Topics in Social Psychology*. Reading, Mass.: Addison-Wesley, 1984.

Goodman, P. S. "Impact of Task and Technology on Group Performance." In P. S. Goodman and Associates, *Designing Effective Work Groups*. San Francisco: Jossey-Bass, 1986.

Goodman, P. S. "Experiments, Institutional Arrangements, and Organizational Design." Paper presented at the Symposium on Knowledge and Institutional Change, University of Minnesota, Oct. 1987.

Goodman, P. S., and Dean, J. W., Jr. "Creating Long-Term Organizational Change." In P. S. Goodman and Associates, *Change in Organizations: New Perspectives on Theory, Research, and Practice*. San Francisco: Jossey-Bass, 1982.

Goodman, P. S., and Griffith, T. L. "The Implementation of New Technology: A Review of the Literature." Unpublished paper, Center for the Management of Technology, Carnegie Mellon University, 1989.

Goodman, P. S., and Miller, S. M. "Designing Effective Vendor/User Training Through the Technological Life Cycle." Unpublished paper, Center for the Management of Technology, Carnegie Mellon University, 1988.

Griffith, T. L. "Monitoring and Performance." Unpublished doctoral dissertation, Graduate School of Industrial Administration, Carnegie Mellon University, 1988.

Hirscheim, R. A. "The Effect of A Priori Views on the Social Implications of Computing: The Case of Office Automation." *Computing Surveys*, 1986, *19* (2), 165–195.

Kiesler, S., and Sproull, L. "The Social Process of Technological Change in Organizations." In S. B. Kiesler and L. S. Sproull (eds.), *Computing and Change on Campus.* New York: Cambridge University Press, 1987.

Kling, R. "Social Analyses of Computing: Theoretical Perspectives in Recent Empirical Research." *Computing Surveys*, 1980, *62* (1), 62–110.

Kling, R., and Scacchi, W. "The Web of Computing: Computer Technology as Social Organization." *Advances in Computers*, 1982, *21*, 1–90.

Louis, M. R. "Surprise and Sense Making: What Newcomers Experience in Entering Unfamiliar Organizational Settings." *Administrative Science Quarterly*, 1980, *25*, 226–251.

Majchrzak, A. *The Human Side of Factory Automation.* San Francisco: Jossey-Bass, 1988.

March, J., and Simon, H. *Organizations.* New York: Wiley, 1958.

Markus, M. L., and Robey, D. "Information Technology and Organizational Change: Causal Structure in Theory and Research." *Management Science*, 1988, *34* (5), 583–598.

Salancik, G. R. "Commitment and the Control of Organizational Behavior and Belief." In B. M. Staw and G. R. Salancik (eds.), *New Directions in Organizational Behavior.* Chicago: St. Clair Press, 1977.

Sproull, L. S., and Hofmeister, K. R. "Thinking About Implementation." *Journal of Management,* 1986, *12,* 43–60.

Sproull, L., Kiesler, S., and Zubrow, D. "Encountering an Alien Culture." In S. B. Kiesler and L. S. Sproull (eds.), *Computing and Change on Campus.* New York: Cambridge University Press, 1987.

Van Maanen, J., and Schein, E. H. "Toward a Theory of Organizational Socialization." In B. M. Staw (ed.), *Research in Organizational Behavior.* Greenwich, Conn.: JAI Press, 1979.

Zuboff, S. *In the Age of the Smart Machine: The Future of Work and Power.* New York: Basic Books, 1988.

3
❈

Work Groups:
Autonomy,
Technology, and Choice

Gerald I. Susman

Advanced manufacturing technology (AMT) is being introduced rapidly into discrete manufacturing industries. Its introduction presents an opportunity to ask whether the new
technology is compatible with work-group autonomy, an
innovation considered to enhance both productivity and the
quality of working life. The answer requires an analysis of
the conditions that are favorable to work-group autonomy
and the impact of advanced manufacturing technology on
those conditions. The analysis that is undertaken in this
chapter suggests that managerial choice is critical in determining the impact of AMT on work-group autonomy. The
primary issues that managers and researchers need to consider
concern the bases on which these choices should be made.

Nature of Work Groups and Their Settings

This chapter will focus on formal work groups in organizations. A formal work group is made up of persons who

The author would like to thank Alison Davis-Blake, Paul Goodman,
Harvey Kolodny, and Lee Sproull for their helpful comments.

are responsible to the same immediate superior. These persons have been assigned to the same superior for one or more of the following reasons: they perform the same types of activities or work with the same product; they work on the same machine, if it is large and complex, or on a cluster of interdependent machines; and they occupy the same area of a building or work on the same shift.

A work group, by definition, has only one hierarchical level (Miller, 1965). If the superior of a work group reports to a more senior person, who is responsible for several work groups, then the larger unit is an organization because it has at least two hierarchical levels. There are usually many work groups in an organization, performing a variety of activities and functions.

A work group is made up of persons who convert raw materials into finished goods. In factories, raw materials are generally physical substances; in offices, they are unorganized data. Conversion may be manual or automated. It is the conscious purpose of the superior to make sure that raw materials are transformed into products that are valued by higher levels of the organization and/or by the organization's customers. This may or may not be the conscious purpose of the work-group members. It is not essential to the definition of formal work groups that their members share a common purpose but only that their immediate superior does. Members of formal work groups are likely to share a common purpose, however, to the degree that their immediate superior delegates decisions to them. Formal work groups are also likely to share properties with "psychological groups" (Schein, 1970); that is, their members interact, are psychologically aware of one another, and perceive themselves to be a group.

This chapter focuses on work groups in discrete manufacturing settings. One reason for this focus is the author's interest and personal experience with such technology. Another reason is that advanced manufacturing technology will profoundly change the kind of work that is performed in discrete manufacturing settings. Further advances in process technology are unlikely to have as profound an effect on work performed in continuous process settings. There is an urgent need, therefore, to understand the impact of advanced manufacturing technology on work because the assumptions about how to design and manage work in discrete manufacturing settings will have to change profoundly to accommodate the impact.

This chapter also focuses on work groups that perform routine activities on a daily basis. It may be easier to understand how new technology affects routine work than how it affects professional work, because much of the technology used for routine work is embedded in machines. The impact of such technology is generally less subtle and more permanent than what resides in workers' heads.

Generalization from factory to office is appropriate when workers in the latter setting perform work that is analogous to factory work—for example, routine entry of raw data into computer terminals (Ranney, 1986). It is also appropriate for some professional support groups that perform routine activities, such as software writing. Generalizations may be limited in scope when applied to ad hoc groups that are formed to complete specific assignments and then disband, or to virtual groups that are formed to communicate via electronic mail (Kiesler, Siegel, and McGuire, 1984). Some similarity exists between ad hoc groups and formal work groups when the latter are solving problems away from the worksite. Some similarity may exist between virtual groups and formal work groups when the latter communicate via electronic media. However, there is minimal evidence to suggest that factory work-group members are communicating yet through electronic media, given the present level of sophistication of advanced manufacturing technology and the degree of its diffusion into industry. They may meet face to face, however, to interpret the meaning of data generated by such media.

Technology

Perspective on Technology. In this chapter, technology is viewed as decisions and actions that produce desired out-

comes (Ellul, 1964; Barrett, 1978). Knowledge of these decisions and actions may be stored in books or in human
memory or may be embedded in machines. In the office, the
desired outcome may be the organization, storage, and retrieval of information. In a factory, the desired outcome
may be the production of finished goods. The decisions and
actions for achieving such outcomes are embedded in some
combination of materials, machines, methods, and manpower. Materials vary in the ease with which they can be
altered or in their capabilities for conductivity, durability,
and so on. Machines vary in their speed, in their tolerance for
meeting specifications, and in their being general purpose or
specialized. Methods vary in their efficiency and in the skills
required to perform them. Finally, workers vary in the skills
and knowledge they possess. Technological progress occurs
as knowledge accumulates about what decisions and actions
taken with various combinations of materials, machines,
methods, and manpower will produce a particular outcome.

Materials, machines, methods, or manpower alone cannot produce desired outcomes; they have to form a technical
system to do that. The system is configured according to
beliefs about what can produce desired outcomes. The system,
once configured, significantly influences the type of work
group that can develop. The influence is more in this direction than in the reverse direction because technology can be
objectified; that is, it has an existence independent of the
user. Even workers' knowledge and skills have this property
because they can be transferred to other persons (Perrow,
1965). When materials, machines, and methods are placed in
a factory, they constrain the options that remain for human
action. Methods and manpower are more alterable than
machines and materials, but knowledge about the most effective way to produce a given product and the skills needed to
produce it do not necessarily change easily.

Engineers and social scientists have different perspectives on technical systems, and they highlight different aspects
of them. Engineers look at the ability of a technical system to
convert raw materials into finished goods in an efficient and

effective manner. Social scientists look at the extent to which the technical system eliminates, enhances, diminishes, or liberates human thinking and action. They also may be interested in what decisions and actions members of work groups have to take in order to keep the technical system operating satisfactorily, as well as in the interdependence between decisions and actions. These are the attributes of technical systems that influence the kinds of work-group structure and process that can develop.

Advanced Manufacturing Technology. This chapter is concerned with advanced manufacturing technology. One type of AMT is computer-aided manufacturing (CAM), which includes robots, flexible manufacturing systems, numerical control machines, automated materials handling systems, and automated storage and retrieval systems. This type of AMT substitutes hardware and/or software for the decisions and actions that work-group members ordinarily take in producing the basic products or services for which the work group is responsible. Instead of taking these decisions and actions, work-group members now monitor the machines to make sure that they operate as they were designed to do.

Three other types of AMT are also being introduced rapidly into the factory. Computer-aided process planning (CAPP) is software that plans the production process. For machined parts, for example, CAPP determines the optimal sequence of operations, selects the machine tools or work station to be employed, and determines the cutting tools, fixtures, speed, and feed rates to be used. This software substitutes for decisions that first-line foremen, manufacturing engineers, and work-group members now make. Once these decisions are made, there is little opportunity for these people to alter those decisions to meet unexpected conditions.

Manufacturing resource planning (MRP) is software that takes data about what products need to be produced within a given time, as well as data about raw materials, machining processes, and labor needed to produce them, and generates a production schedule and information about needed orders for raw materials. MRP systems can reduce inventory and increase delivery reliability. MRP systems reduce uncertainty for work groups about what to produce, how much, and when—that is, as long as the computer-generated schedule is followed. Following the schedule requires discipline from customers, suppliers, and manufacturing management that is difficult to establish and maintain (Anderson and Schroeder, 1984). For example, first-line supervisors either distrust the schedule or are pressured by sales personnel to expedite special orders for customers (Schneider, Howard, and Enispak, 1985).

Computer-aided design (CAD) and computer-aided engineering (CAE) use hardware and software to design products. The process of designing is accelerated by the use of CAD to quickly perform routine drafting, selection of parts, and so on. CAE allows engineers to test their designs without building expensive prototypes. For example, CAE can demonstrate the effects of stress or heat on a given product design. Both CAD and CAE can considerably reduce time for product development and make it easier to design products that can be made simply and reliably. The more successful CAD and CAE are in designing products that are easier to fabricate and assemble, the less uncertainty and complexity work-group members face in converting raw materials into finished goods.

CAM and CAPP are part of the core technology of the work group. They perform some of the basic transformation activities of the work group. MRP is a buffer technology that uses product forecasts to generate schedules for delivery of raw materials and for work performance. CAD and CAE are used by engineers to determine what product the work group is going to produce. They influence the degree of complexity and uncertainty that work-group members face with respect to decisions on the types of materials used, the number of product parts, and so on.

Information systems (IS) include machines that organize, store, and retrieve data and the media that convey data between machines. IS can provide data to organizational personnel about the status of production processes and outcomes.

IS can also provide data to instruct and coordinate other types of AMT. For example, after CAD has designed a product, the design data can be downloaded to CAM through a local-area network, giving instructions to CAM on how to make the product. Local-area networks can be arranged hierarchically, so that a mainframe or minicomputer can direct the activities of several local-area networks. Integration of this kind is called computer-integrated manufacturing (CIM).

Advanced Manufacturing Practices. Several types of advanced manufacturing practices are also being introduced in factories, either as a prelude to introducing one or more of the types of hardware or software just discussed or independently of them because of their own perceived benefits. These practices, being innovations in manufacturing methods, fall within the definition of technology used in this chapter.

Just-in-time (JIT) manufacturing is based on the belief that inventory is wasteful (Schonberger, 1982). Inventory increases costs by requiring space and people to store and retrieve work in process and finished goods. Instead of using time and space buffers to cope with variability, JIT demands that variability be removed at its source by substantial improvement in product and process reliability. The objective of JIT is to produce and deliver goods just in time to be sold, to produce and deliver assemblies and parts just in time for each succeeding production step, and to purchase materials just in time to be transformed into products.

Group technology (GT) is a practice by which similar parts are grouped into families to take advantage of their similarities in design and manufacturing processes (Suresh and Meredith, 1985). On the design side, engineers can avoid designing new parts by examining the GT data base to see if the design for a similar part can be used or modified slightly. On the manufacturing side, the number of different manufacturing methods and layouts can be reduced by use of those that already exist for parts within a particular part family.

Associated with GT is cellular manufacturing, which leads to the clustering of dissimilar machines on the factory floor by similarities in the sequences of operations needed to produce part families. This arrangement eliminates much of the moving and queuing time that characterizes factories that cluster machines by common manufacturing processes.

Total quality control (TQC) (Feigenbaum, 1961) is a methodology by which workers and managers can improve product quality and maximize customer satisfaction. Among TQC's prominent practices is statistical process control (SPC), which workers and managers can use to collect and analyze data on variability in the manufacturing process. SPC improves the reliability of products and their conformance to standards by identifying the sources of variability and suggesting ways to reduce or eliminate it.

The analysis that follows will focus on CAM, CAPP, MRP, JIT, IS, and manufacturing cells. The term *AMT* will be used to refer to these six technologies unless there is a need to mention one or more of them by name. These six technologies have a greater potential impact on work-group autonomy than do the other technologies shown in Figure 3.1. As the figure shows, these types of AMT are embedded in materials, machines, or methods or modify them in some way. Technology that is embedded in materials, machines, or methods has an existence that is independent of the people who use it. As such, it can significantly influence the work-group structures and processes that develop. Choices about these types of AMT are usually made by people far removed from the factory floor; thus, the implications of their choices for work-group autonomy are often overlooked.

The Impact of Advanced Manufacturing Technology on Work-Group Autonomy

According to the perspective on formal work groups introduced in this chapter, every organization has work groups, no matter what kind of technology is employed. If an organization has only one hierarchical level, because few people work in it, then, by definition, the organization and the work group are one and the same. The interesting ques-

Figure 3.1. Types of Advanced Manufacturing Technology
and the Media in Which They Are Embedded.

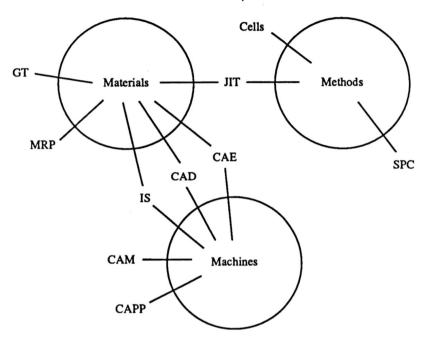

GT = Group technology
MRP = Manufacturing resource planning
IS = Information systems
CAM = Computer-aided manufacturing
CAPP = Computer-aided process planning

CAD = Computer-aided design
CAE = Computer-aided engineering
JIT = Just-in-time manufacturing
Cells = Manufacturing cells
SPC = Statistical process control

tion is the kind of work group that is possible with AMT. Is it a work group in which all decisions are made by the supervisor, or one in which the members have a high degree of autonomy?

Autonomous work groups have become very popular in recent years. Managers introduce them when they believe that group members can make some decisions and coordinate their work as well as or better than their supervisors can. Group members may set production goals, assign tasks, meet to solve problems, assess progress toward their goals, and so on. The organization benefits from better group decisions, fewer hierarchical levels, and more motivated workers. The workers benefit from higher skills, more interesting and challenging work and, perhaps, higher pay (Lawler, 1986). The question is whether advanced manufacturing technology is compatible with such groups.

One way to assess the impact of AMT on work-group autonomy is to assess the impact of AMT on conditions considered to be favorable to work-group autonomy regardless of the technology used. Davis and Wacker (1987) consider conditions to be favorable (1) when work is not entirely unskilled; (2) when the work group can be identified as a meaningful unit of the organization, and when inputs and outputs are definite and clearly identifiable and the groups can be separated by stable buffer areas; (3) when turnover in the group can be kept to a minimum; (4) when there are definite criteria for performance evaluation of the group and group members; (5) when timely feedback is possible; (6) when the group has resources for measuring and controlling its own critical variances in workflow; (7) when tasks are highly interdependent, so that group members must work together; (8) when cross-training is desired by management; and (9) when jobs can be structured to balance group and individual tasks.

The analysis that follows will show that AMT has a direct impact on conditions 1, 2, 5, 7, and 9. The impact may be favorable or unfavorable to work-group autonomy, depending on whether the nature of the impact is understood by those who implement the technology. The impact may be unfavorable if the internal logic of AMT is allowed to prevail over any other consideration. However, as will be shown, managerial choice can ensure that AMT will produce significant economic benefits without sacrificing those derived from work-group autonomy.

Conditions 3, 4, 6, and 8 relate to manpower, the fourth medium in which technology can be embedded. Innovative human resource practices can affect these conditions directly and facilitate work-group autonomy, whether or not AMT is being used. Their impact is presumed to be greater, however, if favorable choices that affect conditions 1, 2, 5, 7, and 9 have been made previously. Since this chapter concerns the impact of advanced manufacturing technology on work-group autonomy, the analysis that follows will focus on conditions 1, 2, 5, 7, and 9 and on the choices about AMT that affect them. The analysis is general enough to be applicable to technology of any sophistication that affects these conditions. The relationship between human resource practices and work-group autonomy has been explored elsewhere (Lawler, 1986; Walton and Susman, 1987; and Majchrzak, 1988); thus, human resource practices and their impacts on conditions 3, 4, 6, and 8 will not be discussed further.

Choices That Influence the Impact of Advanced Manufacturing Technology on Work-Group Tasks

Skill. The evidence suggests that more skill is required to operate and maintain AMT than is required for conventional manufacturing technology (Adler, 1986). A major managerial choice concerns who will have a chance to develop and exercise the increased skill—managers, engineers, or workers.

AMT requires more skill because it demands problem solving from those who operate and maintain it. The worker no longer converts raw material into finished goods. Hardware and software now perform the conversion activities that workers used to perform. The case for increased skill is easier to make for maintenance workers than it is for operators, as judged by the content of the training that maintenance workers generally receive (Ettlie, 1988; Majchrzak, 1988). However, the skill level of operators is also likely to increase. Aside from the few conversion tasks that may remain (for example, setup, removal, and movement of parts), operators generally monitor the production process, identify any deviations from standards, and intervene as necessary to eliminate the deviations. Sometimes such responsibility demands little skill—for example, when an operator on a highly automated assembly line periodically wedges a crowbar between carts carrying products moving between work stations, to prevent the line from jamming. Such monitoring requires vigilance, but deviations are easy to identify, and the correct action is known and easy to execute.

Hayes, Wheelwright, and Clark (1988) would call monitoring and intervention of this type "reactive control." All that is demanded of the worker is that deviations be identified and corrected. If workers were responsible for "preventive control" (preventing deviations from occurring), "progressive control" (eliminating the sources of deviations), or "dynamic control" (raising the overall performance level by introducing new methods, developing new skills, and so on), then increasingly complex and theoretical knowledge of chemistry, physics, electronics, and so on, would be required. If workers were given responsibilities of this nature, they would probably carry them out with supervisors and engineers.

Recent studies (National Academy of Sciences, 1986; Walton and Susman, 1987) suggest that many managements are opting for greater worker involvement in more challenging forms of process control because the workers have valuable firsthand knowledge of the production process that is needed for such problem solving. Competitive pressures from companies that require and reward continuous performance improvement in their plants—notably, Japanese companies (Imai, 1986)—are forcing American management to adopt a similar objective.

Workers can often perform such advanced types of control with little or no assistance from support personnel, as the author learned on a recent visit to Honda's automobile assembly plant in Marysville, Ohio. A group of workers within a highly automated welding department met after work and on weekends to study the cycle time of two robots. The members collected data by observing the robots and then reprogrammed them and succeeded in improving their cycle time by 28 percent.

Further evidence that AMT increases skill is the increased use of data for problem solving that symbolically represents the technical system; that is, the technical system is indirectly observed, by way of an electronic display or paper printout, rather than observed by direct experience. As Zuboff (1988) points out, AMT "informates" work, as well as automating it. The state of the production process and appropriate actions to change it are inferred from data, rather than directly observed. Knowledge of this type is conceptual rather than concrete. It develops by way of reasoning and experimentation, rather than accumulating by experience. Managers and engineers have traditionally used conceptual knowledge in performing their work, but workers have used concrete knowledge much more often. As managers, engineers, and workers increasingly use knowledge of a similar kind for problem solving, a major status barrier between them will be lowered.

AMT increases the skill of those who operate and maintain AMT by increasing the demand for problem solving and increasing the use of symbolically mediated data in such problem solving. Whether workers, engineers, or managers will develop and exercise this skill depends on a managerial choice to share responsibilities for complex problem solving with workers. Choosing not to share these responsibilities may increase overhead support costs enough to nullify any savings in direct labor costs that accrue from replacing workers with machines. Furthermore, managers and engineers are farther removed than workers from the production process and are less likely to identify problems as early as workers can. An important link in the learning loop is also severed when the data that workers can bring to the problem-solving process are ignored.

Task Interdependence. AMT increases task interdependence if two or more workers are responsible for the same machine or for two or more machines that are integrated or clustered into manufacturing cells. If one machine goes down, so may all the others. The workers may need to share information about the system as a whole, even if action has to be taken on only one particular machine. Such sharing of information may be necessary under the crisis conditions of machine downtime, but it also may be necessary under steady-state conditions, when workers are solving problems in order to improve performance continuously. In the latter case, task interdependence may extend to managers and engineers. Thompson (1967) characterizes interdependence of the type described here as reciprocal. Under reciprocal interdependence, the actions taken by one person may modify the conditions under which any other person in a group takes action.

JIT also increases task interdependence by reducing buffers between any two work stations. In such cases, the interdependence may be reciprocal or sequential (Thompson, 1967). In the latter case, the task assigned to one worker cannot begin until tasks assigned to others have been completed.

Timely Feedback. Preventive, progressive, and dynamic control (Hayes, Wheelwright, and Clark, 1988) require much more timely and complex data than does responsibility for reactive control. IS can collect such data on line. The more relevant question is who has direct access to the data. The types of control that require such data are usually considered to be the exclusive responsibility of managers and engineers.

Zuboff (1988) cites the case of an expense-tracking system in a paper pulp mill. Although the technology is continuous process, the lessons from the case are instructive for discrete manufacturing. Management permitted members of a work group to have direct access to expense data that were generated on line by a new information system. As a result, the work-group members were able to get immediate feedback from actions that they believed would reduce costs. The performance results quickly surpassed expectations. However, the results reached a plateau quickly when middle managers began to use the data to check up on the workers and to blame them when performance varied from preset conditions. The managers also began to take unilateral credit for any improvements in performance. These dynamics were generated because the workers were performing activities for which the managers were still held accountable. The successful use of such data by the work group led the middle managers to doubt the value of their own contributions to the organization. Their doubts were not inappropriate, given that many organizations with autonomous work groups have fewer managerial levels (National Academy of Sciences, 1986).

Choices That Influence the Impact of AMT on Work-Group Boundaries

Clarity of Boundaries. The decision about whether to organize work-group tasks by product or process has a significant impact on work-group boundaries. Manufacturing cells are organized according to similar products or similar product parts. Such cells strengthen work groups' boundaries because the task of the cell is to produce an identifiable product. All the materials, machines, methods, and manpower needed to produce the product are contained within the cell. The interdependence among the resources within the cell is greater than among these resources and other resources outside its boundary.

Management may not choose to use manufacturing cells when the variety of products a plant produces on any day is so high that there are virtually no identifiable families of parts or products to assign to cells. One alternative to cells is the assembly line, which may be used at the extremes; that is, variety is so high that lot sizes are equal to one, or variety is so low that dedicated technology is used.

IBM's typewriter plant in Lexington, Kentucky, produces a large variety of typewriters and printers on seven miles of conveyor belt. No two products are likely to be made in sequence. The work stations are far apart, and there is no evidence that autonomous work groups are a basic organizational unit. A number of workers report to a first-line supervisor, who has a greater amount of responsibility than is typical for managers in similar positions. The individual worker is given a great deal of autonomy, however. The job, rather than the work group, is the unit of choice for autonomy in this setting. IBM calls those who hold these broadened jobs "owner-operators." Such workers have responsibility for setup, trouble-shooting, maintenance, and so on.

Another alternative to using cells is to make an entire shift into one large work group. This can be done only when there are very few workers on the shift. Such is the case at the Saginaw Division of General Motors. The $60 million plant manufactures axles. It employs only fifty-four persons, on two shifts, and will eventually produce on a third, unmanned, shift. Twenty-four persons (twelve semiskilled, eight skilled, and four support personnel) make up the Shift Operations Group. Like IBM, Saginaw produces such a high variety of products that there are virtually no families of products or product parts by which to organize cells. The heterogeneity of background and skills among personnel is so great that it may be difficult to maintain a sense of identity and common purpose among work-group members.

Task Meaningfulness. A work group has a meaningful task when all its members can identify with it and see how their own tasks contribute to it. A meaningful task forms a gestalt in that it is clear which tasks belong to the group and which do not, and who contributes to it and who does not. For example, complex problem solving may motivate and challenge individual workers, but it may undermine task meaningfulness for the work group as a whole if there is no interdependence between types of problems. However, if a large number of nonmembers (that is, managers and engineers) are involved in problem solving, the boundaries of the work group may become unclear.

Task meaningfulness can also decrease if the work group cannot control the task it is expected to perform. MRP can decrease task meaningfulness by reducing a work group's control over when inputs cross the group's boundary, the order in which tasks will be performed, when they will be performed, and when outputs will be delivered. The degree to which MRP reduces a work group's control over these decisions depends on the level of detail to which it schedules production. MRP can plan at the level of the individual job or work station, thus removing virtually all work-group discretion over scheduling within the group's boundaries. MRP can also plan effectively at the work-group level. For example, MRP can make all scheduling decisions concerning inputs and outputs to and from the work-group boundary but allow group members to make all scheduling decisions internal to the group.

Digital Equipment Corporation made the decision to protect autonomous work groups at its plant in Enfield, Connecticut. The plant produces printed circuit-board modules for computer storage systems. Management implemented an MRP using the work group as its smallest unit of analysis and rejected the advice of an MRP consultant to use individual work stations as the unit of analysis. The plant currently develops schedules on a weekly basis and has sufficient capacity to meet these schedules. The plant may face pressures to plan at a greater level of detail if the scheduling interval shortens and plant capacity tightens.

Identity of Inputs and Outputs. AMT may not have much impact on the identifiability of inputs and outputs in discrete manufacturing. In continuous process manufacturing, raw materials and work in process cannot be seen because they are stored in tanks and transported through pipes. Inputs and outputs are likely to remain visible in discrete manufacturing, but there will be less control over when they enter and leave the work group.

Manufacturing cells are likely to increase the identity of outputs, in a psychological sense, because the cells produce a complete product or product part. This should increase the perception among cell workers that they are making a meaningful contribution to the goals of the larger organizational unit that contains the cell. Members of work groups that are organized by process are less likely to have this perception.

Decreased Unit Buffers. Just-in-time manufacturing can have a negative impact on work-group autonomy by reducing time and inventory buffers within and between work groups.

JIT demands that work-in-process inventory be reduced to a minimum. Such reduction alone would not necessarily be negative, but JIT also demands reductions in lead time between order receipts and product delivery. In that way, essential work in process remains on the factory floor for the shortest possible time. The combined demand to reduce time and inventory buffers puts continuous pressure on the organization to locate slack of any kind and remove it. Any activity that does not immediately add value to the product is eliminated. From the JIT perspective, the only activities that add value are those that transform raw material into a finished product in the shortest time possible.

The JIT perspective can have a pernicious effect on work-group autonomy if it does not legitimate work-group activities that add value in ways that cannot be assessed in terms of time and space. For example, work-group members need time for problem solving, to reduce sources of variability and to reduce lead time by eliminating non–value-adding activities. Ironically, the more the group successfully does this, the smaller the required buffers within and between work groups; thus some of the time the group has available to solve problems of this kind, or to balance individual tasks against group tasks, is eliminated (see condition 9).

At the Digital Equipment Corporation plant in Enfield, work-group members have sufficient slack time to hold half-hour meetings daily to discuss work problems and for workers to leave their task assignments to help other workers with problems. There are also enough persons in the group for one worker to fill in for an absent worker, or for a worker who is taking a class to enhance skills. There is also enough slack to permit flexible work schedules, so that workers can make medical appointments or deal with problems concerning their children.

The legitimation of time for personal activities is not based on efficiency but on values concerning how workers should use time during normal working hours. The other activities can be legitimated on efficiency and effectiveness criteria if the activities are valued appropriately and the timeframe for expected results is reasonable. The time used for problem solving has to be considered as valuable as time used to produce the product or monitor production process. The timeframe for expected results from activities has to be days, not minutes.

Conclusions

This chapter ends with some questions that managers and researchers should consider in making choices about how AMT is used. These are choices that can significantly influence conditions that are favorable or unfavorable to work-group autonomy.

How can humans most effectively contribute to AMT settings? The answer provided in this chapter is that the most effective way for humans to contribute in AMT settings is to solve problems. Most of the problems that limit optimal AMT performance cannot be known or solved by system designers before technology is operational. AMT transforms the nature of the contributions that humans make to the production process. AMT automates work and eliminates skills, but it simultaneously "informates" work and increases skills for those who use information to solve problems (Zuboff, 1988). The type of problem solving required must go well beyond that required for reactive control, however. The type of problem solving must be able to achieve the higher forms of control about which Hayes, Wheelwright, and Clark (1988) have written.

Who should carry out the higher forms of problem solving? The answer provided in this chapter is that work group members are capable of carrying out the highest forms of problem solving if they are carefully selected for potential ability, adequately trained, and appropriately rewarded. Managers and engineers cannot perform these higher forms of problem solving by themselves as effectively as they can in partnership with work group members. An important segment of the learning loop is severed when work-group members are left out of problem solving.

What should be the focus of problem solving? As AMT increases in the factory, direct labor as a percentage of total costs shrinks dramatically, yet accounting systems still place undue emphasis on reducing labor costs (Kaplan, 1984). With AMT, material and overhead costs are by far the greatest contributors to total costs. Assigning higher forms of problem solving to work groups, rather than to managers and engineers, may lead to a flatter organization and therefore to lower overhead costs. Workers may be able to lower material costs by finding ways to reduce lead time (a major JIT objective) in other ways than by removing slack from their own activities. For example, work-group members at Digital's Enfield plant significantly reduced lead time by solving problems with engineers, to find ways of reducing the burn-in cycle on printed circuit-board modules.

When is the appropriate time to solve problems? The Japanese try to eliminate all forms of slack from the production process. It appears that they give high priority to encouraging and rewarding workers for offering suggestions, but they expect workers to develop suggestions before or after normal working hours or during time set aside from work— for example, in quality circles. Since American managers are enamored these days with Japanese manufacturing techniques, such as JIT, they ought to think about the consequences of implementing them for the other productivity and QWL innovations that they also value. Unless the time that workers take to solve problems is legitimated and protected, it may be swept away in the relentless effort to eliminate slack from the production process. If that were to happen, then one of the most effective ways in which workers can contribute to AMT settings would be destroyed.

References

Adler, P. S. "New Technologies, New Skills." *California Management Review*, 1986, *29*, 9-28.

Anderson, J. C., and Schroeder, R. G. "Getting Results from Your System." *Business Horizons*, 1984, *27*, 57-64.

Barrett, W. *The Illusion of Technique.* New York: Anchor Press/Doubleday, 1978.

Davis, L. E., and Wacker, G. J. "Job Design." In G. Salvendy (ed.), *Handbook of Human Factors.* New York: Wiley, 1987.

Ellul, J. *The Technological Society.* New York: Vantage Books, 1964.

Ettlie, J. E. *Taking Charge of Manufacturing: How Companies Are Combining Technological and Organizational Innovations to Compete Successfully.* San Francisco: Jossey-Bass, 1988.

Feigenbaum, A. V. *Total Quality Control.* New York: McGraw-Hill, 1961.

Hayes, R. H., Wheelwright, S. C., and Clark, K. B. *Dynamic Man Creating the Learning Organization.* New York: Free Press, 1988.

Imai, M. *Kaizen: The Key to Japan's Competitive Success.* New York: Free Press, 1986.

Kaplan, R. S. "Yesterday's Accounting Undermines Production." *Harvard Business Review,* 1984, *62,* 95–101.

Kiesler, S., Siegel, J., and McGuire, T. W. "Social Psychological Aspects of Computer-Mediated Communication." *American Psychologist,* 1984, *39,* 113–121.

Lawler, E. E., III. *High-Involvement Management. Participative Strategies for Improving Organizational Performance.* San Francisco: Jossey-Bass, 1986.

Majchrzak, A. *The Human Side of Factory Automation: Managerial and Human Resource Strategies for Making Automation Succeed.* San Francisco: Jossey-Bass, 1988.

Miller, J. G. "Living Systems: The Group." *Behavioral Science,* 1965, *10,* 302–398.

National Academy of Sciences. *Human Resource Practices for Implementing Advanced Manufacturing Technology.* Washington, D.C.: National Academy Press, 1986.

Perrow, C. B. "Hospitals: Technology, Structure, Goals." In J. G. March (ed.), *Handbook of Organizations.* Skokie, Ill.: Rand-McNally, 1965.

Ranney, J. M. "Bringing Sociotechnical Systems from the

Factory to the Office." *National Productivity Review*, 1986, 5, 124-133.

Schein, E. H. *Organizational Psychology*. (2nd ed.) Englewood Cliffs, N.J.: Prentice-Hall, 1970.

Schneider, L., Howard, R., and Enispak, F. *Office Automation in a Manufacturing Setting*. Washington, D.C.: Office of Technology Assessment, 1985.

Schonberger, R. J. *Japanese Manufacturing Techniques*. New York: Free Press, 1982.

Suresh, N. C., and Meredith, J. R. "Achieving Factory Automation Through Group Technology Principles." *Journal of Operations Management*, 1985, 5, 151-165.

Thompson, J. *Organizations in Action*. New York: McGraw-Hill, 1967.

Walton, R. E., and Susman, G. I. "People Policies for the New Machines." *Harvard Business Review*, 1987, 65, 98-106.

Zuboff, S. *In the Age of the Smart Machine: The Future of Work and Power*. New York: Basic Books, 1988.

4

✕✕

Technology and Structure: An Organizational-Level Perspective

W. Richard Scott

As dramatized by a recent conference theme of the European Group for Organizational Studies, the relation between technology and organizations may be characterized as a two-edged sword. Thrusting in one direction reveals the impact of a given technology on organizational structure and performance. The counterthrust emphasizes that organizational structures vary in their capacity to appropriate or to generate new technologies. The former treats technology variously as a causal agent, a design element, or at least a constraining force shaping organizational structure. The latter reverses the causal arrows, examining how organizational forms support innovative processes—the creation of new technologies or the early adoption of them. Since, under present time and space constraints, it is not possible for me to do justice to both of these directions—each has spawned much research effort, reflected in a large literature—I will give primary attention

I have received helpful comments on earlier drafts of this chapter from Paul S. Adler, Paul S. Goodman, Leonard H. Lynn, Jerry Ross, and Lee Sproull.

to the first theme: technology's cutting edge as shaping organizational structure. This decision is reluctantly made, since the two questions are clearly related, even though their respective literatures are differentiated and tend to be insulated. Further work should strive to bring them into closer correspondence. A narrow, slim, two-edged blade may prove to be a more effective weapon for attacking our subject than a flat, one-sided broad sword.

My review proceeds in three phases. I begin by surveying developments driven by contingency theory, the dominant approach to technology–structure linkages, noting both recent advances and continuing issues. Next, I examine some attempts to reconceptualize technology–structure relations that entail a radical rethinking of what technologies and structures are and how they interact. Some of these revisions have been proposed by theorists; others are suggested by empirical studies of the new technologies. Finally, I review other efforts to pursue the technology–structure linkage at more macro levels of analysis, with attention shifted from the organizational level to that of the population or the community.

The Dominant Contingency Paradigm

Since the mid 1960s, research on the relation between technology and organizational structure has been dominated by contingency theory. In its most general formulation, the theory emphasizes the interdependence of organizations and their environments (Lawrence and Lorsch, 1967). *Environments* are broadly defined to include size (demand), technology, and, increasingly, political and institutional elements. Prominent from the outset, however, has been an emphasis on technology as a central factor shaping organizational structure (Woodward, 1965; Perrow, 1967; Thompson, 1967).

Definitions of *technology* have tended to be broad rather than narrow; few analysts have restricted the term to its colloquial meaning of hardware (tools, implements, machines). Most also include such artifacts as work procedures and techniques. Others incorporate workers' skills, know-how, and knowledge. Broader definitions also include the characteristics of the objects or materials on which work is performed (both inputs and outputs), and the broadest conceptions encompass the task environment within which the organization operates. From the earliest work up to the present, there remains much definitional diversity. Two features of these varying definitions merit comment.

First, since the scope of the concepts varies so widely, the observed effects can also be expected to exhibit a comparable range. Not surprisingly, there is a positive correlation between the breadth of the definition employed and the magnitude of the effects on structure attributed to technology. It is apparent, for example, that the Aston researchers report weaker effects associated with technology than many other researchers do because they employ a relatively narrow conception—workflow integration—and elect to treat other characteristics of the tasks as aspects of the organization's charter (see Pugh, Hickson, Hinings, and Turner, 1969; Hickson, Pugh, and Pheysey, 1969).

Second, the line between technology and structure is blurred in many of the definitions. Such factors as capital investment in equipment or workers' education and experience can as reasonably be treated as attributes of structure as of technology. The overlapping and interpenetration of our notions of technology and structure have recently become, if anything, even greater. (I discuss these developments in the second section of this chapter.)

There is also variation in the structure of the arguments employed. In practice, contingency theory incorporates two modes of argument, which have been labeled by Fry and Schellenberg (1984) as "congruent" and "contingent" propositions. A congruent proposition posits a simple unconditional association; for example, the more routinized the technology, the more formalized the structure. A contingent proposition specifies a conditional relation between two independent variables and a third dependent variable, usually a performance measure; for example, when technologies are routine and structures are highly formalized, performance will be enhanced. Both types of propositions assume the importance of a fit or match between technology and environment, but the assumption is left implicit in the congruent form. Empirical tests of congruent propositions are much more abundant than are tests of contingent propositions; only rarely do analysts attempt to empirically assess the impact of technology–structure match on performance.

Use of one or the other of these two types of arguments tends to be associated with other important differences. Drazin and Van de Ven (1985) point out that congruent arguments are consistent with a selection approach—whether natural or managerial—that posits that appropriate or matched structures are more likely to be selected or to survive. Contingent propositions are consistent with an interaction approach that explains "variations in organizational performance from the interactions of organizational structure and context" (Drazin and Van de Ven, 1985, p. 517). Donaldson (1985, pp. 139–142) observes that congruent propositions are associated with the work of comparative analysts (such as Pugh or Blau) examining the various determinants of organizational structure, while contingent propositions are characteristic of design theorists (such as Woodward or Lawrence and Lorsch), who are seeking to determine which structured arrangements are most conducive to high performance. (While these differences are clearly important, the broader similarities in general assumptions and in level of analysis are such that I will continue to treat both as parts of contingent theory.)

Adding to the diversity of definitions of technology and modes of argument is the large variety of variables identified to capture one or another aspect of the phenomenon. Many of these variables are operationalized in numerous ways, giving rise to an even larger number of indicators. In an earlier review (Scott, 1975) of the confusing jumble of measures utilized to assess technology, I proposed that most could be accommodated within a typology in which Hickson, Pugh, and Pheysey's (1969) distinctions among approaches focusing on materials, operations, or knowledge aspects of technology were cross-classified by the stage of processing emphasized—

input, throughout, or output phases. The table accompanying that review provides specific measures illustrating each of the nine types of variables. Measures employed also vary by whether subjective (based on the perceptions of participants) or objective (based on assessments by the researcher or other experts) judgments are employed.

In spite of this diversity, there has been considerable consensus among contingency theorists on which aspects or dimensions of technology are most significant for predicting structural arrangements. Building on the work of Woodward (1965), Perrow (1967, 1970) and Thompson (1967), most analysts have emphasized the significance of the following three types of variables: *complexity* or *diversity*, referring to the number of different items that must be dealt with at any given time by the organization; *uncertainty* or *unpredictability*, referring to the variability exhibited by materials and/or work procedures or to the extent to which it is possible to predict what problems are to be encountered or what procedures are to be carried out; and *interdependence*, referring to the extent to which the items or elements involved or the work processes themselves are interrelated, so that changes in the state of one element affect the state of the others (Scott, 1987, pp. 212-214).

In one of the most influential contributions to the contingency literature, Galbraith (1973, 1977) points out that these three variables—complexity (or size), uncertainty, and interdependence—all tap a single, deeper underlying dimension: they all pose increasing information-processing demands on the structure if the work is to be accurately and adequately performed. The greater the diversity, uncertainty, and interdependence associated with performing a given type of work, the larger the amount of information that must be processed by those attempting to successfully carry out the work. Organizational structure, in turn, is viewed as a set of mechanisms for processing information—for subduing it, summarizing it, and simplifying it. Assuming the existence of incentives to match information-processing demands with appropriate structural mechanisms, propositions of the following type result (see Scott, 1987, pp. 214-215):

1. The greater the technical complexity, the greater the structural complexity—differentiation of structure by function, level, or location.
2. The greater the technical uncertainty, the lower the formalization and centralization of decision making.
3. The greater the technical interdependence, the more resources must be devoted to coordination mechanisms—rules, schedules, and line and staff officials.

A considerable number of empirical studies have been carried out over the past twenty years to assess these and similar propositions. While many of these studies have been conducted at the level of the individual worker or job, or at the work-group level, I focus here primarily on studies pertaining to the organization as a whole. There have been a number of studies at this level, and it is important to assess the accumulated evidence; but, for reasons to be discussed, I do not believe that this is the optimal level at which to assess technology–structure relations. Such studies entail, of necessity, assessing the character of the technology and of the structure of two or more organizations. Most of these studies have utilized a cross-sectional design and have employed the statistical techniques of regression or partial correlation. The measures of organizational structure—for example, formalization, differentiation, and centralization—focus on the organization's formal aspects and usually rely on indicators that are based on written documents (organizational manuals, job descriptions, charts) or on the reports of key (typically, managerial) informants (see Gerwin, 1981).

The studies conducted vary considerably in terms of breadth or diversity in the types of organizations sampled. Numerous studies have focused on organizations within the same or similar industries (for example, Blau and Schoenherr, 1971; Blau, 1973; Corwin, 1972; Hage and Aiken, 1969; Heydebrand, 1973; Holdaway, Newberry, Hickson, and Heron, 1975; Meyer, 1979). Others have included a broader range of firms but limited their samples to the manufacturing sectors (for example, Blau, Falbe, McKinley, and Tracy, 1976; Hinings and Lee, 1971; Khandwalla, 1974). Still others have attempted to encompass the broad range of employing organizations, including both service and manufacturing sectors and public and private firms (for example, the Aston studies—see Pugh, Hickson, Hinings, and Turner, 1969; Hickson, Pugh, and Pheysey, 1969; Child and Mansfield, 1972; Zwerman, 1970). As a basis for testing technology–structure relations, the first sampling strategy is problematic in that the range of technological variation is necessarily somewhat restricted, with the result that other, less constrained variables, such as size, tend to account for much of the observed variance in structural form (see Scott, 1987, pp. 247-248). The third strategy suffers from the difficulty that many measures of technology are highly correlated with the distinction between service and manufacturing, making it hard to separate out the independent effects of technology (see Aldrich, 1972; Gerwin, 1981). The middle strategy—the "Goldilocks" version, which includes diverse, but not too diverse, types of organizations—appears better suited to examining technology–structure relations.

The cumulative results of the research to date remain in dispute. Two recent surveys of findings draw differing conclusions. Gerwin (1981) reviewed empirical studies at both the job and the organizational levels, assembling the relevant results by variable in a series of tables and, in some cases, recalculating the analyses to render them more comparable. He reports finding more confirmation for the predictions at the job level than at the organization level. On the basis of a review of five studies at the job level, Gerwin (1981, pp. 12-13) concludes, "Overall, the results . . . make a plausible case for structural and technical covariation. Within each of the four structural categories—complexity, formalization, centralization, and configuration—almost all of the correlations are significant and all are in the same direction. Magnitudes are not particularly large, but neither are they small. . . . It appears that as technology becomes more routine, the qualifications of line personnel decrease, rule following becomes more prevalent and employee participation in decision making diminishes." By contrast, reviewing the results of ten studies conducted at the organizational level leads Gerwin (1981, pp. 23-24) to conclude, "There are some relationships between structural and technological characteristics at the organizational level, but not particularly strong ones. As technology becomes more explicit [routinized, automated] in manufacturing, the number of staff specialists increases, overall formalization and formalization of personnel procedures increases, a chief executive's span of control increases, and the subordinate ratio first increases and then decreases. Explicitness is positively related to vertical span in three different types of organizations. . . . However, almost all of these patterns are adversely affected when size is controlled. Other results involving explicitness and variety are either inconsistent or depend on too few data."

Different and more favorable conclusions are reached by Fry (1982), who reviewed forty-eight empirical studies of technology and structure conducted between 1965 and 1980. Fry's primary objective was to determine whether the empirical results reported were influenced by differences in level of analysis, by choice of technology variables, or by the use of subjective versus objective measures. His meta-analysis suggests that studies conducted at the organizational or the subgroup levels—but not at the individual level—revealed a relatively consistent pattern of results supportive of contingency theory's predictions. (This conclusion strongly differs from that reached by Gerwin. However, as Fry notes, most of the findings he summarized at the individual level were drawn from a single study.) Results across the varying technological variables were found to be consistent, with the exception of the Aston measures, which were argued to tap a different dimension of technology. Finally, contrary to earlier results reported by Pennings (1973), the use of objective versus subjective measures was not found to affect the pattern of findings. Fry (1982, pp. 542-546) concludes, "Once the effects of the Aston research and individual-level studies are removed from the body of results in this area . . . there is little doubt that empirical support for technology–structure relationships exists." Specifically, Fry reports that when studies conducted at the individual level and those employing the Aston measures were removed, 69 percent of the relations between technology and structure were in the predicted direction and were statistically significant.

It is interesting that some of the most recent studies of technology and structure have extended the sample of organizations studied to include non-Western forms—in particular, Japanese firms. A study by Marsh and Mannari (1981) of fifty manufacturing establishments in Japan found strong support for the association of technology variables with types of labor input, span of control, and formalization. A study conducted by Lincoln, Hanada and McBride (1986), comparing fifty-five United States and Japanese manufacturing plants, reports that technology was associated, as expected, with specialization, span of control, and formalization. The major relationship distinguishing Japanese from Western firms was the one between technology and centralization: U.S. firms characterized by large-batch production exhibited higher levels of centralization as compared with firms engaged in process or customized production, but this pattern was not found among Japanese firms. Thus, although there is evidence of some important cultural or institutional variations, the results of these studies also provide considerable support for technological contingency-theory arguments.

My own conclusion is that, given the many types of problems cited (multiple conceptions, variables, indicators, samples), the results of empirical studies conducted up to the present provide evidence for linkages among technology and organizational structure. The evidence is reasonably consistent but not particularly strong. Note that these empirical relations rest on studies conducted within both a congruence and a contingent framework and so are consistent with either a selection or an adaptation perspective. My summary judgment implies two further conclusions. First, the work to date has not been useless and does not deserve to be dismissed, as some critics have suggested. For example, Carroll (1988, p. 1) has proclaimed, "Intellectually speaking, contingency theory is dead," and Barley (1986, p. 78) ends his review of the empirical literature on technology and structure with the recommendation that we "embrace the contradictory evidence as a replicated finding." These conclusions appear to me to be premature and overstated. Second, there nevertheless remains much room for improvement in our understanding of technology–structure relations. Several avenues have been proposed along which to seek improved models. These include attempts to *modify* and incrementally improve the contingency formulation at the organizational level, attempts to *loosen* the relation between technology and structure, and attempts to *bound* or *conditionalize* the contingency formulation. I shall briefly consider examples of each proposal.

Modifying Contingency Arguments. Many contemporary analysts continue to embrace the basic contingency formulation that links technology and structure and are currently seeking ways to improve the arguments and strengthen the evidence. An obvious problem is presented by the fact that most organizations employ not one but many technologies. Multiple technologies may be employed in the production departments of firms. For example, having decided to focus on a firm's "dominant" technology, Woodward (1965) had to eliminate twenty of the one hundred firms in her sample because they lacked one dominant technological approach. Similarly, Marsh and Mannari (1981), employing a category scheme of five types of technologies, reported that only twenty-seven of the fifty Japanese factories used only one type, while ten employed three or more. Of course, most firms contain departments other than production (marketing, personnel, finance, research and development), and each of these utilizes one or more distinctive technologies. It is clearly wrong to assume that an organization has only one or even a dominant technology, although this assumption is more realistic for small organizations than for larger ones (see Aldrich, 1972).

It also seems mistaken to attempt to aggregate into a single score measures derived from assessing multiple, specific technologies. For example, the Aston group's measure of workflow integration is based on scores obtained from combining assessments of numerous pieces of equipment and technical processes, as is the Amber and Amber (1962) automation scale. Khandwalla (1974) attempts to take into account the differential importance or prevalence of varying technologies within an organization by utilizing a weighting approach, but this technique still does not address the fundamental problem. The difficulty, of course, is that such averaging approaches ignore the realities of both technological diversity and structural differentiation—the coexistence within organizations of subunits with varying technologies and structures. For this reason, it is my belief that technology-structure arguments are best suited to the subgroup (for example, departmental) level. Most departmental units can be characterized as containing one or at least a dominant technology. Indeed, many organizational theorists posit that departmentalization reflects technological diversity—that departments are structures designed to support and to reflect technological boundaries.

If applications of technology–structure arguments are to be made at the organizational level, I continue to believe that wisdom lies in the direction of respecting their technological and structural diversity, and, as I have previously argued, "Rather than treating the wider organizational structure as some kind of average of the characteristics of its work activities and work units, it would seem more appropriate to treat it as an overarching framework of relations linking subunits of considerable diversity, and to develop measures that capture the distinctive characteristics of this superstructure" (Scott, 1987, p. 226).

A second problem confronting contingency arguments is that most continue to be vague about the form of the relation specified (see Schoonhoven, 1981). Some of the most interesting and consistent findings relate to the nonlinear effects of technology on structure that were first noted by Woodward (1965) (see also Lincoln, Hanada, and McBride, 1986). Woodward observed, for example, that as the extent of complexity

increased from low (batch) through medium (mass) to high
(process production), the span of control exhibited a curvilinear pattern, with narrower spans of control occurring at the
two extremes. Although such curvilinear patterns have been
widely reported for a number of supervisory or control variables (see Lincoln, Hanada, and McBride, 1986), most analyses
continue to apply statistical tests employing assumptions of
linearity. Better-specified theoretical and statistical models are
needed if progress is to be made in accurately mapping the
variety in these relations.

Another limitation of current work on contingency
theory is that most studies examine only one relation at a
time—for example, the relation between uncertainty and formalization—although the theory implies that technologies
and structures consist of multiple-variable, patterned relations. Some progress has been made on this front. Mintzberg
(1979) was among the first to move in this direction, coupling
a series of hypotheses about the congruence between specific
technical and structural factors with a configuration hypothesis "which postulates that effective organizations achieve an
internal consistency among their design parameters" (Mintzberg, 1983, pp. 151-152). Similarly, Miller (1981, p. 3) has proposed that researchers should not be content with ever more
refined measures of single relationships but should instead
"search for different organizational configurations or adaptive
patterns that are richly described by the dynamic interaction
among variables of environment, organization and strategy."
Such configurations or gestalts need to be identified, according to Miller, because they are expected to conditionalize
specific relationships. Taxonomies of technology–structure
configurations are called for as necessary to embed and interpret individual relations. Mintzberg's (1979, 1983) five structural types represent an example of such a taxonomy at the
organizational level, and literature is cited as consistent with
its predictions, but it has not been subjected to direct empirical evaluation.

To my knowledge, the only empirical attempt to evaluate a configurational framework is that conducted by Drazin

and Van de Ven (1985). Their work is sufficiently important to merit comment, even though their units of study were employment security offices, not organizations. In their formulation, they argue that "high-performing units that undertake work at low, medium and high levels of task difficulty and task variability will adopt, respectively, systematized, discretionary and developmental modes of structure and process. Here mode means a logically coherent pattern of structure and process matched to a level of task uncertainty" (Drazin and Van de Ven, 1985, p. 524). Structural variables included specialization, standardization, discretion, and personnel expertise. Process variables focused on coordination mechanisms and included mode of communication and methods of conflict resolution. In all, eleven structural and process measures were assessed, combining data based on responses of individual workers and supervisors in 629 work units. Results of two types of analysis supported the configurational predictions. First, a subset of high-performing units was identified under each of the three task conditions. Most of their mean structure and process scores were found to differ significantly from each other and to exhibit the predicted mode. Second, the three profiles of scores displayed by the high-performing units were then treated as "ideal" patterns, and the discrepancy between the scores of these units and other units performing less well was calculated. As predicted, results indicated that the greater the distance from the respective "ideal" type for each unit, the lower the performance of that unit.

We should not conclude anything from a single study—other than, perhaps, that configurational approaches, albeit difficult to formulate and evaluate, appear to be promising. I look forward with interest to the replication of this type of approach.

Loosening Contingency Arguments. A number of recent investigators have suggested the value of recognizing that the technology–structure linkage need not imply a single, determinant relation. They urge acknowledgment of the possibility of equifinality—the existence of more than one appropriate structural form or mechanism in relation to a given technological process (see Miller, 1981; Drazin and Van de Ven, 1985). In more modern terminology, structure and technology may be *loosely coupled.* To use older language, there may be functional equivalence among several structural forms, so that they are in effect interchangeable. It has been suggested, for example, that increasing uncertainty may be handled either by increased delegation of decision making to individual performers or by increased hierarchical and lateral channels to supply necessary information to specialist performers (see Scott, 1987, p. 236). Some of the weaknesses in existing evidence concerning technology–structure relations may be due to our overly narrow conception of the necessity for a one-to-one correspondence: one technology, one and only one structural form. While this assumption appears questionable, it is incumbent on those advocating this direction to explicitly spell out the family of forms that are to be equated or the criteria to be employed in making such judgments. To date, this work has not been pursued in any systematic fashion.

Bounding Contingency Arguments. Recent work by institutional theorists suggests the possibility of restricting or bounding technology–structure arguments. In one version of this approach, which my colleague John Meyer and I have pursued, it is argued that "many organizations cannot usefully be viewed as technical systems" and that "no organization is merely a technical system" (Meyer and Scott, 1983, p. 13). We emphasize, rather, that organizations are also shaped by their institutional environments—by the wider rules and regulations, belief systems, and legal frameworks that surround, support, and constrain organizational forms. From one point of view, these arguments may appear to contradict or at least compete with technological theories. I prefer to believe, however, that they help to better define these theories by identifying important contextualizing factors that can operate to reduce or constrain technological effects. The institutional approach does not deny the operation of technical influences but sees them as more influential for some types of organizations than for others and as always operating within and being partially shaped by a wider context of institutional arrangements. The latter argument implies that similar technologies can have varying structural effects, depending on the institutional context.

Reconceptualizing Technology–Structure Relationships

During the past decade, a variety of analysts have expressed numerous criticisms of the dominant contingency paradigm. There is much diversity among these critics. Some, including the sort just reviewed, are reformist in orientation, seeking to broaden and deepen the contingency framework; others are more revolutionary in their aims and look to overturning or displacing the dominant paradigm. While there is no clear-cut division among these camps, I turn now to focus the concerns of a set of theorists who are seeking relatively fundamental changes. Their diversity is such that it is not possible at this time to discern a clear alternative model that is being proposed. What is apparent, however, is that these theorists are not calling for minor revisions but for a major rethinking of the technology–structure relation.

At the same time, a number of empirical studies dealing with the new technologies have appeared. These largely descriptive accounts have only just begun to find their way into the mainstream organizational literature, but they clearly pose a set of challenges to previous approaches and understandings. Taken together, the newer theories and empirical accounts raise questions about the concept of technology, the concept of structure, and the relation between technology and structure.

Rethinking Technology. A common thread that runs through the new critical work is that technology is indeterminant or at least much less determinant than it is portrayed in the conventional contingency literature. Thus, Noble (1984, p. xi) argues, "Because of its very concreteness, people tend to confront technology as an irreducible brute fact, a given, a first cause, rather than as hardened history, frozen fragments of human and social endeavor. In short, the appearance here of automaticity and necessity, though plausible and thus ideologically compelling, is false, a product, ultimately, of our own naivete and ignorance. For the process of technological development is essentially social, and thus there is always a large measure of indeterminancy, of freedom, within it. Beyond the very real constraints of energy and matter exists a realm in which human thoughts and actions remain decisive. Therefore, technology does not necessitate. It merely consists of an evolving range of possibilities from which people choose." In this view, technology is socially shaped, containing not only materialist but also social determinants. Davis and Taylor (1976, p. 380) argue that social choices are "contained within the technological design" itself, pointing out, "It is well known that of the many technological alternatives considered in any instance, technical systems planners put forth only one as a solution. . . . Technical systems designs incorporate social system choices, either made intentionally or included accidentally, either casually or as a result of some omission in planning. In this sense, engineers or technologists can be called social system engineers."

Pursuing a similar argument, Perrow (1983, pp. 533–534) concludes, "The design of [technological] systems, and the equipment that is used, is not entirely determined by technical or engineering criteria; designers have significant choices available to them that will foster some types of social structures and operator behaviors rather than others."

In order to demonstrate this argument, a number of recent social analysts have attempted to document how social and political factors influence what types of technologies are developed and adopted. Thus, Noble (1984) argues that numerical-control approaches (NC) won out over record-playback approaches to the design of automatically controlled machine tools because they located control in the hands of programmers and managers rather than among machine operators on the shop floor and so better served the interests of a number of powerful groups, including the U.S. Air Force, aerospace contractors, and the engineering community. As summarized by Powell (1987, p. 191), "The NC model was a realization of the common interests of the scientific, military, and industrial elites, who shared a general disregard for and distrust of workers' skills and a fascination with formal, abstract, complex solutions that eliminated any chance of human error."

From these newer perspectives, in sum, technology is not only strongly shaped by social and political processes but also embodies crucial social assumptions in the so-called technical system.

A related change that characterizes much of the recent literature is the increased emphasis on subjective versus objective views of technology. The early, influential work of Woodward, Perrow, and Thompson treated technology as objective—as empirically measurable features of the work process (for example, the uniformity of inputs encountered or the automaticity of machinery employed). More recent views have given priority to the definitions or interpretations of participants. For example, Dornbusch and I (Dornbusch and Scott, 1975) challenged the assumption of consensus that underlies conventional studies of technology—the assumption that all participants, or that analysts and participants, will agree on the characteristics of a given technology.

Weick (this volume, Chapter One) stresses the value of a subjective view of technology but too quickly assumes that this entails a micro orientation, emphasizing the importance and variability of individual perceptions. By contrast, Dornbusch and I, in developing the notion of task conception, stress a more macro perspective: "Task conceptions are the ways that certain categories or groups of organizational participants view the attributes of their tasks. The term *conception* was chosen as representing a compromise between the notion of task characteristic, which sounds too objective, and the notion of task perception, which places too much emphasis on differences among individual participants. We expect task conceptions to vary as a function of such factors as the current state of technical knowledge, the reference groups used by participants, and the organizational location of par-

ticipants" (Dornbusch and Scott, 1975, p. 79). In our own
analysis, we particularly stressed differences in the determinants and consequences of the task conceptions of administrators and managers versus those of task performers (see also
Scott, 1972). A more macro approach to task conceptions is
also consistent with and reinforced by the recent work of institutional theorists who stress the extraorganizational sources
of cognitive frames and shared definitions of social reality
(see, for example, Meyer and Rowan, 1977; Brown, 1978;
Scott, forthcoming).

Turning attention to the empirical accounts of the new
technologies, what changes, if any, are required in earlier
attempts to isolate the most salient features of technology?
My own incomplete reading of these descriptions suggests
that conclusions such as those reached by Susman and Chase
(1986, p. 257), to the effect that recent innovations in technology and manufacturing methods found in the integrated factory are "radically new," are overstated. Susman and Chase
themselves conclude that the new technologies enable companies that formerly utilized small-batch processing techniques
to move in the direction of continuous process technologies,
with appropriate modifications required in their structures.
In short, the newness entailed does not appear to be of the
sort that requires the introduction of new additional dimensions in our conceptions of technology, but only the reclassi-
fication of selected organizations along existing dimensions.

Similarly, Weick's (this volume, Chapter One) concerns
that existing concepts cannot accommodate significant qualities of newer technologies seem unfounded. His candidates—
stochastic events, continuous events, and mental workload—
appear to be readily incorporated under the dimensions of
uncertainty and complexity. However, the accompanying discussion does suggest the value of developing additional and
more sensitive indicators than are available at present to assess
degrees and types of uncertainty, complexity, and so on.

In general, however, the empirical descriptions of the
new technologies appear to have stronger relevance to current
conceptualizations of structure and of technology–structure

relations than to technology per se. These issues are considered in the next two sections.

Rethinking Structure. Whereas contingency theory views organizational structure as framework or form or configuration—as a static system of normative and/or behavioral relations—an alternative conception began to arise in the 1970s, viewing structure as process. Contributing to this revised conception have been organizational psychologists, such as Weick (1969), who has insisted that it is more useful to speak of organizing than of organization, as well as action theorists, such as Silverman (1971), and symbolic interactionists, such as Goffman (1983) and Strauss (1978). These theorists variously propose that structures are more accurately conceived as interlocked behaviors, as patterned actions that must be continuously produced and reproduced, or as negotiated orders constantly undergoing revision and renegotiation, rather than as stable forms.

Giddens (1979, 1984) has attempted to reconcile the conception of structure as form and structure as process by proposing that structure be viewed as a duality: that action is both "constituted by" and "constitutive of" social organization; "that the structural properties of social systems are both the medium and the outcome of practices that constitute those systems" (Giddens, 1979, p. 69). From Giddens's perspective, although one can emphasize one or the other aspect of the dual reality (action defining structures or structures constraining actions) of greatest importance is the interplay between the two. As amplified by Barley (1986, p. 80), "Through this interplay, called the process of structuring [Giddens employs the term *structuration*], institutional practices shape human actions which, in turn, reaffirm or modify the institutional structure. Thus, the study of structuring involves investigating how the institutional realm and the realm of action configure each other."

The shift from structure to structuring, or structuration, commits the analyst to a longitudinal approach: whether one is accounting for change or for stability, it requires studying the system over time (see Ranson, Hinings, and Greenwood, 1980). Indeed, from Giddens's perspective, one of the most neglected aspects of social organization is the study of temporal order (see also Barley, forthcoming).

On close examination, many of the recent descriptive studies of the new technologies are as much (if not more) concerned with changes in structural forms as with technologies per se. Such innovations as just-in-time (JIT) manufacturing, although dependent on the support of computers for rapid information transfer, entail dramatic increases in interdependence by the relatively simple expedient of doing away with or at least significantly reducing organizational slack in the form of excess inventories. Similarly, design for producibility and production for marketability represent a reduction in buffering mechanisms, as sequential arrangements are exchanged for reciprocal interdependence between, respectively, manufacturing/design and manufacturing/marketing units. These examples underline the importance of the realization that the level of interdependence is determined not only by the state of the technology but also by the nature of the structure—for example, by how extensive the division of labor is (see Scott, 1987, p. 230).

The level of uncertainty encountered is not just a function of technology. Susman and Chase (1986, p. 263) call attention to "boundary transaction uncertainty" and point out that increased responsiveness to customer demands—production for marketability—entails increased uncertainty "over what to produce and when to produce it."

In short, many of the organizational innovations chronicled in the recent literature on new technologies appear on close inspection to represent primarily structural rather than (or in addition to) technological changes.

Rethinking Technology-Structure Relations. Just as the new views emphasize that there are important social choices built into technologies, it is also argued that there are important "social choices contained within the organization design undertaken to use the technology" (Davis and Taylor, 1976,

p. 380). Technologies, once selected, do not necessitate a given social structure but allow a range of possible structures. Choice is possible. This is emphasized in all three types of empirical literature that have developed around this perspective: sociotechnical design studies, historical studies, and case studies of technological change. Note that all three types utilize a longitudinal approach.

Design studies, particularly those stemming from the sociotechnical perspective, would make no sense under an assumption of technological determinism. Regardless of whether the attempt is to design more efficient or more humanized work organizations, the assumption is made that choices are available and that some possible ways of organizing are superior to others (see Galbraith, 1973). Systems design is itself viewed as a process, usually an iterative one, in which work structures and work activities and equipment are designed and redesigned and their effects, both predicted and unexpected, are noted. Design usually proceeds from the bottom up—from tasks and work groups to larger, administrative structures, although it is recognized that the broader structures must be supportive if local changes are to persist (see Jaques, 1951; Miller and Rice, 1967; Trist, 1981). Historical studies, such as those conducted by Hounshell (1984) and Noble (1984), can focus on either relatively narrow and specific or on broader and more general technological change. In either case, it is typical of these new technological histories to emphasize the diversity and unevenness of change—to reject what Sabel (1982, p. 5) labels the assumption of "essentialism," which holds that "what is true for society as a whole is true of each of its parts." An important concern in all of these histories is to uncover "roads not taken" (Noble, 1984)—to document alternative technical solutions and/or organizational arrangements that developed but did not become dominant. Most of these accounts also emphasize the role played by organizational politics, by vested interests, and by institutional arrangements in the shaping and selecting of technologies and in the designing of structures. Indeed, Davis and Taylor (1976, p. 412) argue that much of the consistency that has been observed in technology-structure relations reflects "the assumptions held by the designers of the technological systems about men and social systems" rather than any technological imperative. Detailed case studies of technical change within organizational settings have become a growth industry within recent years. One source of stimulation is the rapid technological changes now occurring in the white-collar realms; not only clerical but also managerial and professional work has been significantly affected. A second important stimulus has been provided by Braverman's (1974) provocative application of Marxist theory to the labor process, in which he argues that industrialization under the capitalist system has resulted in significant deskilling as the basis for continuing managerial control. I will not attempt to review this burgeoning literature but will only note that it is characterized by detailed studies of technological and structural changes occurring in diverse settings, with much attention given to the play of power—among workers as well as among managers—and the importance of context. The studies reveal that skilling and deskilling processes alike vary over occupations, industries, and situations. Results support the general thesis that technologies developed in cooperation with their users are more readily accepted and typically result in enhanced skills and discretion; those guided more by managerial interests are more likely to meet workers' resistance and to result in deskilling and more centralized controls (for reviews, see Attewell, 1987; Form, 1987).

Reflecting on data collected in field investigations of three plants utilizing advanced forms of information technology, Zuboff (1985, p. 105) suggests a distinction that helps to explain why the new technologies have variable effects on structure. Zuboff notes that the technology "can be applied in order to *automate* operations. For example, a numerically controlled machine tool will operate by computerized instructions without the physical intervention of an operator. . . . In its second function, the technology creates information. [It has the] capacity to *informate* the production process. That is, the intelligence of the microprocessor that resides at the base of virtually every application not only applies instructions to equipment but can convert the current state of product or process into information."

Recalling Galbraith's insight that technologies affect structures by determining how much information must be processed during the task sequence, it is possible to see that some aspects of new technologies absorb information: such technologies as automation eliminate the need for the information-processing capacities of structures. By contrast, other aspects of the new technologies generate or create new information: they are able to render "transparent activities that had been either partially or completely opaque" (Zuboff, 1985, p. 104). Depending on which of these effects is emphasized in a given situation, the "same" technology can be expected to have completely different structural ramifications.

A recent study by Barley (1986) exemplifies many aspects of the challenging paradigm. He conducted detailed observations of changes occurring in the social order of two radiology departments at the time when computer tomography (CAT) scanners were introduced. For Barley, the technology introduced is far from determinant and is conceived only as "an occasion" for structuring: "the scanners occasioned change because they became social objects whose meanings were defined by the context of their use" (Barley, 1986, p. 106). His object was to document how the interaction patterns exhibited by radiologists and technicians changed over time by isolating "scripts" that defined identifiable sequences in the changing order. Because of differences in the surrounding contexts, the varying expertise of personnel, and the specific course of interactions, identical technologies gave rise to different structural outcomes. Although "each department changed in similar directions, one department became far more decentralized" (Barley, 1986, p. 105).

In my view, these new conceptions and associated studies provide a useful corrective to those contingency theorists who have embraced an overly materialistic view of technology, have overstated the constraints placed by technology on structure, or have overlooked the dynamic properties of organizational structure. These conceptions also appropriately emphasize the importance of political, ideological, cultural, and institutional factors in shaping these relations. The associated studies go far toward explaining why comparative, cross-sectional studies report, at best, modest associations between technology and structure. Finally, a major contribution from the newer approaches is their emphasis on reverse causality—social structure at various levels—societal, sectoral, organizational, subgroup—influencing technology.

While these are clearly important contributions, there are also deficiencies in the newer work. I believe that many of its practitioners fail to acknowledge the existence of some consistent, albeit small, regularities in technology-structure relations. The existing evidence is inappropriately dismissed (see, for example, Barley, 1986). While it is important to recognize and emphasize diversity and variance, it is equally important to discern general features and consistent relationships. It is also essential to recognize that contingency theory is not a single theory but encompasses a rather diverse range of views. Many versions of contingency theory make allowances for the operation of nonrational factors; many of the arguments tested do not rest exclusively on a rational system framework. Finally, the newer work overstates the process aspects of organizational structure to the same extent that the earlier work overstates the formal aspects. In this sense, the two literatures are better viewed as complementary—the latter supplementing but not supplanting the former.

Higher Levels of Analysis

The recent decade has witnessed another important type of change in efforts directed toward understanding the relation between technology and organizational structure. These approaches vary from the earlier work primarily in the level of analysis at which the relation is approached. Rather than the individual organization being treated as the unit of analysis, attention shifts to the population level or to an examination of the structure of the organizational "community" or "field." I shall now briefly examine examples of work of each type.

Organizational Population Studies. Students of populations of organizations isolate for analysis all organizations of a similar kind. Attention is directed toward examining the mechanisms by which these forms diversify and then selectively persist or die out. A natural-selection model is emphasized, whereby the primary mechanism of change is assumed to be the differential survival of varying types of organizations in response to environmental change (see Hannan and Freeman, 1977; Aldrich, 1979; McKelvey, 1982).

Population ecologists differ from contingency theorists—in particular, from the design group—primarily in their views of the flexibility or adaptability of organizational structure. Individual organizations are viewed as relatively inflexible—as unlikely to embrace new technologies that would require fundamental changes in their structural arrangements. Thus, Nelson and Winter (1982, p. 134) argue, "Efforts to understand the functioning of industries and larger systems should come to grips with the fact that highly flexible adaptation to change is not likely to characterize the behavior of individual firms." Hannan and Freeman (1984, p. 155) concur: "We think it is a reasonable first approximation to think of organizations as possessing relatively fixed repertoires of highly reproducible routines."

Organizations are viewed as exhibiting relatively high levels of structural inertia, and these inertial forces are argued to be strongest among those structures associated with the technical core of the organization (Hannan and Freeman, 1984). Note that this view implies a tight if not rigid connection between technology and structure. Hannan and Freeman have argued that, far from being a defect, the structural inertia of organizations constitutes an important survival mechanism, allowing organizations to achieve high reliability of performance and high levels of accountability—characteristics that are valued under many environmental conditions. Structural inertia is assumed to vary with organizational life cycle and with size, becoming stronger as organizations age and increase in size.

In sum, population ecologists appear to share with contingency theorists the assumption that technologies are an important determinant of organizational structure. If anything, their theoretical models presume an even tighter connection between technology and structure than is posited by many contingency theorists. The relation is so constraining that a given organizational structure is unlikely to embrace or be able to accommodate new technologies. Adaptability is restricted, and adaptation is minimal. As a consequence, ecologists insist that "most organizational change occurring in any historical period is the result of processes of organizational selection and replacement rather than internal transformation and adaptation. Thus, organizational ecology calls for attention to patterns of organizational founding and mortality, the visible outcomes of selection processes" (Carroll, 1988, p. 2).

An important implication of these ecological arguments is that over time the members of an organizational population are likely to become more similar in their technologies and structural features. Competitive processes tend to encourage structural isomorphism. Empirical support for such a process has been provided by Abernathy (1978), as well as by Sahal (1981), who notes that once a branch of industry is established, the core technology on which it is founded tends to remain unchanged. Moreover, there tends to be little transmission of technical know-how among industries, which instead follow what Sahal (1981, p. 57) terms "the principle of technological insularity."

Such arguments and findings have led recent analysts interested in explaining change and diversity to expand the scope of analysis from a focus on single populations to the study of multiple populations, variously defined as organizational communities, industry systems, or fields.

Organizational Community Studies. Theoretical arguments by Astley (1985) and empirical research by Tushman and colleagues (Tushman and Romanelli, 1985; Tushman and Anderson, 1986) support the view that since major technological changes tend to be associated with the creation of new organizational forms, they are better observed at the organizational community or industry level of analysis.

These arguments are based on distinctions first suggested by Abernathy (1978) and by Mensch (1979), who noted that technological innovations tend to be characterized by small, incremental improvements that refine a given technology until there is a sudden breakthrough that represents a quantum leap. Mensch distinguishes between improvement and basic innovations. More graphically, Abernathy and Clark (1985) and Tushman and Anderson (1986) characterize these types as competence-enhancing and competence-destroying technological shifts, since "they either destroy or enhance the competence of existing firms in an industry" (Tushman and Anderson, 1986, p. 442).

In studies of innovations within the minicomputer, cement, and airline industries from their inception until 1980, Tushman and Anderson (1986, p. 444) assemble evidence in support of their predictions: "Competence-enhancing discontinuities tend to consolidate industry leadership: the rich are likely to get richer. Competence-destroying discontinuities, in contrast, disrupt industry structure." Because of structural inertia, basic innovations are unlikely to stem from or be embraced by existing organizations but rather give rise to new organizational forms that challenge and disrupt existing industry structures.

In order to track and explain such developments, a number of analysts have argued that it is necessary to forsake the conventional category of *industry*, which limits attention to competitive firms producing products that are close substitutes for each other and to enlarge our conception to include both the wider system of diverse, interdependent organizations that compete and exchange vital resources and those agents that provide financing, supply legitimacy, exercise regulation, and so on (see Hirsch, 1972, 1985; DiMaggio and Powell, 1983; Scott and Meyer, 1983; Astley, 1985; Van de Ven and Garud, 1987). Although the terminology proposed for this new conceptual category is varied—*industry system, organizational field, societal sector, ecological community, industry social system*—all of these new approaches are in agreement on three fundamentals: the desirability of moving to a higher level of analysis that encompasses diverse types of interrelated organizations; the importance of surveying change processes over relatively longer time periods; and the necessity of attending to institutional arrangements that support and constrain technological processes.

Conclusions

While it is always imprudent to be overly sanguine about recent developments in any arena of social science, it does seem to me that the past two decades of work—both theoretical and empirical—examining the relation of technology and organizational structure do provide evidence of some progress. From the early days, when our comparative results were based on the study of a handful of organizations, we can now examine results based on sizable and diverse samples. After much dissension over variables and measurements, we can now point to some convergence on both, so that it is possible to draw some conclusions about the effects of technical uncertainty and complexity on structural features of organizations, on the basis of thirty or more empirical investigations. Contingency models, broadly defined, continue to provide the dominant theoretical paradigm.

In my view, attempts to radically reformulate our notions of both structure and technology have not so much undermined as supplemented and enriched knowledge based on earlier comparative research. It is helpful to be made aware of the diversity, both in forms and processes, but the evidence from such micro-level studies is not necessarily inconsistent with the broader patterns discerned by the macro-level investigations.

Recent work that shifts attention to organizational populations and communities provides new insights into technology–structure linkages and into the mechanisms of change in these systems. To date, studies of technology development and structural change at this level have been highly revealing and, it is hoped, will stimulate many imitators.

Characteristic of the newer work—both the micro case studies and the investigations of organizational populations and fields—is the transition from cross-sectional to longitudinal approaches. This is clearly a step in the right direction and must be regarded as a welcome indication of the maturation of research in this arena.

References

Abernathy, W. *The Productivity Dilemma.* Baltimore, Md.: Johns Hopkins University Press, 1978.

Abernathy, W., and Clark, K. B. "Innovation: Mapping the Winds of Creative Destruction." *Research Policy,* 1985, *14,* 3–22.

Aldrich, H. E. "Technology and Organizational Structure: A Reexamination of the Findings of the Aston Group." *Administrative Science Quarterly,* 1972, *17,* 26–43.

Aldrich, H. E. *Organizations and Environments.* Englewood Cliffs, N.J.: Prentice-Hall, 1979.

Amber, G. H., and Amber, P. S. *Anatomy of Automation.* Englewood Cliffs, N.J.: Prentice-Hall, 1962.

Astley, G. W. "The Two Ecologies: Population and Community Perspectives on Organizational Evolution." *Administrative Science Quarterly,* 1985, *30,* 224–241.

Attewell, P. "Big Brother and the Sweatshop: Computer Surveillance in the Automated Office." *Sociological Theory,* 1987, *5,* 87–99.

Barley, S. R. "Technology as an Occasion for Structuring: Evidence from Observations of CT Scanners and the Social Order of Radiology Departments." *Administrative Science Quarterly,* 1986, *31,* 78–108.

Barley, S. R. "On Technology, Time and Social Order: Technically Induced Change in the Temporal Organization of Radiological Work." In Frank Dubinskas (ed.), *Making*

Time: Anthropologies of Time in High-Technology Environments. Philadelphia: Temple University Press, forthcoming.

Blau, P. M. *The Organization of Academic Work.* New York: Wiley, 1973.

Blau, P. M., Falbe, C. M., McKinley, W., and Tracy, P. K. "Technology and Organization in Manufacturing." *Administrative Science Quarterly,* 1976, *21,* 20-40.

Blau, P. M., and Schoenherr, R. A. *The Structure of Organizations.* New York: Basic Books, 1971.

Braverman, H. *Labor and Monopoly Capital.* New York: Monthly Review Press, 1974.

Brown, R. H. "Bureaucracy as Praxis: Toward a Political Phenomenology of Formal Organizations." *Administrative Science Quarterly,* 1978, *23,* 365-382.

Carroll, G. R. "Organizational Ecology in Theoretical Perspective." In G. R. Carroll (ed.), *Ecological Models of Organizations.* Cambridge, Mass.: Ballinger, 1988.

Child, J., and Mansfield, R. "Technology, Size, and Organization Structure." *Sociology,* 1972, *6,* 369-393.

Corwin, R. G. "Strategies for Organizational Innovation: An Empirical Comparison." *American Sociological Review,* 1972, *37,* 441-454.

Davis, L. E., and Taylor, J. C. "Technology, Organization, and Job Structure." In R. Dubin (ed.), *Handbook of Work, Organization, and Society.* Skokie, Ill.: Rand-McNally, 1976.

DiMaggio, P. J., and Powell, W. W. "The Iron Cage Revisited: Institutional Isomorphism and Collective Rationality in Organizational Fields." *American Sociological Review,* 1983, *48,* 147-160.

Donaldson, L. *In Defence of Organization Theory.* Cambridge, England: Cambridge University Press, 1985.

Dornbusch, S. M., and Scott, W. R. *Evaluation and the Exercise of Authority.* San Francisco: Jossey-Bass, 1975.

Drazin, R., and Van de Ven, A. H. "Alternative Forms of Fit in Contingency Theory." *Administrative Science Quarterly,* 1985, *30,* 514-539.

Form, W. "On the Degradation of Skills." *Annual Review of Sociology,* 1987, *13,* 29-47.

Fry, L. W. "Technology-Structure Research: Three Critical Issues." *Academy of Management Journal*, 1982, *25*, 532–552.

Fry, L. W., and Schellenberg, D. "Congruence, Contingency, and Theory Building: An Integrative Perspective." Unpublished manuscript, University of Washington, 1984.

Galbraith, J. *Designing Complex Organizations.* Reading, Mass.: Addison-Wesley, 1973.

Galbraith, J. *Organization Design.* Reading, Mass.: Addison-Wesley, 1977.

Gerwin, D. "Relationships Between Structure and Technology." In P. Nystrom and W. Starbuck (eds.), *Handbook of Organizational Design.* Cambridge, England: Cambridge University Press, 1981.

Giddens, A. *Central Problems in Social Theory.* Berkeley: University of California Press, 1979.

Giddens, A. *The Constitution of Society.* Berkeley: University of California Press, 1984.

Goffman, E. "The Interaction Order." *American Sociological Review*, 1983, *48*, 1–17.

Hage, J., and Aiken, M. "Routine Technology, Social Structure, and Organization Goals." *Administrative Science Quarterly*, 1969, *14*, 279–290.

Hannan, M. T., and Freeman, J. "The Population Ecology of Organizations." *American Journal of Sociology*, 1977, *82*, 929–964.

Hannan, M. T., and Freeman, J. "Structural Inertia and Organizational Change." *American Sociological Review*, 1984, *49*, 149–164.

Heydebrand, W. *Hospital Bureaucracy.* New York: Dunellen, 1973.

Hickson, D. J., Pugh, D. S., and Pheysey, D. C. "Operations Technology and Organization Structure: An Empirical Reappraisal." *Administrative Science Quarterly*, 1969, *14*, 378–397.

Hinings, C. R., and Lee, G. L. "Dimensions of Organization Structure and Their Context: A Replication." *Sociology*, 1971, *5*, 83–93.

Hirsch, P. M. "Processing Fads and Fashions: An Organization-Set Analysis of Cultural Industry Systems." *American Journal of Sociology*, 1972, *77*, 639-659.

Hirsch, P. M. "The Study of Industries." In S. B. Bacharach and S. M. Mitchell (eds.), *Research in the Sociology of Organizations*. Vol. 4. Greenwich, Conn.: JAI Press, 1985.

Holdaway, E. A., Newberry, J. F., Hickson, D. J., and Heron, R. P. "Dimensions of Organizations in Complex Societies: The Educational Sector." *Administrative Science Quarterly*, 1975, *20*, 37-58.

Hounshell, D. A. *From the American System to Mass Production, 1800-1932: The Development of Manufacturing Technology in the United States*. Baltimore, Md.: Johns Hopkins University Press, 1984.

Jaques, E. *The Changing Culture of a Factory*. London: Tavistock, 1951.

Khandwalla, P. N. "Mass-Output Orientation of Operations Technology and Organizational Structure." *Administrative Science Quarterly*, 1974, *19*, 74-97.

Lawrence, P. R., and Lorsch, J. W. *Organization and Environment: Managing Differentiation and Integration*. Boston: Graduate School of Business Administration, Harvard University, 1967.

Lincoln, J. R., Hanada, M., and McBride, K. "Organizational Structures in Japanese and U.S. Manufacturing." *Administrative Science Quarterly*, 1986, *31*, 338-364.

McKelvey, B. *Organizational Systematics*. Berkeley: University of California Press, 1982.

Marsh, R. M., and Mannari, H. "Technology and Size as Determinants of the Organizational Structure of Japanese Factories." *Administrative Science Quarterly*, 1981, *26*, 33-57.

Mensch, G. *Stalemate in Technology: Innovations Overcome the Depression*. Cambridge, Mass.: Ballinger, 1979.

Meyer, J. W., and Rowan, B. "Institutionalized Organizations: Formal Structure as Myth and Ceremony." *American Journal of Sociology*, 1977, *83*, 340-363.

Meyer, J. W., and Scott, W. R. *Organizational Environments: Ritual and Rationality*. Newbury Park, Calif.: Sage, 1983.

Meyer, M. W. *Change in Public Bureaucracies.* Cambridge, England: Cambridge University Press, 1979.

Miller, D. "Toward a New Contingency Approach." *Journal of Management Studies,* 1981, *18,* 1-26.

Miller, E. J., and Rice, A. K. *Systems of Organization.* London: Tavistock, 1967.

Mintzberg, H. *The Structure of Organizations.* Englewood Cliffs, N.J.: Prentice-Hall, 1979.

Mintzberg, H. *Structure in Fives: Designing Effective Organizations.* Englewood Cliffs, N.J.: Prentice-Hall, 1983.

Nelson, R. R., and Winter, S. G. *An Evolutionary Theory of Economic Change.* Cambridge, Mass.: Harvard University Press, 1982.

Noble, D. *Forces of Production: A Social History of Industrial Automation.* New York: Knopf, 1984.

Pennings, H. J. "Measures of Organizational Structure: A Methodological Note." *American Journal of Sociology,* 1973, *79,* 686-704.

Perrow, C. "A Framework for the Comparative Analysis of Organizations." *American Sociological Review,* 1967, *32,* 194-208.

Perrow, C. *Organizational Analysis: A Sociological View.* Belmont, Calif.: Wadsworth, 1970.

Perrow, C. "The Organizational Context of Human Factors Engineering." *Administrative Science Quarterly,* 1983, *28,* 521-541.

Powell, W. W. "Review Essay: Explaining Technological Change." *American Journal of Sociology,* 1987, *93,* 185-197.

Pugh, D. S., Hickson, D. J., Hinings, C. R., and Turner, C. "The Context of Organization Structures." *Administrative Science Quarterly,* 1969, *14,* 91-114.

Ranson, S., Hinings, B., and Greenwood, R. "The Structuring of Organizational Structures." *Administrative Science Quarterly,* 1980, *25,* 1-17.

Sabel, C. F. *Work and Politics.* New York: Cambridge University Press, 1982.

Sahal, D. *Patterns of Technological Innovation.* Reading, Mass.: Addison-Wesley, 1981.

Schoonhoven, C. B. "Problems with Contingency Theory: Testing Assumptions Hidden Within the Language of Contingency Theory." *Administrative Science Quarterly,* 1981, *26,* 349–377.

Scott, W. R. "Professionals in Hospitals: Technology and the Organization of Work." In B. S. Georgopoulos (ed.), *Organization Research on Health Institutions.* Ann Arbor: Institute for Social Research, University of Michigan, 1972.

Scott, W. R. "Organizational Structure." *Annual Review of Sociology,* 1975, *1,* 1–20.

Scott, W. R. *Organizations: Rational, Natural, and Open Systems.* (2nd ed.) Englewood Cliffs, N.J.: Prentice-Hall, 1987.

Scott, W. R. "Symbols and Organizations: From Barnard to the Institutionalists." In O. E. Williamson (ed.), *Organizational Theory: From Barnard to the Present and Beyond.* New York: Oxford University Press, forthcoming.

Scott, W. R., and Meyer, J. W. "The Organization of Societal Sectors." In J. W. Meyer and W. R. Scott (eds.), *Organizational Environments: Ritual and Rationality.* Newbury Park, Calif.: Sage, 1983.

Silverman, D. *The Theory of Organizations.* New York: Basic Books, 1971.

Strauss, A. *Negotiations: Varieties, Contexts, Processes, and Social Order.* San Francisco: Jossey-Bass, 1978.

Susman, G. I., and Chase, R. B. "A Sociotechnical Analysis of the Integrated Factory." *Journal of Applied Behavioral Science,* 1986, *22,* 257–270.

Thompson, J. D. *Organizations in Action.* New York: McGraw-Hill, 1967.

Trist, E. L. "The Evolution of Sociotechnical Systems as a Conceptual Framework and as an Action Research Program." In A. H. Van de Ven and W. F. Joyce (eds.), *Perspectives on Organization Design and Behavior.* New York: Wiley, 1981.

Tushman, M. L., and Anderson, P. "Technological Discontinuities and Organizational Environments." *Administrative Science Quarterly,* 1986, *31,* 439–465.

Tushman, M. L., and Romanelli, E. "Organizational Evolution: A Metamorphosis Model of Convergence and Re-orientation." In L. L. Cummings and B. M. Staw (eds.), *Research in Organizational Behavior.* Vol. 7. Greenwich, Conn.: JAI Press, 1985.

Van de Ven, A. H., and Garud, R. *Framework for Understanding the Emergence of New Industries.* Discussion paper no. 66. Strategic Management Research Center, University of Minnesota, 1987.

Weick, K. E. *The Social Psychology of Organizing.* Reading, Mass.: Addison-Wesley, 1969.

Woodward, J. *Industrial Organization: Theory and Practice.* London: Oxford University Press, 1965.

Zuboff, S. "Technologies That Informate: Implications for Human Resource Management in the Computerized Industrial Workplace." In R. E. Walton and P. R. Lawrence (eds.), *Human Resource Management Trends and Challenges.* Boston: Harvard Business School Press, 1985.

Zwerman, W. L. *New Perspectives on Organization Theory.* Westport, Conn.: Greenwood, 1970.

5

✖

Technology, Management, and Competitive Advantage

James G. March
Lee S. Sproull

In the standard theory of technological change, competition is seen as resulting in the survival and growth of organizations able to exploit superior technologies. Environmental demands combine with individual and organizational attributes to generate requirements for competitive success. Technologies that match those needs survive and thrive; technologies that do not match those needs fail. Thus, it is a theory of change that emphasizes competitive advantages and disadvantages associated with using a new technology. In this chapter, we examine this general theory of technological change, using the special case of modern information technology in management.

Information technology includes the machines, artifacts, and procedures used to gather, store, analyze, and disseminate information. Thus, it includes a variety of techniques, including human thought, for making inferences and

This research was supported by grants from the Spencer Foundation, the System Development Foundation, the Stanford Graduate School of Business, and the Stanford Hoover Institution.

manipulating flows of information. For example, for over forty years, from the early 1920s to the late 1960s, DuPont senior executives gathered at least once a month in the Chart Room. The Chart Room represented a primitive form of information technology. It had (Yates, 1985, p. 18) "a ceiling covered with tracks and switches adapted from equipment designed to move heavy bales of hay in barns. From these tracks hung metal frames holding large (30″ × 40″) charts that represented each department's contribution to the elements of a complex return on investment (ROI) formula. The tracks allowed any of the 350 charts in the room to be brought up to the center front position where it could be viewed by the semicircle of DuPont executives making up the Executive Committee (or less frequently, the Finance Committee and the Board of Directors)."

Since the days of the Chart Room, there have been significant developments in information technology, particularly in those forms based on computing hardware and software. Despite these developments, it is a conspicuous fact of contemporary organizations that the offices of senior managers are not often filled with computer-based information technology. To be sure, the language and perspectives of information-based analyses are important in modern management; but we observe that managers, if given a choice, often avoid direct interaction with technology, leaving it to staff members and subordinates. This is particularly the case at the top. The overwhelming majority of senior administrators do not use computer-based information technology directly (Moore, 1986). A few senior executives use electronic mail, a technology that resembles a combination telephone, answering machine, and dictating machine. A few, particularly financial executives, use spreadsheets. Such executives are, however, exceptions. Managers have access to computers and an array of related equipment capable of dealing with information and decision making, but these technologies are rarely found in senior managers' offices. They are used extensively by managers' staffs or consultants, not by managers themselves (Dutton and Kraemer, 1980; Mittman and Moore, 1986; Siegel, 1988).

Senior executives also spend relatively little time reading the output from these technologies (Mintzberg, 1973; Sproull, 1984). When they do attend to it, they rate it as relatively unimportant (Jones and McLeod, 1986; Hannaway, 1988).

The limited direct attention to information technology by senior managers does not stem from a lack of resources or power. Executives decide how to invest in and manage research and development (Rosenberg, 1982; Cohen, Levin, and Mowery, 1987). They decide what technologies to build or develop and how to manage those processes (Brooks, 1975; Kidder, 1981). They decide what technology to acquire and how to deploy it (Cyert, Simon, and Trow, 1956; Pettigrew, 1972; Lynn, 1982; Argote, Goodman, and Schkade, 1983; Hickson and others, 1986; Kiesler and Sproull, 1987; Pennings and Buitendam, 1987). For the most part, however, the same managers who invest billions of dollars in technology, for use by the people and systems they manage, rarely invest in or use technology for themselves. The decision and information technologies actually used by senior administrators are mostly limited to telephones and dictating machines.

In the remainder of this chapter, we explore why managers have not embraced new information technology more enthusiastically. Our primary intention, however, is neither to explain the particulars of the relation between managers and information technology nor to forecast its future development. Rather, we wish to use this episode in the history of technology as a springboard for examining the relationships among technology, management, and competitive advantage more generally.

Technological Innovations and Their Adoption

Some technological innovations spread through a population of potential users fairly rapidly. Although it was originally conceived as an aid to printing and was unsuccessful in that role, the typewriter spread rather rapidly through offices once it was introduced to them (Monaco, 1988). The telephone also spread rapidly among businesses, although it was resisted quite vigorously by polite society (Aronson, 1977; Perry, 1977).

However, most new technologies fail to spread at all (Mansfield, 1968b). The world of technology is littered with commercial failures of technologies, including many that were patented and some that were highly touted. In the management literature, management by objectives and zero-based budgeting were popular technologies of the later 1960s and early 1970s. They were intended to make decision making more systematic and rational. They had their successes, but they were not widely used and, when used, were not particularly successful or were transformed into rituals (Wildavsky, 1974; Nystrom, 1977). Computer-based financial planning models fared similarly (Dutton, 1981). So did video conferences (Egido, 1988) and Delphi techniques (Sackman, 1975).

Since histories of technological success often include periods of failure, and since histories of technological failure often include periods of success, interpretations made by prophets of contemporary technologies tend to vary with the technological prejudices of historians. Enthusiasts for a new technology are likely to attribute slowness in adoption either to correctable faults of the technology or to various forms of irrational resistance. Skeptics are likely to attribute failures to the fact that the technology either addresses a real need poorly or solves a problem that does not exist.

Enthusiasts and skeptics differ in interpretations, but they share a common theory of technological adoption. It is a theory of competition among technologies and survival of the better. The standard stylized script for a successful technology has three acts. In the first act, society endures the problems attributable to the inadequacy of existing technology and is often unconscious of them. In the second act, a new technology is discovered or invented. It is resisted at first, partly because it is imperfect and partly because of inertia. In the third act, the advantages of the new technology are gradually established, and it comes into general use.

In the standard script, success may come slowly. Suppose that a new generation of decision technology, aimed at executives, were potentially helpful. That technology is not likely to match current procedures for considering alternatives or for developing consensus. This procedural mismatch may cause most managers to avoid the technology entirely. However, some executives will use it, improve it, and become more successful. As that success is observed, or as it reflects itself in reduced performance by others, the new technology will gradually gain converts.

This stylized success story has an implicit "shadow story" of technological failure. In the story of failure, a new technology secures a few adherents for a while but ultimately loses in the competition. Suppose that a new generation of decision technology aimed at executives were to emphasize the relatively more programmed aspects of executive work, perhaps proclaiming the necessity of freeing an executive for more important, unprogrammable activities. Suppose further that, as seems possible, the replaced activities are those that maintain social relationships, keeping channels of communication exercised so that if they are needed in a crisis or for an unexpected opportunity they are ready at hand. Then the changes have long-run negative consequences. Embracing the technology will diminish rather than increase an executive's capacity for action and thus reduce competitive advantage. The result will be a short-run success, followed by a gradual failure of the technology and of those managers who have embraced it.

These stories and the simple theory they reflect attribute the limited use of modern information technology by senior executives to a mismatch between them that makes the technology ineffective in providing competitive advantage to a manager who uses it (Huber, 1984). The speculation that information technology is poorly designed for modern managers, and vice versa, is supported by observations that attitudes toward computers in the office are less positive among managers who use them than they are among those who do not (Weisband, 1987), and that fewer than half the executives who use the technology describe their use as increasing with time (Moore, 1986).

Information Technology and Managerial Needs

Contemporary theories of organizations distinguish two aspects of the match between new technologies and the needs of potential users that affect the diffusion of a technology. The first aspect is the extent to which the innovation improves technical efficiency. It is generally observed that new technologies offering substantial improvements in technical performance spread more rapidly than those that do not (Mansfield, 1968a; Von Hippel, 1988). The second aspect is the extent to which the innovation contributes to institutional legitimacy and reputation. In general, changes that meet these institutional needs spread more rapidly than do those that do not (Meyer and Rowan, 1977; DiMaggio and Powell, 1983; Tolbert and Zucker, 1983). Both arguments are basically competitive-advantage arguments. In the first case, competitive advantage comes from gains in technical capabilities. In the second case, competitive advantage comes from gains in social position. In many cases, of course, the distinction between the two is somewhat arbitrary.

Information Technology and Technical Efficiency. Assertions that effective information management is a cornerstone of effective administration were common long before the advent of electronic computers, but they have become particularly frequent in the contemporary literature on information and expert systems. It has been observed that managers invest substantial resources in systems of organizational intelligence (Wilensky, 1967; Daft and Lengel, 1986). Managers are seen as using information to assess alternatives, make decisions, and implement them, and those activities are seen as central to their roles (Aguilar, 1967; Huber and McDaniel, 1986). It is primarily within such a context that information-processing technology is portrayed as the technology of administrative intelligence, promising substantial competitive advantage to administrators who master and use its power (Simon, 1973; Keen and Scott-Morton, 1978; Demski, 1980; Sprague and Carlson, 1982; Huber, 1984).

Decision technologies, like other managerial nostrums, are loosely based on a commonly held theory of managerial decision making. In this theory, preferences are stable, problems and premises precede solutions and conclusions, information is neutral, and managers make decisions by considering alternatives in terms of their anticipated consequences for prior objectives. Observation of actual managerial behavior calls into question each of these tenets (March and Olsen, 1976; Sproull, Weiner, and Wolf, 1978; March, 1988; Feldman, 1989), and thereby suggests an imperfect match between decision technologies and managerial needs.

For example, El Sawy and El Sherif (1989) have argued that the failure of senior political executives to use modern information technology stems from the fact that conventional decision-support systems mistake the nature of both the strategic decision-making process and the role of senior executives in that process. In particular, they have noted that the process is often murky; that it is usually a group effort involving negotiation and consensus building; that it involves a variety of stakeholders, with different assumptions and values; that it takes place in an emergent fashion, exploiting serendipitous discovery; that there is a great deal of information, but much of it is qualitative, oral, or poorly recorded; that the significance of the stakes involved leads both to political maneuvering and to stress; and that top managers are short of time, resistant to change, comfortable with intuition, and powerful enough to enforce quick responses to their needs.

The problems are general. Values and beliefs change over time, but decision-support systems normally are designed in a way that assumes that preferences or tastes are stable over time. They often require decision makers to know today the preferences they will have tomorrow. While decision makers can often specify at least some of what they would like to know today, they recognize that their tastes or needs for information are likely to change over time in ways that they cannot specify (March, 1978, 1987).

Consider an "intelligent" communication system, a technology intended to protect managers from junk mail while allowing important information through (Malone and others, 1987). In these systems, managers specify topics about which they would like to receive mail. In order for managers to receive mail on particular topics, they must be able to specify those topics in advance; but if managers cannot know what they will find interesting in the future, they cannot include those topics in their filters. If a primary way in which they discover new interests is through reading the mail, and if they read only mail that has passed through topic filters defined in terms of existing interests, then they will be unlikely to elaborate their lists of topics. The problem is familiar to the design of libraries (for example, in the "new acquisitions" shelf or list) and to students of rationality (March, 1981; March and Sevón, 1984).

Conclusions and solutions often precede problems and premises (March, 1988), but decision technologies usually assume that problems precede solutions. The technologies generally ask managers to state their premises or their rules, and then the technologies provide the conclusions. In some cases, they automatically implement them as decisions. But managers often do not want to give up control over their conclusions. Often they already know the answers and are looking for justification. Solutions intrude on their consciousness as aggressively as problems do. Technologies that ask managers to give up solution control do not match the world in which they live.

Information in organizations is not innocent; rather, it is shaped by expectations of its consequences (Feldman and March, 1981). When the decision relevance of information is made explicit, the information can be corrupted by strategic actors. For example, revealing the decision rule for relating information on costs and benefits to investment decisions is an invitation to biased estimates. Establishing a criterion or acceptable risk makes the assessment of risk a political process. These complications are well known to managers, but decision-support technologies often require managers to make their decision rules explicit. Thus, they often increase decision makers' vulnerability to strategic manipulation.

As a minor example from managerial life, consider a computer-supported calendar system, a technology intended to help managers make better decisions about how to spend their time. Managers who use them have to specify their time constraints, a priority list of people to whom they wish to be accessible, and their "bumping" rules—their decisions about whom to accommodate if time requests from equal-priority people collide. When this information is made explicit, as these systems require, other people are able to act strategically with respect to a manager's schedule. For example, they can sign up for large blocks of low-priority time, trade time, "sell" their places in the queue, and so forth. "Intelligent" mail filters are subject to the same kinds of strategic manipulation. People who want to reach a manager will discover the filtering rules and disguise their mail to slip through the filters.

Furthermore, sounding out is eliminated from these systems. The delicate process by which two people discover (and transform) their mutual importance is inadmissible. Graceful face-saving fictions disappear. "I'd love to see you, but I'm completely booked for the next six weeks" becomes "Schedule X only if someone more important doesn't want to see me. All of the following people are more important than X." Finally, a priority system imposes a particular kind of decision structure on the process, one that may be quite distant from a manager's view of what is sensible.

Objectives do not always precede action, but decision-support systems ordinarily assume that they do. Goals are discovered in decision processes as much as they are acted upon (March, 1978; Hauschildt, 1986; Dornblaser, Lin, and Van de Ven, 1988), and senior executives may be goal developers more than decision makers (Barnard, 1938; Selznick, 1957; Burns, 1978). Information technologies that allow managers to track performance over time (historical analyses) or over competitors (market analyses) may be helpful in setting aspiration levels or in tuning existing goals, but goal development also entails discovering new goal dimensions and directing attention to them.

Executives often discover new ideas and information through weak-tie systems rather than through strong-tie systems (Granovetter, 1973). In a strong-tie system, characterized by frequent and dense interaction, most people know what everyone else knows. A weak-tie system is characterized by infrequent and sparse interaction, with barely overlapping areas of knowledge and information. To develop their weak ties, executives engage in multinational scanning (Keegan, 1974). They cultivate social contacts (Dalton, 1959; Domhoff, 1974). They join the boards of other organizations (Pfeffer, 1972; Allen, 1974). They take deliberate steps designed to turn their attention away from the familiar and the routine within their own organizations. They participate in brainstorming sessions. They go on retreats. They hold open-door days.

If technology can contribute to executives' goal discovery, it is not likely to be through special-purpose and goal-discovery systems, which are subject to the irrelevancies noted above. General-purpose electronic monitoring or communication systems may be more helpful. Computer-mediated communication technologies may make it possible for executives to weaken the influence of existing strong ties and construct some new, weak ones in order to increase variation in the pool of goal possibilities (Sproull and Kiesler, 1986; Feldman, 1987; Finholt and Sproull, 1990). For instance, managers mostly engage in near-neighborhood search, but these technologies weaken the hold of physical and social proximity on attention and interaction. Thus, technology may allow physically distant or socially distant people to compete more equally for managerial attention, thereby providing greater variation. It should be noted, however, that any technology has its own "distance" metric that it imposes on search, and so the advantages of a new technology are likely to be transient. During the transition period, it adds variety; after the transition, it is different but probably not more variable.

Information Technology and Institutional Legitimacy.
Modern information technologies are marketed partly on the basis of their contributions to institutional reputation and

legitimacy. Computers symbolize modernity and competitiveness (Anderson, Hassen, Johnson, and Klassen, 1979; Bikson, Gutek, and Mankin, 1981; Moshowitz, 1981; Danziger, Dutton, Kling, and Kraemer, 1982). Their use signals competence and rationality (Feldman and March, 1981; March, 1987). For example, early computation facilities were often treated more as sacred temples than as parts of the technical environment. They were displayed behind glass windows and shown to schoolchildren.

Some of the more common stories about information technology are stories about the purchase of hardware that was displayed but not used, or about the introduction of software that was made available but never accessed (Kling and Scacchi, 1982; Gasser, 1986). Managers have developed small bits of software to exercise computers in their names, so that they would not be routinely logged out, by a priority system that they had installed, from a system that they did not use much (Blackwell, 1987). These stories suggest that some of the benefits of information technologies are derived simply from possessing, adopting, or claiming access to them; they need not be used. In such situations, we would expect to see organizations investing in technology and gaining advantage from such adoption, even if there is little or no managerial use of the technology. Whether a technology adopted on such a basis ultimately becomes technically important depends on the interaction between symbols and behavior (Feldman and March, 1981).

The symbolic significance of managers' use of decision and information technology is, however, not guaranteed to be positive. Managerial use of information and decision technology evokes the classic struggle between conflicting ideologies of management: scientific management versus charismatic leadership. Contemporary culture is mixed. On the one hand, today's popular culture seems to glorify the techno-macho hero, the leader who masters technology sufficiently to dominate both the technology and others who are less competent (Wolfe, 1979). On the other hand, the substitution of electronic gear for senior executives conjures images of managerial routinization that seem to demean managerial functions.

Historically, the actual practice of scientific management entailed managers' adopting new technologies for other people to use. The primary objects of these management practices were laborers, production workers, and clerical personnel. The adopted technologies rarely impinged directly on the everyday behavior of managers. Thus, charismatic leaders could practice scientific management of other people, but not of themselves, with no necessary ideological conflict. But decision technologies—unlike shovels with longer handles, robotic paintsprayers, or keystroke models of transaction processing—are intended to affect the daily behavior of managers themselves. Technology already appears to have made significant inroads into the prerogatives and prestige of middle management. Modern advertising terminology for computers, with its metaphors of artificial intelligence and expert systems, is an open challenge to the status of senior executives. Managers may find it difficult to create or sustain charisma if they rely on technology or if it is known that they rely on technology.

The symbolic significance of technology in management is closely related to the more general issue of the relation between technology and human decision-making intelligence. Technology has supplanted many activities formerly performed by people. Some of these substitutions have improved human safety and spirit by easing work in noxious environments and work demanding extreme physical effort (Florman, 1977). Some technologies have impoverished and endangered human existence (Roszak, 1973; Perrow, 1984). In all cases, however, human beings could take comfort in the belief that their ability to make complex decisions, drawing on both reason and emotion, made them unique (Weizenbaum, 1976). Beliefs in a distinctive human decision-making ability undergird modern conceptions of the uniqueness of human beings and their superiority to nature, other species, and technology. Some aspects of information technology and computers have long been seen as threats to such beliefs (McCorduck, 1979).

In that sense, they symbolize and elicit what is base and inhuman about people (Hawthorne, 1844; Melville, 1855). In the executive suite today, if managers believe that what makes them uniquely human (or distinctively managerial) is their role as decision makers, they will be slow to abdicate that uniqueness in favor of technology.

Others will also be slow to encourage them to do so. One of the primary functions of organization and of a decision process is the allocation of responsibility for events in a world in which allocating responsibility is in fact difficult (Brunsson, forthcoming). When there are multiple, interacting causes for events, and when the role of human intention is obscured by its interaction with numerous other factors, technology (like other forms of knowledge and organization) is more attractive if it reinforces not only a general vision of human control over destiny but also the precise allocation of individual responsibility, by which most humans are absolved. This suggests that information technology designed to support executive communication or the monitoring of events is likely to spread more quickly among executives than is technology linked directly to decision making.

Complications in Competitive Advantage

The general argument is that technologies will thrive if they contribute to technical or institutional needs of the organizations that use them. As we have seen, even the simple form of such an argument provides some clue to the relative failure of computer-based technologies among senior executives, as well as some clue to the circumstances under which such technologies can be expected to be adopted by top-level managers. Nevertheless, the simple argument needs to be complicated a bit. In this section, we will be suggesting some consequences of interdependencies in diffusion, as well as some difficulties in forecasting technological success from the present characteristics of a technology. In the following major section, we will turn to some issues concerning the inefficiencies of using history for rendering technological judgments.

Interdependencies in Diffusion. Understanding the match between information technologies and managerial needs is not simply a case of understanding the technical and institutional match between individual technologies and individual executives. Technologies and executives are each connected to other technologies and other executives. The interdependencies make a difference to competitive advantage.

Consider, for example, the case of technical efficiency. For many technologies, the gain from adopting one technology depends critically on the other technologies one is currently using. A nineteenth-century example illustrates the point. Carbon paper was available in the United States as early as 1823, but it was largely irrelevant to the writing tools (quill, steel, or gold pens) of the time. Only after the typewriter was patented (1868) and marketed extensively (in the 1880s) did businesses begin using carbon paper to reproduce documents (Yates, 1987).

The gain from adoption also depends on whether competitors and collaborators are using the same technology. The nature of the links is technology-specific; that is, the gains from a new technology, under some circumstances, are augmented by the fact that others are using it. Many kinds of communication technology fall into such a category. For example, the advantage to an executive of using electronic mail or a fax transmission system depends critically on whether other executives are also using it. Thus, success in inducing an executive to invest in such a technology for his or her own use is likely to be minimal until others also invest. One of the reasons lower levels in an organization use such technologies is that their collective use can be coerced and coordinated by organizational authority.

Under other circumstances, the gains from a new technology are decreased by the fact that others are using it. Many kinds of production technology fall into such a category. Information technology devoted to providing competitive advantage through advance information on movements in a market seems a prototype of this second case. Advance information is particularly valuable if others do not have it; not having it is particularly disadvantageous when others do.

Interdependencies in ideological and symbolic significance are also clear. Whether the adoption of a particular technology increases or decreases institutional legitimacy depends on who else is using it. Standard discussions of diffusion in the institutionalization literature assume that gains in legitimacy or reputation from adoption of a new technology increase with the number and status of other users. Thus, it is argued that early adopters of a technology are driven more by technical considerations than are later adopters (Tolbert and Zucker, 1983), and that as an innovation gains adherents it becomes normatively irresistible. Where standing is established by differentiation, as in the case of fashion leaders, the effects work in the opposite direction.

These interdependencies make analysis more complicated than it would otherwise be. They also suggest why the spread of technology may look decidedly imitative. It is frequently true that as a new technology becomes more common among others, adoption becomes more advantageous. It is also frequently the case that the process will generate a technological "armaments race," in which new technology spreads quickly, even though no user is better off when all are using the technology than when none was.

Present Technologies, Future Technologies. Much of the foregoing analysis suggests that there is not a strong match between the competitive needs of contemporary top management and the current capabilities of information technology. Indeed, some modern designers of decision-support systems have built systems that assume little or no direct use of information technology by senior executives (El Sawy and El Sherif, 1989). Technology does change, however, and the history of information technology shows a rate of change that makes the future unlikely to resemble the present. As information technology and its symbolic meaning change, the match between that technology and managerial needs also changes.

Technology optimists believe that executives eschew current technology primarily because at present it is neither good enough technically nor acceptable enough ideologically. Optimists believe that it will improve on both counts and that the improvements will lead managers to adopt it and use it (Gray, 1987; Henderson, Rockart, and Sifonis, 1987). They observe that the scarce use of technology by senior executives in the late 1980s reflects a substantial increase over the minuscule use earlier (Moore, 1986).

With respect to the more mundane technical aspects, it is argued that managers are reluctant to use a keyboard as an input device, but that when voice recognition becomes practical, managers will use computer technology. It is also noted that expert systems are currently too small, too slow, and too crude in their inferences and decision rules to be very useful, but that when they become bigger, faster, and more subtle, managers will use them. Undoubtedly, technology will continue to improve, although possibly not at the rate anticipated by technology prophets. Any argument of the form "the future lies ahead" is difficult to refute, but past improvements in technology have not always led to increased use by managers. In the case of the telephone and the photocopier, some improvements—pictures in the first case, color in the second—led to almost no use at all.

Similarly, it is possible to argue that information technology will improve its ideological position with respect to senior executives. As information technology spreads through the rest of the world, some of the negative meanings with which it is saddled will presumably be discarded. The history of ideological resistance to technology is, for the most part, a history of defeat; and more effective ideologists of expert systems and artificial intelligence will presumably come to prominence and build an ideology and a symbolic structure attractive not only to hackers and science fiction writers but also to others.

This "brave new world" ideological forecast is, like its cousin with respect to technical improvements, hard to refute; but it is not obvious, either. Articulate proponents of information technology have been aware of the ideological problems for many years and have fought them with semantic

imagination, philosophical elegance, and elements of success
(Hofstadter, 1979; Simon, 1981; Lenat, 1983). It remains true,
however, that relatively few of those successes have been seen
among executives or their publicists, with the possible exception of some military commanders (and success among military commanders is a mixed ideological blessing).

The Inefficiencies of Competitive History

In the simple theory of technological competition,
assessing the match between modern information technology
and the job of modern senior executives is all that is required
to understand and anticipate technological history. Those
technologies that provide technical or institutional advantages will survive. Such a theory is, however, notably flawed.
The future development of the use of information technology
by executives cannot be predicted from a simple theory of
technical efficacy. Historical processes do not move reliably
to better technologies. It is not difficult to specify courses of
history that culminate in the widespread adoption of technically inefficient technologies or the widespread rejection of
efficient ones (Nelson and Winter, 1982; Hansen and Samuelson, 1988). Even in situations in which the relative superiority
of alternative technologies is clear, there can be circumstances
in which poorer technologies survive and better ones die
(Arthur, 1984).

The standard example is the QWERTY keyboard.
Other keyboard arrangements are demonstrably superior, but
QWERTY has become so widespread and so deeply embedded
in social and technological practice that superior technologies
go unused. It is not the only example. The United States, a
modern, developed country, maintains a system of measurements built on such quaint units as inches, feet, and miles.
Computer technologies exhibit a similar persistence. The
United States Social Security Administration produces forty
million checks per month on a computer system developed
in the 1950s, running programs written in Autocoder. The
current telephone system, which ties telephone numbers to

physical locations, was developed when mechanical source-routing technology made that link necessary. Today, computerized switching technology makes it just as easy to tie phone numbers to people, wherever they may be, as to physical locations; but the old technology prevails.

The history of technology is filled with such examples. There is no reason to believe that the evolution of information technology will be any different. Executives will come to use some technologies that turn out to be suboptimal. They will persist in them. In the present case, the success or failure, with senior executives, of computer-based information technology provides little conclusive evidence about the fit between that technology and executive roles. It is entirely possible that the technology will fail to conquer the executive suite, even if its use is advantageous, and it is entirely possible that the technology may come to be a standard feature of executive life, even if it is not optimal.

History is inefficient in that it often has multiple equilibria; and even when an equilibrium is unique, the path is slow and somewhat tortuous. The course of technological history affects the outcome. Different organizations and different managers persist in different technologies—not because their conditions are different, but because their histories are. Understanding technological change involves capturing these inefficiencies in history. We note here two of the more obvious inefficiencies relevant to our argument: the problem of specialization in competence, and the problem of conflict of interest.

Competence Traps. Increasing competence within an existing technology (or other knowledge structure, such as a scientific paradigm) makes it difficult to shift to new and potentially better technologies. In effect, learning drives out the experimentation on which it depends. As competence is gained with a particular technology, that technology is, sensibly enough, used more often. Increased use further increases competence and reduces competence on other technologies. Thus, an organization or an individual may become so expert at an old technology that shifting to a newer (and, in principle, better) technology will lead to decreased performance, in the short run (March, 1981; Herriott, Levinthal, and March, 1985; Levitt and March, 1988). Large differences between the potential of a new technology and that of the existing one are ordinarily associated with a level of incompetence at the new technology that results in lower (early) performance than was realized with the older technology (within which competence was higher).

A variant of the competence-trap argument is common among those students of technology who see the current absence of information technology among senior managers as temporary. It is observed that current senior managers did not grow up with sophisticated information technology; they do not appreciate its benefits. Indeed, because they are sufficiently competent at the technologies they use, it is unreasonable to expect them to reach the same level of competence at new technologies within a relatively short period of time. Younger managers who have grown up with these technologies use them more extensively and comfortably (Moore, 1986). As these younger managers mature and enter the senior executive ranks, the argument goes, they will naturally take their competences and their technologies with them. The argument is plausible, although it requires some fine-tuning to accommodate the fact that changes in information technology may continue to be more rapid than changes in the technological socialization of generations.

Competence traps inhibit organizations and the individuals in them from adopting technologies that have superior potential. Such reluctance is not entirely foolish. A shift in technology is likely to produce short-run decrements in performance that reduce the competitiveness of the organization. Frequent shifts are likely to prolong the period in which an organization is vulnerable to competition. Thus, organizations that seek to be perpetually up to date may have difficulty surviving long enough to secure the benefits of their progressiveness.

Institutional Frictions. The simple theory of competitive advantage is built on the notion that historical processes differentially sustain those technologies that are "optimal," but optimality is an ambiguous concept to apply to adaptive processes in a naturally evolving, nested system (Maynard Smith, 1978; Dawkins, 1980). In simple terms, optimality involves poorly specified trade-offs across time and across segments of the system (Levitt and March, 1988). What is good in the short run is not good in the long run; what is good for the individual is not good for the collectivity; and so on. The intuitively appealing link between the idea of optimality and the idea of evolutionary, stable strategies is difficult to sustain as a general principle (Hansen and Samuelson, 1988).

Thus, theories of competitive equilibria need to be attentive to the many ways in which equilibria are either unstable or nonoptimal, in the sense that a nontautological meaning of *optimality* is difficult to establish. What is good for the country is not necessarily good for General Motors, and vice versa. For example, most formal organizations are hierarchies. Some people (bosses) make decisions about the technologies to be used by other people (workers). Hierarchies allocate responsibilities and authority in ways that presumably contribute elements of efficiency to the system. They also allocate perquisites, power, and position in a chain of domination and subordination that contributes elements of pleasure (and pain) to the individuals who are part of the system.

In a hierarchy, the competitive advantage of a technology is simultaneously assessed for its contribution to the survival of the organization and for its contribution to the survival of the social order within the organization. New technologies that alter attention patterns disrupt existing organizational systems. Such disruptions in procedures, role relationships, hierarchies, incentives, and memories are not neutral with respect to their impacts on the social order of an organization. It is the rare executive who embraces revolution in order to increase efficiency. Technologies perceived by managers to increase their control, or the stability of systems under their control, are more likely to be adopted by them than ones that are perceived to undermine the social order (Bariff and Galbraith, 1978; Bjørn-Andersen and Pedersen, 1980).

Thus, technology proponents, who want technology adopted and who recognize this reluctance, often try to position technology conservatively. They announce, reassuringly, that it will simply improve old ways of doing business; the status quo remains intact and may even be strengthened. This strategy increases the likelihood of executives' accepting the technology, but it also decreases the likelihood of their discovering new (and potentially better) ways of using the technology once it has been adopted. The alternative strategy is to preach revolution and directly challenge the status quo. This strategy is usually pursued from outside the organization rather than from within; or, if pursued from within, it is rarely successful (Emmett, 1981; Zuboff, 1988).

Hierarchical relations are one of the many important sets of relations in organizations. There are others—for example, the communication structure, the coalition structure, and the temporal structure. Numerous individuals are organized into numerous overlapping and nested groups. It is not necessary that a particular technology be optimal from every point of view, but the processes of competition have to fit all of these structures together. It would be quite misleading to assume that a technology that provided a competitive advantage for some organizations in their competition with other organizations, or for bosses in their competition with workers, or for workers in their competition with bosses, or for clients in their competition with professionals, or for professionals in their competition with clients (and so on) would necessarily be adopted. In order for a particular technology to thrive, it must fit into this mosaic of conflict and cooperation.

Conclusions

We began by trying to understand why most senior executives are not currently firsthand users of information technology based on modern computers. We have tried to indicate why that result is not too surprising. It is not clear that current technologies particularly match current executives' technical or institutional needs, nor is it clear that these technologies strengthen the hierarchical position of senior executives.

Our main intent, however, has not been to clarify the present and probable future of information technology and top management. Rather, we have tried to sketch a theory of technological competitive advantage that can be used to consider the utilization of technology in organizations. That theory presumes that competitive advantage includes both technical and institutional components, that interdependencies among technologies and changes in technologies over time complicate the understanding of competitive outcomes, and that there are substantial historical inefficiencies in the process of realizing competitive dominance.

As a consequence, simple theories of technological competitive advantage are likely to be misleading. They tend to exaggerate both the necessity and the intelligence of the outcomes of technological competition, thus exaggerating the link between evolutionary equilibria and optimality. A more adequate theory would have to cope with two major difficulties: first, how to describe the fit between a particular technology and the complicated structure of evolving needs within an organization; and, second, how to accommodate the multiple equilibria of competitive processes and their history dependence, the ways in which routes to equilibria affect the equilibria that are achieved.

References

Aguilar, F. *Scanning the Business Environment.* New York: Macmillan, 1967.

Allen, M. P. "The Structure of Interorganizational Elite Cooptation: Interlocking Corporate Directorates." *American Sociological Review*, 1974, *39*, 393–406.

Anderson, R. E., Hassen, T., Johnson, D. C., and Klassen, D. L. "Instructional Computing: Acceptance and Rejection by Secondary School Teachers." *Sociology of Work and Occupations,* 1979, *6,* 227–250.

Argote, L., Goodman, P. S., and Schkade, D. "The Human Side of Robotics: How Workers React to a Robot." *Sloan Management Review,* 1983, *24* (3), 31–41.

Aronson, S. H. "Bell's Electrical Toy: What's the Use? The Sociology of Early Telephone Usage." In I. de Sola Pool (ed.), *The Social Impact of the Telephone.* Cambridge, Mass.: MIT Press, 1977.

Arthur, W. B. "Competing Technologies and Economic Prediction." *IIASA Options,* 1984, *2,* 10–13.

Bariff, M. L., and Galbraith, J. R. "Interorganizational Power Considerations for Designing Information Systems." *Accounting, Organizations, and Society,* 1978, *3,* 15–27.

Barnard, C. *The Functions of the Executive.* Cambridge, Mass.: Harvard University Press, 1938.

Bikson, T., Gutek, B., and Mankin, D. *Implementation of Information Technology in Office Settings: Review of Relevant Literature.* Santa Monica, Calif.: Rand Corporation, 1981.

Bjørn-Andersen, N., and Pedersen, P. H. "Computer-Facilitated Changes in the Management Power Structure." *Accounting, Organizations, and Society,* 1980, *5,* 203–216.

Blackwell, M. "Electronic Observations of Computer User Behavior." In S. B. Kiesler and L. S. Sproull (eds.), *Computing and Change on Campus.* New York: Cambridge University Press, 1987.

Brooks, F. *The Mythical Man Month.* Reading, Mass.: Addison-Wesley, 1975.

Burns, J. M. *Leadership.* New York: Harper & Row, 1978.

Brunsson, N. *The Organization of Hypocrisy.* New York: Wiley, forthcoming.

Cohen, W., Levin, R., and Mowery, D. "Firm Size and R&D Investment: A Reexamination." *Journal of Industrial Economics,* 1987, *35,* 543–565.

Cyert, R. M., Simon, H. A., and Trow, D. B. "Observation of a Business Decision." *Journal of Business,* 1956, *29,* 237–248.

Daft, R., and Lengel, R. L. "Organizational Information Requirements, Media Richness, and Structural Design." *Management Science*, 1986, *32*, 554–571.

Dalton, M. *Men Who Manage.* New York: Wiley, 1959.

Danziger, J., Dutton, W., Kling, R., and Kraemer, K. *Computers and Politics.* New York: Columbia University Press, 1982.

Dawkins, R. "Good Strategy or Evolutionary Stable Strategy?" In G. W. Barlow and J. Silverberg (eds.), *Sociobiology: Beyond Nature/Nurture.* Boulder, Colo.: Westview, 1980.

Demski, J. *Information Analysis.* Reading, Mass.: Addison-Wesley, 1980.

DiMaggio, P. J., and Powell, W. W. "The Iron Cage Revisited: Institutional Isomorphism and Collective Rationality in Organizational Fields." *American Sociological Review*, 1983, *48*, 147–160.

Domhoff, G. W. *The Bohemian Grove and Other Retreats: A Study of Ruling-Class Consciousness.* New York: Harper & Row, 1974.

Dornblaser, B. M., Lin, T., and Van de Ven, A. H. "Innovation Outcomes, Learning, and Action Loops." In A. H. Van de Ven, H. Angle, and M. S. Poole (eds.), *Research on the Management of Innovation.* Cambridge, Mass.: Ballinger, 1988.

Dutton, W. "The Rejection of an Innovation: The Political Environment of a Computer-Based Model." *Systems, Objectives, Solutions*, 1981, *1*, 179–201.

Dutton, W., and Kraemer, K. "Automating Bias." *Society*, 1980, *17*, 36–41.

Egido, C. "Video Conferencing as a Technology to Support Group Work: A Review of the Failures." In *Proceedings of the Conference on Computer-Supported Cooperative Work.* New York: Association for Computing Machinery, 1988.

El Sawy, O. A., and El Sherif, H. "Issue-Based Decision-Support Systems for the Egyptian Cabinet." *MIS Quarterly*, 1989, *13*.

Emmett, V. "VNET or Gripenet?" *Datamation*, 1981, *27*, 48–58.

Feldman, M. "Electronic Mail and Weak Ties in Organizations." *Office: Technology and People*, 1987, *3*, 83–101.

Feldman, M. *Order Without Design: Information Production and Policy Making*. Stanford, Calif.: Stanford University Press, 1989.

Feldman, M., and March, J. G. "Information as Signal and Symbol." *Administrative Science Quarterly*, 1981, *26*, 171–186.

Finholt, T., and Sproull, L. S. "Electronic Groups at Work." *Organization Science*, 1990, *1*.

Florman, S. C. *The Existential Pleasures of Computing*. New York: St. Martin's Press, 1977.

Gasser, L. "The Integration of Computing and Routine Work." *ACM Transactions on Office Information Systems*, 1986, *4*, 205–225.

Granovetter, M. "The Strength of Weak Ties." *American Sociological Review*, 1973, *68*, 1360–1380.

Gray, P. "Group Decision Support Systems." *Decision Support Systems*, 1987, *3*, 233–242.

Hannaway, J. *Signals and Signalling: The Workings of an Administrative System*. Oxford, England: Oxford University Press, 1988.

Hansen, R. G., and Samuelson, W. F. "Evolution in Economic Games." *Journal of Economic Behavior and Organization*, 1988, *10*, 315–338.

Hauschildt, J. "Goals and Problem Solving in Innovative Decisions." In E. Witte and H.-J. Zimmermann (eds.), *Empirical Research on Organizational Decision Making*. Amsterdam: Elsevier, 1986.

Hawthorne, N. "Rappaccini's Daughter." *Democratic Review*, 1844, *15*, 545–560.

Henderson, J., Rockart, J., and Sifonis, J. "Integrating Management-Support Systems into Strategic Information Systems Planning." *Journal of MIS*, 1987, *4*, 5–24.

Herriott, S. R., Levinthal, D., and March, J. G. "Learning from Experience in Organizations." *American Economic Review*, 1985, *75*, 298–302.

Hickson, D. J., and others. *Top Decisions: Strategic Decision Making in Organizations*. San Francisco: Jossey-Bass, 1986.

Hofstadter, D. R. *Godel, Escher, Bach: An Eternal Golden Braid.* New York: Basic Books, 1979.

Huber, G. "The Nature and Design of Postindustrial Organizations." *Management Science,* 1984, *30,* 928–951.

Huber, G., and McDaniel, R. "The Decision-Making Paradigm of Organizational Design." *Management Science,* 1986, *32,* 572–589.

Jones, J. W., and McLeod, R., Jr. "The Structure of Executive Information Systems: An Exploratory Analysis." *Decision Sciences,* 1986, *17,* 220–249.

Keegan, W. J. "Multinational Scanning: A Study of Information Sources Utilized by Headquarters Executives in Multinational Companies." *Administrative Science Quarterly,* 1974, *19,* 411–421.

Keen, P., and Scott-Morton, M. *Decision Support Systems: An Organizational Perspective.* Reading, Mass.: Addison-Wesley, 1978.

Kidder, T. *Soul of a New Machine.* New York: Avon, 1981.

Kiesler, S. B., and Sproull, L. S. (eds.). *Computing and Change on Campus.* New York: Cambridge University Press, 1987.

Kling, R., and Scacchi, W. "The Web of Computing: Computer Technology as Social Organization." *Advances in Computers,* 1982, *21,* 1–90.

Lenat, D. B. *Building Expert Systems.* Reading, Mass.: Addison-Wesley, 1983.

Levitt, B., and March, J. G. "Organizational Learning." *Annual Review of Sociology,* 1988, *14,* 319–340.

Lynn, L. H. *How Japan Innovates: A Comparison with the United States in the Case of Oxygen Steelmaking.* Boulder, Colo.: Westview Press, 1982.

McCorduck, P. *Machines Who Think.* New York: W. H. Freeman, 1979.

Malone, T., and others. "Intelligent Information-Sharing Systems." *Communications of the ACM,* 1987, *30,* 390–402.

Mansfield, E. P. *The Economics of Technological Change.* New York: Norton, 1968a.

Mansfield, E. P. *Industrial Research and Technological Innovation.* New York: Norton, 1968b.

March, J. G. "Bounded Rationality, Ambiguity, and the Engineering of Choice." *Bell Journal of Economics*, 1978, *9*, 587–608.

March, J. G. "Footnotes to Organizational Change." *Administrative Science Quarterly*, 1981, *26*, 563–577.

March, J. G. "Old Colleges, New Technology." In S. B. Kiesler and L. S. Sproull (eds.), *Computing and Change on Campus*. New York: Cambridge University Press, 1987.

March, J. G. *Decisions and Organizations*. Oxford, England: Basil Blackwell, 1988.

March, J. G., and Olsen, J. P. *Ambiguity and Change in Organizations*. Bergen, Norway: Universitetsforlaget, 1976.

March, J. G., and Sevón, G. "Gossip, Information, and Decision Making." In L. S. Sproull and P. D. Larkey (eds.), *Advances in Information Processing in Organizations*. Vol. 1. Greenwich, Conn.: JAI Press, 1984.

Maynard Smith, J. "Optimizing Theory in Evolution." *Annual Review of Ecological Systems*, 1978, *9*, 31–56.

Melville, H. "The Paradise of Bachelors and the Tartarus of Maids." *Harper's New Monthly Magazine*, 1855, *10*, 670–678.

Meyer, J. W., and Rowan, B. "Institutionalized Organizations: Formal Structure as Myth and Ceremony." *American Journal of Sociology*, 1977, *83*, 340–363.

Mintzberg, H. *The Nature of Managerial Work*. New York: Harper & Row, 1973.

Mittman, B., and Moore, J. "Senior Management Computer Use: Implications for DSS Design and Goals." In R. Sprague and B. McNurlin (eds.), *Information Systems: Management in Practice*. Englewood Cliffs, N.J.: Prentice-Hall, 1986.

Monaco, C. "The Difficult Birth of the Typewriter." *Invention and Technology*, 1988, *4*, 11–21.

Moore, J. "Senior Executive Computer Use." Unpublished manuscript, 1986.

Moshowitz, A. "On Approaches to the Study of Social Issues in Computing." *Communications of the ACM*, 1981, *24*, 146–155.

Nelson, R. R., and Winter, S. G. *An Evolutionary Theory of*

Economic Change. Cambridge, Mass.: Harvard University Press, 1982.

Nystrom, P. "Managerial Resistance to a Management System." *Accounting, Organization, and Society,* 1977, *2,* 317–322.

Pennings, J., and Buitendam, A. (eds.). *New Technology as Organizational Innovation: The Development and Diffusion of Microelectronics.* Cambridge, Mass.: Ballinger, 1987.

Perrow, C. *Normal Accidents: Living with High-Risk Technologies.* New York: Basic Books, 1984.

Perry, C. R. "The British Experience, 1876–1912: The Impact of the Telephone During the Years of Delay." In I. de Sola Pool (ed.), *The Social Impact of the Telephone.* Cambridge, Mass.: MIT Press, 1977.

Pettigrew, A. "Information Control as a Power Resource." *Sociology,* 1972, *6,* 187–204.

Pfeffer, J. "Size and Composition of Corporate Boards of Directors: The Organization and Its Environment." *Administrative Science Quarterly,* 1972, *17,* 333–363.

Rosenberg, N. (ed.). *Inside the Black Box.* Cambridge, England: Cambridge University Press, 1982.

Roszak, T. *Where the Wasteland Ends: Politics and Transcendence in Postindustrial Society.* New York: Doubleday, 1973.

Sackman, H. *Delphi Critique.* Lexington, Mass.: Lexington Books, 1975.

Selznick, P. *Leadership in Administration.* New York: Harper & Row, 1957.

Siegel, J. "Managers' Communication and Telecommunications Technology Use." Unpublished doctoral dissertation, Carnegie Mellon University, 1988.

Simon, H. A. "Applying Information Technology to Organization Design." *Public Administration Review,* 1973, *33,* 268–278.

Simon, H. A. *The Sciences of the Artificial.* (2nd ed.) Cambridge, Mass.: MIT Press, 1981.

Sprague, R., and Carlson, E. *Building Effective Decision Support Systems.* Englewood Cliffs, N.J.: Prentice-Hall, 1982.

Sproull, L. S. "The Nature of Managerial Attention." In L. S.

Sproull and P. Larkey (eds.), *Advances in Information Processing in Organizations.* Vol. 1. Greenwich, Conn.: JAI Press, 1984.

Sproull, L. S., and Kiesler, S. B. "Reducing Social Context Cues: The Case of Electronic Mail." *Management Science,* 1986, *32,* 1492–1512.

Sproull, L. S., Weiner, S., and Wolf, D. *Organizing an Anarchy: Beliefs, Bureaucracy, and Politics in the National Institute of Education.* Chicago: University of Chicago Press, 1978.

Tolbert, P. S., and Zucker, L. G. "Institutional Sources of Change in the Formal Structure of Organizations: The Diffusion of Civil Service Reform, 1880–1935." *Administrative Science Quarterly,* 1983, *28,* 22–39.

Von Hippel, E. A. *The Sources of Innovation.* New York: Oxford University Press, 1988.

Weisband, S. "Instrumental and Symbolic Aspects of an Executive Information System." In S. B. Kiesler and L. S. Sproull (eds.), *Computing and Change on Campus.* New York: Cambridge University Press, 1987.

Weizenbaum, J. *Computer Power and Human Reason.* New York: W. H. Freeman, 1976.

Wildavsky, A. *The Politics of the Budgetary Process.* (2nd ed.) Boston: Little, Brown, 1974.

Wilensky, H. *Organizational Intelligence: Knowledge and Policy in Government and Industry.* New York: Basic Books, 1967.

Wolfe, T. *The Right Stuff.* New York: Farrar, Straus & Giroux, 1979.

Yates, J. "Graphs as a Managerial Tool: A Case Study of DuPont's Use of Graphs in the Early Twentieth Century." *Journal of Business Communication,* 1985, *22,* 5–33.

Yates, J. "From Hand Copy to Xerox Copy: The Effects of Duplicating Technology on Organizational Communication in American Firms in the Nineteenth and Twentieth Centuries." In L. Thayer (ed.), *Organizational Communication: Emerging Perspectives.* Vol. 2. Norwood, N.J.: Ablex, 1987.

Zuboff, S. *In the Age of the Smart Machine: The Future of Work and Power.* New York: Basic Books, 1988.

6

❊

Technology and Organizations: A Cross-National Analysis

Leonard H. Lynn

A cross-national perspective on technology and organizations can help illuminate questions that are of both intellectual and policy interest. One such question is what causes some societies to excel or lag in using new technology. In the 1950s and 1960s, many scholars came to this question out of a concern with the institutional changes Third World countries would have to make to become modern. A common notion was that certain managerial styles and organizational forms were required to exploit modern technology effectively. American business was seen as providing the model of appropriate organizational forms and managerial styles. This literature contained a note of pathos: if there is one best way to manage technologies, pressures to compete militarily and economically may engender a technological imperative that is forcing a "Coca-Colonization" of the world. Now, for Americans, there is the more immediate fear that competitive pressures to use technology effectively will tempt us to jettison parts of the American normative and value system. Some fear, for example, that the import of Japanese workplace practices, such as quality circles and just-in-time inventory control, could subvert traditional American values of individualism.

A cross-national approach to technology and organizations can lend insight to this issue, but the major task of untangling the existing literature and developing new streams of research lies before us. Complicating this task is that cross-national differences in how organizations use technology can occur because of national differences in the economic or political environment, in the social or institutional environment, or in the norms and values held by organizational members. One could argue, for example, that steel firms in Japan were generally faster than those in the United States to adopt new technology in the postwar years because of any of the following factors:

1. Aspects of the economic environment, such as the more rapid growth of the Japanese industry or lower Japanese sunk costs in older technologies
2. Aspects of the political environment, such as government targeting of the steel industry, or government help in procuring foreign technology
3. Aspects of the social environment, such as the existence of specialized information-collecting organizations in Japan that allowed a relatively faster and more accurate evaluation of new technology by the Japanese
4. Aspects of the institutional environment in Japan, such as permanent employment, which reduced labor's fears of technologically based unemployment and thus facilitated technological change
5. Aspects of the cultural environment, such as a stronger Japanese emphasis on values like hard work, norms of thorough preparation through collecting information, norms of bottom-up decision making, or perhaps a generalized national determination in the 1950s and 1960s to catch up with the West (Lynn, 1982).

Economic, political, social, and institutional explanations of technological innovation in organizations are relatively compatible, and efforts have been made to integrate them. There has not, however, been much systematic effort to integrate cultural variables into a broader explanation (for a very limited effort in this direction, see Walton, 1987), nor has there been much effort to look at the interaction between the cultural and noncultural factors affecting how technology is used by organizations in different countries. Those emphasizing economic, political, institutional, and many sociological variables tend to assume that people do not differ from country to country in significant ways. These scholars may concede the possible existence of cultural differences but implicitly regard such differences as being of only slight importance. In any case, such differences are felt to be declining under the pressure of technological imperatives. To assume otherwise is considered an act of virtual nihilism by some of these scholars. As Hickson, McMillan, Azumi, and Horvath (1979, p. 29) put it, the notion that organizations may differ between countries, because they have different scores on the standard variables of concern to organization theorists, is "interesting," but the notion that cultural factors may cause the relationships between organizational variables to differ from country to country is "terrifying."

Those emphasizing cultural variables assume, conversely, that individuals socialized in different cultures differ from one another in how they interact with one another, what they value, and how they think things should be done. These differences are seen as causing organizations in different countries to have whatever unique qualities are associated with their cultures. Most of the scholars in this group are not much interested in the political systems, organizational structures, or other institutional arrangements associated with organizations in different countries. These structures are seen as more or less empty shells, in which culturally based processes are occurring.

If we are to gain a sense of the degree to which organizations in different countries can and will come to resemble one another, as well as of the nature of the struggles they may have along the way, we need to learn much more about the relationship between cultural and other variables. We may find that cultural differences are irrelevant to how organizations use technology in different countries. This would seem counterintuitive and, as such, an interesting intellectual puzzle. We may find that different cultures are more or less equal in providing the raw materials for the efficient use of technology by organizations. The processes by which this happens would be of very great interest. But if culture does make a difference, the implications lead to both policy and intellectual questions. One of these questions is whether nations can justify protection against international competition to protect their own core values.

Culture and Organizational Orientations
Toward Technology

Social scientists commonly regard technology as systems of physical objects (hardware), knowledge (software), and human activities by which humans act on their environment (Drucker, 1977; MacKenzie and Wajcman, 1985). This concept is fine for many purposes but somewhat unwieldy in a discussion of the relationships between cultural and societal variables and technology in organizations. Our emphasis will be on the hardware component of technology, since a central issue in much of our discussion is the extent to which hardware requires that human activities be structured in certain ways. While much of our discussion of technology is abstract, our major concern is with how organizations in different societies handle technological innovation and the management of technology.

Culture, according to Tyler's classic definition, is "that complex whole which includes knowledge, belief, art, morals, law, customs, and any other capabilities and habits acquired by man as a member of society" (cited in Ogburn, 1964, p. 3). Putting the concept into less global (and more tractable) terms has proved difficult. Indeed, a widespread criticism of so-called cross-cultural studies of organizations has been that very few of them define what they mean by *culture* (Roberts, 1970; Ajiferuke and Boddewyn, 1970; Nath, 1985). At the broadest level, culture is typically thought of as a socially

transmitted system of norms and values. In transferring the
concept of culture from the societal to the organizational
level, Schein (1985, p. 6) defines *cultures* as *"basic assumptions*
and *beliefs* that are shared by members of an organization,
that operate unconsciously, and that define in a basic 'taken-
for-granted' fashion an organization's view of itself and its
environment."* In attempting to compare cultures, some scholars have sought to look at cultures or societies as a whole,
while others have started with examinations of individuals.

Max Weber, of course, is the most prominent among
those taking a macro approach. Although Weber (1958
[1904–1905]) was most concerned with showing that some of
the values associated with the Protestant ethic were conducive
to the initial development of capitalism, these values also
imply a certain orientation toward technology. The value system associated with the Protestant ethic eschews traditional-
ism and favors the constant seeking of new ways of doing
things. Organizations where these values hold sway should
manage technology with great care and attention to detail,
so as to maximize economic acquisition. They should also be
constantly seeking new technologies and constantly seeking
incremental improvements in existing technologies.

The economic success of Japan and other countries of
East Asia has led to a search for elements of a so-called spirit
of capitalism in the value systems of those countries. Bellah
(1957) found analogous values in Tokugawa, Japan. More
recently, Morishima (1982) has argued that the Japanese value
system is not merely functionally equivalent to the spirit of
capitalism engendered by the Protestant ethic but is actually
more efficiently directed toward attaining economic progress.
Berger (1986) speculates that Confucianism is playing an
important role in the economic development of several East
Asian societies.

The claim that a certain value orientation led to the
development of capitalism or is necessary to economic development is very much in dispute (Wallerstein, 1979). We need
not give cultural values such a central role in economic
change, however, to believe that cultural values may influence

how technology is used. A greater difficulty with the approach taken by Weber, Bellah, Morishima, and Berger is that it leaves too many empirical gaps between the identification of philosophical doctrines and evidence that these doctrines influence the behavior of individuals in systematic ways. Another approach is to focus on modal differences in attitudes or beliefs among the members of different cultures. Less attention is paid to the philosophical roots of these attitudes and beliefs. Perhaps the most ambitious attempt in this vein has been that by Hofstede (1980) and his associates.

Hofstede sees people as carrying mental programs that contain components of their national cultures. These mental programs are developed in the family during early childhood and are reinforced in schools and other organizations. The mental programs allow social systems to exist by making behavior predictable within them. Culture, then, is a kind of collective programming that distinguishes one group from another. The program includes *values*, which Hofstede thinks of as a broad tendency to prefer some states of affairs over others. Values are nonrational because they are programmed early in life; what the majority in a culture desire is a *norm*.

Hofstede bases his analysis on the results of a survey given to employees of subsidiaries of a multinational company in forty different advanced nations. He uses four dimensions to differentiate national cultures. *Power distance* includes norms related to the acceptance of differences in the power of bosses and subordinates. *Uncertainty avoidance* describes how the members of a culture cope with uncertainty. *Individualism* is defined by the relative importance members of an organization attach to people and events outside the organization. *Masculinity* norms include being assertive, being acquisitive, exhibiting dominance, showing little concern about people or the quality of life, and emphasizing the instrumental over the expressive.

These dimensions may plausibly explain some differences in how organizations in different cultures use technology. A lower degree of power distance could allow the freer flow of communication within an organization, thus facilitating technological innovativeness. Indeed, this may be taken as part of the rationale for the Japanese development of quality circles; nor is this the only area where the Japanese seem to manifest low power distance, so as to enhance their utilization of technology. Japanese organizations routinely assign university-trained engineers to jobs as production workers at the beginning of their careers. This seems to improve the flow of information within Japanese firms (Lynn, Piehler, and Zahray, 1988). Anecdotal evidence also suggests that Japanese engineers are willing to undertake routine maintenance, cleaning, and other jobs that Americans consider to be the province of those without university degrees. One apparent result is that American machinery is less well maintained. An American engineer working at a Japanese laboratory was surprised at the extent to which Japanese research scientists performed their own low-level technical-support services (Bhasavanich, 1985). Japanese engineers who were involved in the transfer of the basic oxygen-furnace steelmaking technology from Austria to Japan, and who later helped in the transfer of technology to South America, stressed the value of having lower-level employees involved in the transfer process because of the unique perspectives on technology they provided (Lynn, 1982). One could speculate, further, that this lower power distance in Japan is manifested (and fostered) in a school system where students are expected to take care of janitorial and cafeteria duties (Duke, 1986). Thus, low power distance in the Japanese value system could help explain the much observed proficient use of technology by the Japanese. Unfortunately for this analysis, however, Japan ranks higher than the United States on Hofstede's dimension of power distance. The attitudes on power distance reported in Hofstede's questionnaire do not seem to reflect observed behavior.

Uncertainty avoidance also seems potentially relevant to the introduction and use of technology. The Japanese were far more averse to uncertainty than Americans were, according to Hofstede's scale. This, of course, is consistent with such widely noted aspects of the Japanese employment system as permanent employment, preference for employment at large firms, and an emphasis on group decision making and long-term planning. One might also suppose, however, that a predisposition to avoid uncertainty would cause Japanese organizations to be extremely slow to adopt new technology, a characteristic that has not been much evident. This apparent contradiction may be worthy of further exploration. Perhaps Japanese individuals avoid uncertainty, but Japanese groups do not. Perhaps the predisposition to long-term planning includes planning for technological innovation, but primarily incremental rather than radical innovation.

Much has been written about the individualism of Americans versus the group orientation of the Japanese. Hofstede's data seem consistent with this contrast. Japan was twenty-second in individualism, and the United States was first. Hofstede sees an incompatibility between the collectivist bent of the Japanese (as well as that of the Chinese, Soviets, and Yugoslavs) and modern technology. He suggests that modern technology is causing an increased individualism in Japan, but he does not indicate why he thinks individualism is necessary for modern technology. An emerging literature suggests some of the advantages of the less individualistic Japanese approach toward developing modern technology (Lynn, Piehler, and Zahray, 1988; Lynn and McKeown, 1988; Lynn, 1986; Westney and Sakakibara, 1986; Vogel, 1985). A more explicit examination of the relationship between individualism and technology may tell us when and where (and if) a collectivist bent is truly a handicap.

Japan had a higher score than any other country on Hofstede's masculinity index; the United States was thirteenth. One consequence of this, according to Hofstede (1980, pp. 297–298), is that in Asia "masculine Japan has huge pollution problems with which it seems to be unable to cope." Here, Hofstede is reaching too far for evidence. Pollution seems much less a problem in Japan in 1988 than it did fifteen years ago. Adler (1986, p. 43) interprets Hofstede's conclusion that Japan is a highly masculine society, while Sweden is highly feminine, as having important implications for motivation in the workplace: "Japanese 'quality cir-

cles,' for example, primarily strive to achieve maximum quality (masculinity/uncertainty avoidance) while the innovative
Swedish work groups at Volvo attempt to enhance job satisfaction and flexibility (femininity/low uncertainty avoidance)." While it is probably incorrect to characterize Japanese
quality circles as primarily striving to achieve maximum quality (other common goals include productivity and workers'
safety), it may be that there is less emphasis on job satisfaction
as a goal in Japan than in Sweden. Yet our stereotypical
images of Japanese organizations seem to suggest that they
are strongly concerned about people and the quality of work
life. American observers also seem impressed by the high level
of expressive behavior in Japanese organizations, such as the
heavy use of ceremonies and symbolism, even at the apparent
cost of such instrumental values as efficiency.

Hofstede's conceptualization of the dimensions of culture is provocative as a starting point for thinking about how
organizations in different cultures may differ in the use of
technology. One problem is that Hofstede frequently uses the
approach of finding a statistical pattern and then scrambling
through various literatures to find anecdotes that he thinks
illustrate the patterns he thinks he has identified. Such ex
post facto speculation is easy, but it is also easily deceptive.
Perhaps this problem could be ameliorated by having experts
on the various countries involved in Hofstede's study systematically go over the questions and data. It may be too late for
that, however. Those knowledgeable about Japan, for example, may wonder about the implications of a sample that is
based on managers of foreign multinationals. Until recently,
the Japanese most likely to take such jobs were likely to be
people whose values deviated from the norms of their society.
Foreign firms were seen as being more congenial to individ-
ualists but also as providing less security and social status.
One would assume, therefore, that Japanese managers likely
to rank high on individualism (for their society) but low on
uncertainty avoidance would be working for foreign multinationals. A more serious problem is the difficulty in drawing
inferences about how attitudes, as captured on a question-

naire, may influence patterns of organizational behavior. The relationship between individual attitudes and actions is ambiguous enough, and the ambiguity is sharply increased by uncertainty about the relationship between individual and group behavior.

Other forms of research are required. It may be well to begin by accepting the notion that culture be viewed, not as a system of preferences, but rather as "a 'tool kit' of symbols, stories, rituals, and world-views, which people may use in varying configurations to solve different kinds of problems" (Swidler, 1986, p. 273). These, at least, are observable. One could, for example, observe how organizations in different cultures use technology, attending particularly to how cultural "tool kits" are used to construct standard operating procedures and strategies of action.

One may even find it possible to draw on the national character studies pioneered by Ruth Benedict (1934). Benedict tried to offer a scientific approach to the analysis of differences between people in different countries. Such distinguished scholars as Clyde Kluckhohn, Gregory Bateson, Margaret Mead, Marion Levy, Jr., and Geoffrey Gorer have also produced national character studies—of the United States, Japan, Germany, Burma, Thailand, Rumania, and Russia. Benedict herself undertook a study of Japan. She sought out the rules and values of Japanese culture by what she called the "what-is-wrong-with-this-picture technique." By this, she meant that she looked for what surprised her in Japanese books, movies, history, and so forth. She then asked Japanese informants to explain the logic behind these surprises. In the summer of 1945, she produced a sixty-page report based on this research. This later became the classic *The Chrysanthemum and the Sword* (Benedict, 1946).

Benedict begins that book by saying, "The Japanese were the most alien enemy the United States had ever fought in an all-out struggle. In no other war with a major foe had it been necessary to take into account such exceedingly different habits of acting and thinking. . . . We had to understand their behavior in order to cope with it. . . . What would the

Japanese do? Was capitulation possible without invasion? Should we bomb the emperor's palace? What could we expect of Japanese prisoners of war? What should we say in our propaganda to Japanese troops and to the Japanese homeland which could save the lives of Americans and lessen Japanese determination to fight to the last man?" (Benedict, 1946, pp. 1–3).

While these questions seem almost quaint in what they imply about the expectations for this research, the work by Benedict and others is widely credited with giving the U.S. forces insights that both facilitated the surrender of Japan and made the American occupation highly successful. While *The Chrysanthemum and the Sword* now seems dated because of its concern with wartime questions, many still find it useful in interpreting what Westerners see as "wrong" in the picture of life in Japanese organizations.

Studies in the spirit of Benedict's have been out of fashion for about a generation. The authors of these studies have been criticized for inappropriately using a phraseology usually associated with primitive and tribal peoples. This is presumably because those crafting the national character studies were most often anthropologists who were accustomed to writing about primitive and tribal people. They have also been attacked for stressing childishness and immaturity in discussing the Japanese, Germans, Russians, and others under study, and for using a clinical vocabulary usually associated with mental and emotional illness. The emphasis on child-rearing practices seems to require the assumption of too many conceptual linkages—some of which are obscure, to say the least. A recent text suggests another reason for the demise of national character studies: "A graduate student would have to think twice before committing himself to writing a doctoral dissertation on a culture-and-personality topic when there are simpler, more manageable subjects available" (Barnouw, 1985, p. 458).

Working at a time of wartime hysteria that must have made objective thinking about the Japanese very difficult, unable to visit Japan, using informants who had been "contaminated" by time spent outside Japan, and hindered by a faulty conceptual basis, Benedict nevertheless was able to produce major insights. Some of these insights even had apparent practical implications. This suggests that her "what-is-wrong-with-this-picture technique" may be a very powerful one. Suppose a modern researcher used this technique in an effort to identify the cultural tools used in technological innovation and management in organizations in different countries. Do Japanese and Chinese managers really refer to Sun Tsu in plotting strategy? Do they draw on philosophical doctrines of the sort examined by Weber and others in making decisions? Our researcher would be unhampered by the need to produce militarily relevant findings, could visit the countries of interest, and would be free of simplistic Freudian explanations requiring that everything be linked to childrearing practices. Perhaps this modern Benedict would look at materials from the broader society in which values and norms are reinforced (books, magazines, films, television programs, newspapers), with an eye to incongruities and a sensitive ear to explanations of them by people from that culture. For years, children's programs in Japan have featured personable and mischief-prone robots (sometimes in league with children against their parents). What should be made of this? How common are themes in which technology is seen as presenting answers to problems, rather than as posing problems? (Do these resonate with traditional stories?) Is a cross-national convergence in values and norms occurring as a result of the internationalization of the entertainment industry? (Are U.S. children being influenced by alien values as they watch Saturday-morning cartoons produced in the Far East?) The core of the research, however, would be the observation of the cultural tools used in organizations.

Technology and the Convergence of Organizational Structures and Processes

So far, our discussion has centered on how researchers can identify culturally based differences in how technology is

handled by organizations in different countries. We now turn
to arguments that technological imperatives may be leveling
these differences. Perhaps the most influential statement of
this argument was made by Kerr, Dunlop, Harbison, and
Myers (1964). They argued that differences in the methods of
production between more and less highly industrialized countries would decrease over time because modern technology
requires institutional arrangements of the sort prevalent in
the West. The non-Western world could either model itself
after the West or face being left out of the modern world. The
result, according to Drucker (1977, p. 54), is "the disappear-
ance of all non-Western societies and cultures under the
inundation of Western technology."

If this convergence hypothesis is valid for societies, it
should also apply to complex organizations. Indeed, one
might suppose that technological imperatives would have
even greater force in business organizations, where the pressures of competition are more apparent and more immediate
than is true at the societal level. Hickson, McMillan, Azumi,
and Horvath (1979) argue that if the convergence hypothesis
is not valid, organizational theory can have little claim to
generality. Whether or not others would argue the point this
strongly, many seem to share the assumptions it is based on.
This has been true of management theorists, as well as of
organization theorists. Farmer and Richman (1965, p. 400)
put the conventional wisdom succinctly: "As the general
similarity of men everywhere is recognized, and as managerial and technological necessity presses all types of cultures
toward a common road, nations everywhere become more
similar. . . . Studies in comparative management . . . will be
largely obsolete. . . . Instead of differences, we shall find similarities, because the logic of technology and management
will lead all to the same general position."

Empirical support was offered for the convergence
argument by Harbison and Myers (1959) in a landmark study
of management in twelve different industrialized countries.
Harbison and Myers conclude that as societies advance, their
institutions and organizational forms go through stages that

are more related to level of advance than to the cultural starting points. Harbison and Myers describe four stages of development, from the agrarian-feudalistic to the industrial-democratic, and conclude that a certain managerial philosophy is appropriate for each. All societies, when they advance sufficiently, will end up, according to these authors, with a democratic form of management. In brief, the needs of modern management will overcome cultural differences.

Harbison and Myers (1959) predicted that Japan, the most notably deviant of the advanced industrial nations, would either change some of its eccentric managerial practices or fall behind. As Japan's level of economic development approached that of many Western countries in the 1960s, a number of sociologists and anthropologists watched closely for signs of a convergence in managerial practices, particularly a diminution of what many of them saw as feudalistic remnants, such as permanent employment, seniority-based promotions, and an emphasis on group problem solving, with rewards going to groups rather than to individuals. Many Japanese observers have strongly advocated that Japanese management abandon these practices, and some scholars have reported seeing signs of convergence (Dunphy, 1987).

Evidence of convergence has also been reported in studies of developing countries. For example, Negandhi, from his study of Argentina, Brazil, India, the Philippines, Taiwan, and Uruguay, concludes that similarities in managerial practices lead to similar organizational effectiveness and, more generally, that "the logic of technology is taking over man's differing beliefs and value orientations" (Negandhi, 1979, p. 332).

A growing number of studies, however, have offered evidence that is interpreted as being inconsistent with the convergence hypothesis. Haire, Ghiselli, and Porter (1966, p. 11) conclude from their survey of 3,600 managers in fourteen countries that there are intelligible patterns in national differences in managerial attitudes about leadership, managerial roles, and the motives managers want to satisfy on the job; they find that countries cluster and that what "emerges most clearly from the clusters is the strong pattern of cultural influence on the data." This clustering showed a "remarkably poor fit" with the hypothesis that it was due to level of industrialization.

Gallie (1978) sought a more finely grained comparison by comparing technologically identical plants in the United Kingdom and France. Although the plants used the same technology and were in countries that were both from the same Western cultural tradition, Gallie found major differences in how the plants were organized with respect to the level of social integration of the work force, the structure of managerial power, and the nature of trade unionism.

Several scholars suggest that the convergence literature exaggerates national similarities because it concentrates on organizational structure. Much of the cultural influence, according to these scholars, is more evident in such processes as recruitment, promotions, suggestions for innovation, and the dominant mechanisms of social control. Aiken and Bacharach (1979) offer evidence for this position based on a study of bureaucracies in two districts of Belgium. Child and Kieser (1979, p. 253) argue that organizations in different societies, even if they face similar contingencies and have similar formal structures, will differ because deep-rooted "cultural forces will still re-assert themselves in the way people actually behave and relate to each other. Structure will remain purely formal if it is not consonant with culturally derived expectations."

In a comparative study of Britain and West Germany, Nicholas (1985) emphasizes what he sees as three key dimensions of the social culture: the training and education systems, task characteristics, and working relationships. He sees the training systems of the two countries as being differently structured toward similar technical ends. Nicholas attributes the difference in structure to history. He notes that the industrial revolution in Britain was more dependent on raw materials and capital than on skill. As a result, little attention was given to either vocational or professional training. The craft unions and professional associations, however, sought to protect their members by defining and bounding qualifications.

The universities and other schools kept their distance by remaining carefully nonprofessional in what they taught. Things were very different in Germany when the industrial revolution took place there. To speed economic development, the German states promoted vocational and professional education. Thus, German technical training has tended to be more highly integrated, giving more stress to the relationship between manufacturing and design. One current implication of this difference in history is that there is less use of formally qualified engineers in the United Kingdom. Moreover, the relationship between being formally qualified for a task and actually having the skills to do it is weaker in Britain. Attitudes toward new technologies also differ between the two countries. In Nicholas's study, the British saw computer-controlled machine tools as deskilling, while the Germans saw these tools as requiring constant training. British foremen were bypassed when the new technology was introduced; German foremen were central to the process of introduction.

What, then, of arguments that the competitive pressure on organizations to use technology with maximum efficiency leads to the abandonment of culturally distinctive ways of doing things? Cole (1973) offers one explanation of why this convergence has not occurred. He argues that a reasonable level of ability to exploit modern technology can be arrived at via a variety of functionally equivalent paths. The Japanese permanent-employment system, for example, may meet the needs of industrialism as well as the more fluid U.S. system does. Cole adds the observation that permanent employment does not have the same meaning to the Japanese as it would to Americans, and vice versa. Thus, the Japanese system of employment may very well meet the technological imperatives of modern industry in Japan, but it will not necessarily satisfy these imperatives in the United States.

Systems theorists sometimes use the term *equifinality* to refer to systems reaching the same final state from different initial conditions and by different routes. Different cultures may sometimes reach comparable levels of efficiency by different combinations of technologies and systems of management. One example may be that of facsimiles and electronic mail in Japan and the United States. The two technologies have partially overlapping functions. Americans seem to prefer electronic mail as a device for avoiding "telephone tag" (although, of course, they also use it for other reasons). The Japanese (being uncomfortable with keyboards) seem to prefer facsimiles for this purpose. One result has been that facsimiles were commonplace in Japan several years before they were in the United States, while the reverse was true of electronic mail. It appears that patterns of usage still differ between the two countries in organizations that seem approximately equal in their technological levels.

It would be useful to identify other examples of technologies that seem more or less compatible with different societies. Particularly interesting might be technologies that seemed to evolve out of cultural preferences in different countries. There are cases that claim to show that certain technologies were developed and became prevalent, not because of technical or economical superiority, but because they embodied the values of those who decided which lines of research to pursue. Thus, Noble (1985) argues that numerically controlled machine tools came into use in place of an alternative technology because they enhanced managerial control over the workplace and did not require managers to trust machinists as much as the other technology did. Cowan (1985) suggests that electric refrigerators prevailed over gas refrigerators because General Electric and other powerful companies wanted to promote the use of electricity.

There is a somewhat different explanation, with very different implications, for why differences persist in organizational practice related to the use of technology. This explanation is that all societies have their inefficiencies, which partially offset one another to ameliorate technological and competitive imperatives. The earlier advocates of the convergence hypothesis tended to assume that the United States provides the ultimate model of tradition-free managerial and organizational practices. Gusfield (1967), Portes (1976), Cole (1979), and others have pointed out the fallacy of this position; it now seems unbelievably (almost quaintly) ethno-centric. Crozier (1964) notes the dysfunctions of French bureaucracy but then points out that the U.S. and Russian bureaucracies also each have their own peculiar, culturally engendered sets of dysfunctions. These dysfunctional differences may persist, in part, because they have been counterbalanced by dysfunctions in competing organizations. Further, the exposure to competition from other organizations has not been intense.

If one accepts Cole's notion of functional equivalence, one can easily envision a world in which each culture's organizations follow a separate path of evolution. This may involve the development of specific technologies tailored to the cultural proclivities of each society. But what if there really is one most efficient technology for most given purposes, and what if there is one most efficient way of structuring organizations to develop and use that technology? Will organizations be able to maintain the eccentricities associated with their cultures as international competition reaches levels that would have been difficult to imagine a few years ago? A generation ago, American workers in the auto and steel industries could insist on and receive large salaries and long vacations; now it seems that they cannot. Observers now tell us that American management and labor must give up their adversarial relationship.

It may be that the various national differences cited as refuting the convergence hypothesis are only transitional. The British may resist more technically efficient methods of ensuring that the most qualified people manage technology in their plants, but this may be an unsustainable luxury after 1992. Living in isolation, the Japanese managed to maintain their cultural preference for swords over guns for some two and a half centuries, but not when they came under competitive pressure from foreigners using guns (Perrin, 1980).

While language and writing systems are somewhat different from the aspects of culture we have discussed, some examples of the interaction between writing systems and technologies is suggestive. At several points during this century,

most recently in the aftermath of World War II, many scholars
in China and Japan strongly advocated the abandonment of
the traditional idiographic writing systems in those countries.
Writing systems based on thousands of characters did not
permit the ready use of what was then modern office technology. Such devices as typewriters and telexes, which required
the use of relatively small keyboards, were simply impractical.
It was extremely difficult to develop efficient, easy-to-use
filing systems. The great civilizations of the East could never
compete with those in the West as long as they relied on their
antiquated writing systems—or so the argument went. (Not
much has been said about the possible advantages of idiographically based language for an information-intensive
world. One is that idiographs are much more information-
rich than Latin letters and may permit a more rapid acquisition of information.) The idiographically based writing systems were not abandoned, but they were simplified, and when
the Japanese began using computers, they found it necessary
to use keyboards developed for the Latin alphabet as input
devices. Indeed, Japanese software even came to use substantial numbers of English words, simply because this was easier.
To a very limited degree, then, there was convergence. There
has also been an intensive search on the part of the Japanese
to find ways of overcoming the disadvantages that their
language gives them in using computers and related technologies. One result has been the development of Japanese
word-processing equipment (which is, however, much more
difficult to use and much slower than the English counterparts). Further advances (possibly including greater use of
voice input) may completely eliminate the disadvantages of
the Japanese language in word processing.

    This anecdote suggests three responses to the challenge
posed by foreign cultures that are better structured to use
technology. First, abandon the weak elements of your own
culture (a response that has been proposed but not followed).
Second, make limited changes in your own culture (a response that has been followed, although only with marginally
satisfactory results). Third, develop a technology more com-

patible with your own culture, and thus eliminate any competitive disadvantage (the response the Japanese are now attempting). The third of these alternatives is the least threatening; but what determines whether a society will be able to create a technology adapted to its own culture, rather than being pressured to adapt to a technology created by foreign cultures?

Part of the answer to this question seems to inhere in the possibilities allowed by technology at any given time. The Japanese had no serious prospects of developing alternative technologies to cope with their written language until computers reached a certain stage of development. Today's conventional wisdom seems to be that the technologies now emerging have fewer imperatives than those of the past. As Hirschhorn (1984) notes, mechanically organized machines (that is, those based on an interplay of masses, forces, torques, and linkages) became less and less flexible as they became more and more productive and automatic. The introduction of electric motors increased flexibility to a degree (since it separated the transformation from the transmission system), and the vacuum tube increased flexibility still more. A bigger jump, however, has come with the development of microprocessors. Even office work has seen the introduction of new technologies that greatly reduce the need for groups of workers to work at the same time and in the same place. The upshot may be that enhanced flexibility with regard to work arrangements may also allow enhanced flexibility with regard to technological imperatives that crush cultural differences. This speculation, however, is not much informed by research.

A related set of issues involves national abilities to develop culturally compatible technologies in response to foreign challenges. The development of such abilities has clearly been a major part of the Japanese policy agenda for over a century. Japanese leaders felt threatened by the implications of Japan's need to adopt technologies that had originated in very foreign milieus. The ways in which they managed to cope with this threat should be studied closely by those apprehensive about unwanted convergencies.

Conclusions and Implications for Research

A number of issues have been raised here, issues that are likely to be of increasing importance as trade barriers, transportation costs, and various other buffers to international competition continue to lose strength. Writing on organizational culture, Schein (1985) and others assume that culture is highly malleable—something to be manipulated by managers. As Adler and Jelinek (1986) comment, it is ironic that culture is treated in this literature as being extremely important in its effect on organizational outcomes and yet is taken to be of such little importance for its own sake. We need to develop a far better understanding of cultural change in organizations. We need to know not only how to change culture for some desired organizational outcome but also what consequences these changes have for individuals.

We need to look closely at the relationship between organizational culture and national culture. Are national cultures as malleable as organizational cultures are supposed to be? The evidence at this point is very thin. In a recent study of innovative change in the shipping industries of eight countries, Walton (1987) concluded that if other factors were sufficiently favorable to produce action, then the action itself could modify the culture (which Walton refers to as a social context). But if our national culture is supposed to be part of our identity, should we so blithely accept changes in it? What do the changes amount to? One recalls the Weberian image of bureaucracies destroying competing organizational forms that were less efficient but that might have better embodied the values prevalent at the time. Is something similar happening today? In the last few years, large numbers of U.S. firms have adopted quality circles, just-in-time inventory control, modified labor–management systems, new decision-making mechanisms, flatter organizational structures, and other organizational innovations from Japan. These changes have largely occurred under the pressure of an unprecedentedly high level of international competition. There is little to criticize in the diffusion of good ideas, but is there a risk that core values may be subverted in the process of borrowing? The converse question is also of interest. What happens when organizational culture is incompatible with national culture? Is there room for a contingency theory of organizations that includes national culture as a contingency?

Are there functionally equivalent paths to equal levels of efficiency in the development and use of technology? We have suggested that, in some instances, a culture may adapt a technology to its own needs. What are the limitations of this process? How does it happen? What about cultures finding alternative materials from within themselves that allow the creation of new organizational forms to cope with competitive challenges in the use of technology? How do economic factors and institutional arrangements constrain or facilitate the processes of adaptation?

In short, we need organizational theories and organizational research that better encompass national and organizational culture, technology, organizational structure, and performance. What type of research is most likely to take us farthest toward reaching these new understandings? The first need is for exploratory case studies, simply because we know so little about the relationships among these variables. The case studies, for reasons argued very well by Cole (1979), should be explicitly comparative. The research should be carried out by multinational teams of researchers studying technology in organizations in different countries. This would not simply be the adaptation of some U.S. study to foreign domains, using foreign research assistants; it would start from the assumption that even the research questions U.S. researchers are likely to begin with include a certain amount of cultural contamination, and that an early phase of international cooperation should include a sorting out of these ethnocentricities. This would best be done by scholars from the different countries participating as equals. A wrinkle—not much pursued, but possibly interesting—would be to have researchers study only organizations not in their own societies. This would allow them to use Benedict's "what's-wrong-with-this-picture technique." The case studies would be oriented toward issues related to organizational adaptation to and utilization of technology.

The scholars would not only study organizational structures and processes but also seek to trace the historical, political, and/or economic origins of these structures and processes. Aside from providing context, this would also allow a preliminary assessment of how generalizable the findings of the study were. A survey approach would then be used to address the issue of how typical the findings were and what the nature of intranational variation might be.

References

Adler, N. J. *International Dimensions of Organizational Behavior.* Boston: Kent Publishing, 1986.

Adler, N. J., and Jelinek, M. "Is Organization 'Culture' Culture Bound?" *Human Resource Management,* 1986, *25* (1), 73–90.

Aiken, M., and Bacharach, S. B. "Culture and Organizational Structure and Process: A Comparative Study of Local Government Administrative Bureaucracies in the Walloon and Flemish Regions of Belgium." In C. J. Lammers and D. J. Hickson (eds.), *Organizations Alike and Unlike: International and Interinstitutional Studies in the Sociology of Organizations.* London: Routledge & Kegan Paul, 1979.

Ajiferuke, M., and Boddewyn, J. "Culture and Other Explanatory Variables in Comparative Management Studies." *Academy of Management Journal,* 1970, *13,* 153–163.

Barnouw, V. *Culture and Personality.* Homewood, Ill.: Dorsey Press, 1985.

Bellah, R. N. *Tokugawa Religion.* Boston: Beacon Press, 1957.

Benedict, R. *Patterns of Culture.* Boston: Houghton Mifflin, 1934.

Benedict, R. *The Chrysanthemum and the Sword.* Boston: Houghton Mifflin, 1946.

Berger, P. L. *The Capitalist Revolution: Fifty Propositions About Prosperity, Equality, & Labor.* New York: Basic Books, 1986.

Bhasavanich, D. "An American in Tokyo: Jumping to the Japanese Beat." *IEEE Spectrum,* 1985, *22,* 72-81.

Child, J., and Kieser, A. "Organizational and Managerial Roles in British and West German Companies: An Examination of the Culture-Free Thesis." In C. J. Lammers and D. J. Hickson (eds.), *Organizations Alike and Unlike: International and Interinstitutional Studies in the Sociology of Organizations.* London: Routledge & Kegan Paul, 1979.

Cole, R. E. "Functional Alternatives and Economic Development: An Empirical Example of Permanent Employment in Japan." *American Sociological Review,* 1973, *38,* 323-345.

Cole, R. E. *Work, Mobility, and Participation.* Berkeley: University of California Press, 1979.

Cowan, R. S. "How the Refrigerator Got Its Hum." In D. MacKenzie and J. Wajcman (eds.), *The Social Shaping of Technology.* Philadelphia: Open University Press, 1985.

Crozier, M. *The Bureaucratic Phenomenon.* London: Tavistock, 1964.

Drucker, P. *Technology, Management, and Society.* New York: Harper & Row, 1977.

Duke, B. *The Japanese School: Lessons for Industrial America.* New York: Praeger, 1986.

Dunphy, D. "Convergence/Divergence: A Temporal Review of the Japanese Enterprise and Its Management." *Academy of Management Review,* 1987, *12,* 445-459.

Farmer, R., and Richman, B. A. *Comparative Management and Economic Progress.* Homewood, Ill.: R. D. Irwin, 1965.

Gallie, D. *In Search of the New Working Class: Automation and Social Integration with Capitalist Enterprise.* Cambridge, England: Cambridge University Press, 1978.

Gusfield, J. "Tradition and Modernity: Misplaced Polarities in the Study of Social Change." *American Journal of Sociology,* 1967, *72,* 351-362.

Haire, M., Ghiselli, E. E., and Porter, L. W. *Managerial Thinking: An International Study.* New York: Wiley, 1966.

Harbison, F., and Myers, C. A. *Management in the Industrial World.* New York: McGraw-Hill, 1959.

Hickson, D. J., McMillan, C. J., Azumi, K., and Horvath, D. "Grounds for Comparative Organization Theory: Quicksands or Hard Core." In C. J. Lammers and D. J. Hickson (eds.), *Organizations Alike and Unlike: International and Interinstitutional Studies in the Sociology of Organizations.* London: Routledge & Kegan Paul, 1979.

Hirschhorn, L. *Beyond Mechanization.* Cambridge, Mass.: MIT Press, 1984.

Hofstede, G. *Culture's Consequences: National Differences in Thinking and Organizing.* Newbury Park, Calif.: Sage, 1980.

Kerr, C., Dunlop, J. T., Harbison, F., and Myers, C. A. *Industrialism and Industrial Man.* New York: Oxford University Press, 1964.

Lynn, L. H. *How Japan Innovates: A Comparison with the United States in the Case of Oxygen Steelmaking.* Boulder, Colo.: Westview Press, 1982.

Lynn, L. H. "Japanese Research and Technology Policy." *Science,* 1986, *233,* 296–301.

Lynn, L. H., and McKeown, T. J. *Organizing Business: Trade Associations in America and Japan.* Washington, D.C.: American Enterprise Institute and University Press of America, 1988.

Lynn, L. H., Piehler, H. R., and Zahray, W. P. *Engineers in the United States and Japan: A Comparison of Their Number, and an Empirical Study of Their Careers and Methods of Information Transfer.* National Science Foundation, 1988.

MacKenzie, D., and Wajcman, J. (eds.). *The Social Shaping of Technology.* Philadelphia: Open University Press, 1985.

Morishima, M. *Why Has Japan "Succeeded"?: Western Technology and the Japanese Ethos.* Cambridge, England: Cambridge University Press, 1982.

Nath, R. "Role of Culture in Cross-Cultural and Organizational Research." Paper presented at the 45th annual meeting of the Academy of Management, San Diego, Aug. 1985.

Negandhi, A. R. "Convergence in Organizational Practices: An Empirical Study of Industrial Enterprises in Developing Countries." In C. J. Lammers and D. J. Hickson (eds.), *Organizations Alike and Unlike: International and Inter-*

institutional Studies in the Sociology of Organizations. London: Routledge & Kegan Paul, 1979.

Nicholas, I. "Cross-Cultural Research, Technological Change, and Vocational Training." In P. Joynt and M. Warner (eds.), *Managing in Different Cultures.* Oslo, Norway: Universitetsforlaget, 1985.

Noble, D. F. "'Social Choice in Machine Design: The Case of Automatically Controlled Machine Tools." In D. MacKenzie and J. Wajcman (eds.), *The Social Shaping of Technology.* Philadelphia: Open University Press, 1985.

Ogburn, W. F. *On Culture and Social Change.* Chicago: University of Chicago Press, 1964.

Perrin, N. *Giving up the Gun: Japan's Reversion to the Sword, 1543–1879.* Boston: Shambhala, 1980.

Portes, A. "On the Sociology of National Development: Theories and Issues." *American Journal of Sociology,* 1976, *82,* 55–85.

Roberts, K. "On Looking at an Elephant: An Evaluation of Cross-Cultural Research Related to Organizations." *Psychological Bulletin,* 1970, *74,* 327–350.

Schein, E. H. *Organizational Culture and Leadership: A Dynamic View.* San Francisco: Jossey-Bass, 1985.

Swidler, A. "Culture in Action." *American Sociological Review,* 1986, *51,* 273–286.

Vogel, E. F. *Comeback.* New York: Simon & Schuster, 1985.

Wallerstein, I. *The Capitalist World Economy.* Cambridge, England: Cambridge University Press, 1979.

Walton, R. E. *Innovating to Compete: Lessons for Diffusing and Managing Change in the Workplace.* San Francisco: Jossey-Bass, 1987.

Weber, M. *The Protestant Ethic and the Spirit of Capitalism.* New York: Scribner's, 1958. (Originally published 1904–1905.)

Westney, D., and Sakakibara, K. "Designing the Designers: Computer R&D in the United States and Japan." *Technology Review,* 1986, *89,* 24–31, 68–69.

7

⚟

Technology and Organizations: An Economic/Institutional Analysis

David C. Mowery

In recent years, research and discussion of the role of technological change in economic development and competitiveness have identified a number of important empirical phenomena, including the following:

1. Management of product development by Japanese automobile firms differs sharply from U.S. firms' product-development performance in a mature industry with stable technology and similar technological staff and skills in both groups of firms. According to Clark, Chew, and Fujimoto (1987), Japanese firms are able to bring a new automobile design to market in half the time required by U.S. firms.
2. Labor productivity and the quality of the products of U.S. and Japanese auto firms with access to identical production technologies also differ considerably. In the best-known "transplant" of Japanese management to a U.S. automobile plant (the Toyota–General Motors NUMMI joint venture), Toyota dramatically improved productivity

I am grateful to Dan Levinthal, Richard Scott, and Lee Sproull for comments and suggestions on this chapter.

and quality with a work force that previously had ranked among the least productive and most fractious within General Motors.

3. The development of the modern industrial economy of the United States is widely hailed (see Rosenberg and Birdzell, 1986) as a testament to the allocative efficiency and dynamism of a market-based system. Yet one of the central institutions in U.S. economic growth during the past century—organized industrial research—historically has been situated largely within the nonmarket portion of this nation's economy, within large, diversified corporations.

4. The U.S. national research system now is undergoing rapid and wrenching structural change. Major corporations have sold, closed, reorganized, or reduced the size of corporate research facilities that formerly were showcases for advanced research. Examples include the central research laboratories of General Electric, DuPont, RCA, and AT&T. These and other firms now are exploring a diverse array of organizational structures for industrial research, including domestic and international collaboration with other firms or universities. Why is this change occurring? How are these new and complex hybrid cooperative organizations to be organized and managed?

All of these issues concern the interaction of technological change and the institutions of economic life—factories, laboratories, and corporations. They have major implications for public policy, private managers, and (according to some) even the national security of this nation, affecting as they do the living standards and wealth of the United States. What light can economic theory and empirical economic research shed on these interactions? What are the implications for the public and private sectors of these insights? This chapter examines the economic perspective on the interaction of organizations and technology.

The numerous and important contributions of economics to the analysis of technology and organizations draw only modestly on mainstream ("neoclassical") economic theory.

As I note in the next section, neoclassical theory devotes little
or no attention to the intrafirm issues, including those just
described, that are critical to an understanding of the interaction of technology and organizations. Nevertheless, the
empirical research of economists and economic historians
has made important contributions to the study of technology
and organizations, describing and analyzing the phenomenon
of technological change and its interaction with economic
institutions.

Partly as a result of the continual uncovering by empirical research of phenomena (again, including those just
noted) that are not easily explained with mainstream theory,
several alternative theoretical frameworks for the analysis of
economic institutions have been developed by economists.
These alternative frameworks, one of which is similar to the
"population ecology" framework described by Scott in this
volume, have important implications for the study of technology and organizations. These alternatives to neoclassical
theory may produce significant revisions or extensions of the
dominant theoretical framework. None of these alternative
analytical frameworks provides a satisfactory treatment of the
links between technological and organizational change, however, nor have empirical applications of these frameworks
advanced such an understanding. For example, Williamson's
(1975, 1985) searching analysis of transaction costs and the
organization of economic activity devotes little attention to
technology. Nelson and Winter's (1982) work, which contains
rich descriptive portraits of the evolution of organizational
capabilities and of technological change, has yielded few
novel empirical implications.

Neoclassical Economic Theory

The vast economics literature on technology and the
structure of the firm and its markets is reviewed in Kamien
and Schwartz (1981) and Cohen and Levin (1988). A discussion of the economic analysis of the interaction between technology and organizations highlights two weak areas within

mainstream economic theory: the analysis of the internal organization of the firm, and the analysis of technological change. The economist's theory of the firm is actually a theory of markets; theoretical understanding of the basis for the existence of the firm, to say nothing of the factors that determine its boundaries, is not well advanced, despite important work by Coase (1937), Williamson (1975, 1985), Chandler (1962, 1977, 1989), and Teece (1982, 1986), which will be discussed shortly. A large literature has appeared in recent years on the economics of information and organization, including contributions by Ross (1973), Marschak and Radner (1972), Sah and Stiglitz (1985) and Herriott, Levinthal, and March (1985), and others. This literature is not concerned with the interaction of technological and organizational change, however, nor has it yielded significant empirical results on the interaction between technology and organizations. I therefore do not consider it in detail in this chapter. This theoretical deficiency is particularly significant in the analysis of the organization of research and development, the source of new technologies in modern economies. Neoclassical theory's emphasis on the appropriability of the results of research investment, which underpins its neoclassical analysis of research and development, must be complemented with an analysis of the conditions supporting the utilization of these results. In the absence of an analysis of the utilization of the fruits of research and development (R&D), economic theory is hard pressed to provide answers to a number of increasingly urgent policy questions.

Technological change itself also challenges this body of theory. Although economists have done a great deal to document the contribution of new technology to economic growth and development, economic theory has been less successful in incorporating technological change, Much of the neoclassical analysis of R&D investment deals with the "public good" character of scientific and technological knowledge. Other characteristics of technology, however, have proved more difficult to incorporate into the neoclassical corpus. Neoclassical theory is poorly equipped to analyze product innovation (the prediction of demand conditions and producer structure for industries producing entirely new products is beyond the capabilities of current theory), the extensive modification of new technologies following their introduction, the accumulation of organization-specific technological assets, and the learning and spillover effects that characterize innovation.

Technology and the Firm. Although neoclassical economic theory has devoted little attention to the organizational structure of the business enterprise, technology plays a central role in the theory of the firm. Economic theory treats the firm as an optimizing "black box." The processes by which output and price decisions are made are not specified, since a rigorous selection environment is assumed to prevent any but efficient firms with identical production technologies and decision rules from surviving (Friedman, 1953, provides a strong statement of this position, as does Becker, 1962). The boundaries of the surviving and therefore efficient firms are determined largely by the technology of production, which determines cost conditions and optimal firm size. *Technology* is defined largely as production techniques, embodied in a "book of blueprints" that is known to all firms. The representative firm has complete knowledge of all possible production techniques that allow it to combine capital and labor at all relative prices for these factors to produce its output at minimum cost.

Technology is assumed to be fixed. Firms respond to changes in relative prices of inputs or demand for output by varying their combinations of capital and labor, drawn from the book of blueprints. The neoclassical theory of the firm denies a major role for the interaction of technology and organizational structure. The theory specifies successive equilibrium states and says little about the process of transition from one to another equilibrium. Economic theory's inattention to the internal structure of the firm limits its ability to explain changes in firm structure. The theory cannot easily account for the rise of diversified, multifunction firms in the late nineteenth century or for the growth of multinational enterprises in the late twentieth century. The prediction of this theoretical apparatus—that all firms within an industry employ identical technologies and face similar cost curves—also does not fit well with substantial interfirm differences in performance (Leibenstein, 1966) and in the choice of technology (Piore, 1968), nor has this conceptual framework addressed the evidence that identical production technologies often are implemented in radically different ways within different plants, resulting in contrasting structures of work organization for the production of similar products within similar process technologies (Cyert and Mowery, 1987; Spenner, 1988; Hirschhorn, 1988).

Economic Theory and the Organization of Innovation. Neoclassical theorists also have considered the innovation process itself. The key elements of the neoclassical economic theory of R&D are contained in papers by Nelson (1959) and Arrow (1962), which considered the economics of knowledge production through investment in industrial research (see Mowery, 1983a, for a more extended discussion). Research was portrayed in these papers as an investment decision made by the profit-maximizing firm. Nelson and Arrow argued that the social returns to research investment exceeded the private returns faced by the firm, a condition leading to underinvestment by the firm (from the social point of view) in research.

This theory's description of market failure illustrates the deficiencies of the neoclassical economic framework for the study of technology and organizations. Arrow (1962), in particular, argued that although firms incurred costs in producing scientific or technical knowledge, the costs of transferring this knowledge, once discovered, were effectively zero. The consumption by another firm of the knowledge produced by a firm does not diminish or degrade the information; thus, it becomes a public good. From the social point of view, the widest possible diffusion of this knowledge is optimal. The price necessary to achieve this goal, however, a price equal to the costs of transfer, is so low as to bankrupt the discoverer.

The supply of socially beneficial research in civilian technologies, basic research in particular, is insufficient because of the disjunction between the privately and socially optimal prices for the results: "Thus basic research, the output of which is only used as an informational input into other inventive activities, is especially unlikely to be rewarded. In fact, it is likely to be of commercial value to the firm undertaking it only if other firms are prevented from using the information. But such restriction reduces the efficiency of inventive activity in general, and will therefore reduce its quantity also" (Arrow, 1962, p. 618).

Although this theoretical analysis identifies a central market failure in the generation of new knowledge through private means, it is deficient. The fruits of research do not consist solely of information that can be utilized at minimal cost for innovation. As Pavitt (1987) and others (Rosenberg, 1982; Mowery, 1983a; Cohen and Levinthal, 1989) have noted, transferring and exploiting the technical and scientific information that is necessary for innovation is costly and knowledge-intensive. The neoclassical analysis of innovation focuses largely on the conditions of appropriability of the returns to innovation and argues that market failure results in insufficient R&D. The critical factor for commercially successful innovation, however, is the utilization of the results of R&D. In neoclassical analysis, the identification of market failure in the supply of R&D is an important but insufficient insight. The market-failure analysis must be supplemented by an analysis of the conditions affecting the utilization of the results of research.

Explaining R&D Organization and Policy with Neoclassical Theory

The neoclassical analysis of R&D investment cannot explain why most U.S. industrial research laboratories are part of manufacturing firms. Why did U.S. industrial research develop in this fashion, rather than being provided via contract by independent firms (see Mowery, 1981, 1983b)? The growth of industrial research within U.S. manufacturing was associated with the progressive absorption by large manufacturing firms of functions previously carried out and organized via market institutions, as well as with the development of entirely new activities within the firm (see Chandler, 1977). In-house research allowed for the development and exploitation of firm-specific knowledge, reflecting the superiority of the quality and quantity of intrafirm communications to those between contractual partners, as well as the fact that production and the acquisition of detailed technical knowledge frequently are joint activities.

The uncertainty associated with R&D makes it difficult to write complete contracts (that is, contracts that cover all contingencies and possible outcomes) for a research project. Moreover, the fact that much of the knowledge relevant to a specific industrial research problem is highly firm-specific means that the research services needed by many firms simply are unavailable from independent contractors. Finally, as already noted, the transfer of knowledge, research findings, and research results from research contractor to client is a knowledge-intensive activity. All of these factors make contractual provision of all but the simplest and least uncertain activities very difficult, increase the level of intrafirm expertise needed to absorb the results of externally performed research, and limit the ability of external research organizations to substitute for in-house research.

Empirical research (Mowery, 1983b) supports these observations. The share of industrial research personnel employed in independent research laboratories not affiliated with manufacturing firms—that is, organizations engaged in the sale of R&D services via contract—declined during the formative period of U.S. industrial research. The activities of these independent research organizations largely complemented (rather than substituted for) the in-house research activities of industrial firms during the 1900–1940 period. Independent research organizations conducted low-risk projects for analyzing chemicals and materials, rather than performing pathbreaking R&D. These findings contradict the predictions of at least one Nobel laureate and proponent of the neoclassical theory of research and development, who notes that "with the growth of research, new firms will emerge to provide specialized facilities for small firms. It is only to be expected that, when a new kind of research develops, at first it will be conducted chiefly as an ancillary activity by existing firms. . . . We may expect the rapid expansion of the specialized research laboratory, selling its services generally. The specialized laboratories need not be in the least inferior to 'captive' laboratories" (Stigler, 1956, p. 281).

The success and failure of cooperative research and development programs sponsored by the U.S. government and other governments provide additional illustrations of the weak policy guidance provided by the neoclassical framework. Programs of support for cooperative research in industries where firms pursue little or no internal R&D have yielded disappointing results (Mowery, 1983a). In Great Britain, public support of cooperative research establishments has been utilized since World War I in an effort to improve the innovative performance of industry. Most analysts and scholars, however, agree that these cooperative laboratories (known as research associations) have not substituted effectively for the in-house research facilities that are lacking in many British firms: "The main value of the research association scheme, as it turned out, is probably in industries with at least some research of their own and not, as originally thought, in industries with virtually no research of their own. Research associations serving industries composed of small units with no private research may be valuable but their contribution is usually different and somewhat limited" (Organization for Economic Cooperation and Development, 1968, p. 124).

Policy experiments in the United States have produced similar results. The University-Industry Cooperative Research Centers Program of the National Science Foundation was an experiment designed "to determine if federal cost-sharing during a five-year period would enable the creation of industry-funded permanent cooperative research centers" (National Science Foundation, 1979, p. v). Program designers appear to have viewed cooperative research organizations as substitutes for in-house research facilities in industries whose poor innovative performance stemmed from insufficient interfirm R&D, a conceptual scheme similar to that underpinning the British research associations. Of the three cooperative programs established in the National Science Foundation (NSF) program in the 1970s, only the program serving a research-intensive industry survived a five-year trial period: "The Polymer Processing Program at MIT is continuing with solid industry support. The Furniture R&D Applications Institute at NCSU [North Carolina State University] is being forced to retrench with termination [of NSF funding] but may obtain continuity in modified form [the Institute currently appears to be moribund]. The New England Energy Development Systems (NEEDS) Center, which was operated with Mitre Corporation providing the university-industry interface, has identified weaknesses associated with this intermediary form of center operation and will cease its operations" (National Science Foundation, 1979, p. v). The NSF evaluation concluded that "substantial participation [in the cooperative programs] has come from the large research-oriented companies that can understand and use the research outputs of the cooperative efforts. Companies with little research background, such as the utilities and furniture companies, are traditionally conservative with respect to new technology and are traditionally dependent on their suppliers for whatever changes they adopt" (National Science Foundation, 1979, p. 30).

The complexities of the relationship between intrafirm and external research also may affect the operations of privately financed research consortia, a number of which have been formed during the past fifteen years by U.S. firms. In many cases, the stated intention of these consortia is to increase basic research investment within an industry. Basic research, however, may require a larger in-house investment in the capacity to utilize the results of research performed outside the firm (Cohen and Levinthal, 1989). As a result, participants in cooperative research programs often shift the collaborative research agenda away from basic research. These pressures

appear to have led such well-known cooperative research
institutions as the Electric Power Research Institute (EPRI)
and the Microelectronics and Computer Technology Corporation (MCC), to reduce their basic research commitment.

The Electric Power Research Institute primarily serves
electric utilities, which support modest in-house research staff
and facilities. Historically, EPRI member firms have not been
direct competitors, serving different geographical areas. This
factor contributed to the formation of EPRI in 1973. EPRI
originally was charged with focusing on "a small number of
large, long-range projects. This was in part due to the industry's concern that EPRI not duplicate or compete with the
product development work of the commercial vendors, for
fear of undermining their incentives to pursue R&D. The
intention was to complement the work of others" (Barker,
1983, p. 6). Since its foundation, however, EPRI appears to
have adopted a shorter time horizon for its research agenda.
In 1976, short-, medium-, and long-term research, respectively,
accounted for 45 percent, 45 percent, and 10 percent of total
R&D expenditures. By 1981, short-term R&D had risen to 50
percent of the total, and medium-term research had been cut
to 40 percent. In 1982, short-term research accounted for 69
percent of the total EPRI research budget, long-term research
absorbed 3 percent, and medium-term research accounted for
28 percent of the total. MCC is experiencing a similar shift.
A recent article on the new chairman of MCC, Grant Dove,
noted his concern with developing applications more rapidly
for members: "To carry out Dove's directive, MCC is restructuring its largest program—Advanced Computer Architec-
ture—to enable its members to focus resources on areas that
promise immediate paybacks" (Lineback, 1987, p. 32).

Positive Contributions of Economics
to the Analysis of Technology and Organizations

Although the neoclassical framework provides little or
no guidance for the structure of research or for the design of
policies to encourage research and commercial innovation,

the larger body of microeconomic theory and applied work (loosely) in this tradition contains important insights into the role and characteristics of technological change. These characteristics mean that considerable care must be taken not to overstate the role of technology in causing changes in employment, organizational structure, or work processes.

The economic theory of technological change emphasizes the range and flexibility of mechanisms that mediate the impact of new technologies on the demand for these quantities. Reductions in labor requirements per unit of output (the definition of increases in labor productivity) that result from new technologies frequently lower the production costs and price of output, inducing (assuming appropriate demand elasticities) an increase in the demand for goods sufficient to offset the employment consequences of the reduction in unit-labor requirements (see Levy, Bowes, and Jondrow, 1984, for an empirical analysis of this possibility). Even where demand for a specific good does not respond sufficiently to offset the employment consequences of productivity growth, reductions in the cost of this good may increase demand for other products, creating employment opportunities in other economic sectors.

Some economic analyses of the employment effects of new technologies have minimized the role of these adjustment mechanisms. For example, the effects of increased productivity and lower costs on the demand for goods or services whose production incorporates new technologies are overlooked in most fixed-coefficient input-output models that forecast dire employment consequences as a result of increased office automation (Leontief and Duchin, 1985; Roessner and others, 1985). Economic theory's focus on comparative statics and successive equilibria inaccurately implies that adjustment to new technologies is frictionless; theory is silent on the speed with which adjustment occurs. Nevertheless, the offsetting influences identified by theory do appear to operate with sufficient consistency to undercut the predictions of large-scale technological unemployment made during the 1930s, 1950s, 1960s, and 1980s.

A critical influence on the relationship between technology and organizations is the adoption of a new technology by an organization. Obviously, the economic or organizational effects of new technologies cannot be realized until the technology has been adopted by the organization. Although the study of the diffusion of new technologies is an area to which noneconomists have made major contributions (the investigations by rural sociologists Ryan and Gross, 1943, of hybrid corn adoption formed the basis for the work of Griliches, 1957, 1960), the empirical investigations of economists have yielded several "stylized facts" that must be incorporated into any study of the interaction of technology and organizations. The first and possibly most important characteristic of the diffusion process is its lengthy duration. Mansfield (1963, 1966) and others have pointed out that the adoption of a new technique by 50 percent of the firms in an industry may take more than a decade. The rate of diffusion of new technologies is affected by the rate of investment, by learning and modification of new technologies, and by the gradual accumulation of improved information about the operation and economic payoffs of these technologies. All of these factors lengthen the process of adoption. An organizational characteristic consistently associated with earlier adoption in these empirical studies is size: larger firms are often early adopters of new technologies. As in the empirical studies of the Schumpeterian hypotheses, however (see the following section), this empirical work provides no rigorous explanation of why large size is associated with early adoption.

Compared with the effects of other sources of economic, organizational, and employment change, the effects of new technologies are felt gradually. Studies that assume nearly instantaneous diffusion, such as those by Ayres and Miller (1983), Leontief and Duchin (1985), and Roessner and others (1985), arrive at dramatic predictions of the magnitude and rate of realization of the employment effects of new technologies that are not well-supported by current or historical experience (for further discussion, see Cyert and Mowery, 1987). As already noted, however, these important empirical contributions of economics to the analysis of technology diffusion and adoption are not easily accommodated by neoclassical theory.

Alternative Perspectives on Technology and Organizations

Although neoclassical theory provides few insights into the relationship between technology and organizations, other theoretical and empirical work in economics has made important contributions. Unfortunately, none of these alternative approaches yet integrates the study of technological and organizational change into a framework that has yielded significant empirical advances. In this section, I consider the pathbreaking work of Schumpeter (1950) on the innovation process and on the structure of firms and markets; the work of Williamson (1975, 1985), Teece (1986), and Chandler (1962, 1977, 1989) on the relationship between technology and organizational structure; and the evolutionary theories of economic change of Nelson and Winter (1982), which have influenced recent theoretical and historical research by David (1985, 1987) and Arthur (1987, 1988). Many of the empirical insights in this eclectic tradition have been reached simultaneously with or in advance of the theoretical advances. Much of the most fruitful empirical work has been historical in focus and methodology.

Schumpeter. Schumpeter (1950) set forth an analysis of the changing organization of the process of innovation that influenced a generation of empirical researchers in economics. It is important, however, to distinguish between Schumpeter's original statement and the hypotheses that have been tested empirically by economists (Fisher and Temin, 1973; see also Cohen and Levin, 1988, who discuss this point in their review of the vast empirical literature spawned by Schumpeter). Writing in the early years of World War II, which would radically change the structure of industrially and publicly financed R&D within the United States, Schumpeter argued that the innovation process had been transformed during the twentieth century and that "innovation is being reduced to routine. Technological progress is increasingly becoming the business of teams of trained specialists who turn out what is required and make it work in predictable ways. The romance of earlier commercial adventure is rapidly wearing away" (Schumpeter, 1950, p. 132). This bureaucratization of the R&D process, Schumpeter asserted, meant the end of an era of heroic entrepreneurship that had produced "gales of creative destruction" (Schumpeter, 1950, p. 84), which periodically revolutionized the technologies and structure of industries and firms. Large firms, operating within concentrated markets, now would play a far more important role in innovation. The giant firm was the "most powerful engine of progress . . . perfect competition is inferior, and has no title to being set up as a model of ideal efficiency" (Schumpeter, 1950, p. 106).

Schumpeter (1934 [1911]) already had argued that radical innovations, combined with the efforts of individual entrepreneurs, had repeatedly transformed market structure via creative destruction. Schumpeter's later analysis considers the implications of the change in the innovation process, from one dominated by individual entrepreneurs and creative destruction to a process controlled by large corporations and organized industrial research. The two descriptions of innovation are not contradictory but refer to different historical epochs in Schumpeter's schema.

Schumpeter's statements have been interpreted by subsequent scholars to mean that large firms are superior innovators and that concentrated markets are conducive to innovation. As Cohen and Levin (1988) note, these hypotheses attracted considerable attention among postwar scholars because they implied the existence of a trade-off between the enforcement of antitrust laws (during the 1940s, major antitrust suits were pursued against AT&T, Alcoa, and DuPont, among others, as a legacy of the Roosevelt administration's "second New Deal" of the late 1930s; see Hawley, 1966) and the innovative performance of the overall economy. Could "trustbusting" reduce social welfare? According to Schumpeter (1950, p. 106), "perfect competition is not only impossible but inferior, and has no title to being set up as a model of ideal efficiency. It is hence a mistake to base the theory of government regulation of industry on the principle that big business should be made to work as the respective industry would work in perfect competition."

The extensive empirical literature that has attempted to test the so-called Schumpeterian hypotheses has been reviewed extensively, and I do not propose to provide yet another survey. The empirical literature on both hypotheses has focused largely on the relationship between innovative inputs (for example, the level of R&D employment or investment), rather than on outputs (innovations), and has yielded mixed results. Recent contributions to this literature, however (Levin, Cohen, and Mowery, 1985; Cohen, Levin, and Mowery, 1987), suggest that characteristics of the technological environment within different industries or firms (for example, the level of technological opportunity, the payoff of R&D investment within a specific technology) are more important than firm or market structure in explaining R&D investment. Size, in particular, does not explain cross-sectional differences in R&D investment at the level of the firm or of the individual product line.

Surprisingly, in view of the vast effort devoted to (largely inconclusive) statistical investigation of these hypotheses, far less research has been done on the basis for the existence of a linkage between market structure and innovative performance or between firm size and innovative performance. Recent work by Cohen and Mowery (1988) on the relationship between R&D investment and such correlates of firm size as diversification or cash flow (correlates that could yield a richer portrait of the relationship between research investment and organizational structure) suggests that the current list of variables employed by economists as measures of organizational structure perform poorly in explaining interfirm differences in R&D investment. Scott in Chapter Four of this volume reports similarly disappointing results from cross-sectional studies by scholars of organizational behavior on the relationship between characteristics of technology and organizational structure.

Investigation of the Schumpeterian hypotheses has also been hampered by the lack of theoretical or empirical work on the underlying characteristics of different technologies and on the relationship of these characteristics to differences in firm structure (for example, size) or performance. This omission is due in part to the fact that, with the exception of the survey compiled by Levin, Klevorick, Nelson, and Winter (1987), there exist virtually no data that allow us to characterize the technological environment of firms and industries.

Schumpeter's analysis of the role of innovation, as well as his speculations concerning the changing structure of the innovation process, remain important conceptual advances in the study of technology and organizations. Analyses and tests of interpretations of Schumpeter's work, however, have been limited by a lack of data that capture the key dimensions of the relationship between economic enterprises and the technological environment. These problems also have hampered empirical work in the other analytical frameworks discussed in this section.

Chandler, Williamson, and Teece. In view of the inability of neoclassical theory to deal with the interaction of technology and organizational structure and the inconclusive findings of many cross-sectional empirical studies, it is not surprising that one of the most influential contributions to this topic within an eclectic tradition of economic analysis has been made by a historian, Alfred Chandler. In a series of important studies of the development of the organizational structure of the modern firm in the United States and other industrial economies, Chandler (1962, 1977, 1989) argued that the internal structure of the firm affects its competitive performance, and that much of this internal structure has been determined by technological change. Chandler's historical work has influenced theorists and empirical scholars working within the neoclassical tradition (see Caves, 1980) and also has affected the development of alternative theories of the structure of the firm, notably Williamson's (1975, 1985).

Chandler's (1962) work argued for the importance of a match between the internal structure of the firm and its product mix and markets—its strategy—in determining profitability and performance. In particular, Chandler argued, the development of multidivisional corporate structures, with decentralized operating responsibilities for different products, made feasible the growth of diversified firms of unprecedented scale. Technological change, although acknowledged as a factor, received little attention in this work. Chandler's (1977) analysis of the rise of the modern U.S. corporation, however, placed technological change in the foreground. Changes in the technologies of production and communication in the U.S. economy of the late nineteenth century transformed the relative costs of interfirm and intrafirm coordination of transactions, expanding both the range of functions carried out within the manufacturing firm and the range of products. For Chandler, unlike the neoclassical economic theorists, technological change brought about change in the internal structure of the firm. Chandler's (1989) work extends this analysis to examine and compare the development of modern corporate structure in Great Britain, the United States, and Germany.

Chandler's analysis departs from the neoclassical tradition in focusing on the internal structure of the firm and in considering market and nonmarket modes for the control of transactions as alternatives, the choice among which may change in response to the development of technology and markets. His analysis is consistent with at least one strand of the neoclassical tradition however, in emphasizing the efficiency-enhancing motivation for and results of this transformation in corporate structure. Like the neoclassical theorists, Chandler sees natural selection as a force that results in the survival and dominance of firms with lower costs and superior performance. The strategic employment of size or diversification to increase the monopoly power of firms (Caves, Fortunato, and Ghemawat, 1984), or to expand their political power, receives short shrift. Chandler's portrait of corporate evolution as a process that only the swift and the efficient

survive contrasts with his scathing critique of the performance of U.S. corporate managers in the 1970s and 1980s, the
product of a century of evolution that presumably rewarded
the corporate "best and brightest" (Chandler, 1989).

The work of Williamson (1975, 1985) has been influenced by and has influenced Chandler's historical research.
Williamson draws on Chandler (1962) and on work by Coase
(1937), March and Simon (1958), and Cyert and March (1963)
in developing one of the few economic theories of the internal
structure of the firm. For Williamson, as for Chandler, firm
structure results from an evolutionary process that is efficiency-enhancing—in this case, minimizing transaction costs
(defined by Arrow, 1969, p. 48, as the "costs of running the
economic system"). Rather than taking the boundaries of the
firm as a datum determined uniquely by cost conditions and
production technology, Williamson (1985, p. 2) focuses on
"the comparative costs of planning, adapting, and monitoring task completion under alternative governance structures."

Bounded rationality, limited information, uncertainty,
and the opportunistic behavior of economic actors may restrict the use of contracts among firms and individuals under
certain circumstances (for example, a small-numbers bargain-
ing situation, that is, one in which assets or investments are
highly specific to a given function or transaction) and therefore make intrafirm forms of governance preferable to market
institutions. Williamson (1975) also devotes considerable attention to the optimal internal structure of the firm, arguing
that Chandler's multidivisional structure (the M-form) had
advantages that stemmed from the superiority of intrafirm
capital allocation decisions over those of capital markets:

> The capital market in an environment of U-form firms
> was earlier regarded as a less than efficacious surveillance
> and correction mechanism for three reasons: its external
> relation to the firm places it at a serious information
> disadvantage; it is restricted to nonmarginal adjustments;
> it experiences nontrivial displacement costs. The general
> office of the M-form organization has superior properties

in each of these respects. First, it is an internal rather than external control mechanism with the constitutional authority and expertise to make detailed evaluations of the performance of each of its operating parts. Second, it can make fine-tuning as well as discrete adjustments. This permits it both to intervene early in a selective, preventative way (a capability which the capital market lacks altogether), as well as to perform *ex post* corrective adjustments, in response to evidence of performance failure, with a surgical precision that the capital market lacks (the scalpel versus the ax is an appropriate analogy). Finally, the costs of intervention by the general office are relatively low. Altogether, therefore, a profit-oriented general office in an M-form enterprise might be expected to secure superior performance to that which the unassisted capital market can enforce. The M-form organization might thus be viewed as capitalism's creative response to the evident limits which the capital market experiences in its relations to the firm [Williamson, 1975, pp. 158–159].

According to Williamson, these advantages of the multidivisional corporation explained the rise and superior performance of conglomerates and other diversified corporations of the 1960s and 1970s.

Although he acknowledges an intellectual debt to Chandler, Williamson (1985, p. 87) denies that technology is an important influence on firms' internal structure: "Technology is fully determinative of economic organization only if (1) there is a single technology that is decisively superior to all others and (2) that technology implies a unique organization form. Rarely, I submit, is there only a single feasible technology, and even more rarely is the choice among alternative organization forms determined by technology."

Transaction-cost analysis has proved useful in explaining some recent developments in the structure of the firm, such as multinational enterprises. (Although Williamson, 1985, minimizes technology's role, transaction-cost explanations for the development of multinational firms have focused on the ability of these governance structures to manage the international transfer of technology, enabling U.S. multinationals to exploit technology-based advantages through direct foreign investment; see Caves, 1982, or Teece, 1976, for further discussion.) Nevertheless, transaction-cost analysis's predictions of the superior performance of intrafirm capital allocation decisions have not been uniformly supported by the recent performance of a number of conglomerates (see Mueller, 1985, or Ravenscraft and Scherer, 1987, p. 214, for a more detailed discussion). Indeed, one recent account suggesting that the cognitive and analytical limitations that Williamson argued could be overcome through M-form conglomerates in fact contributed to the poor performance of many diversified firms during the 1970s:

> Only 20 years ago senior managers spent their time building conglomerates through acquisition. . . .
>
> Companies became trapped in the worst of all worlds. Some 7 out of 10 acquisitions turned out poorly. Management often failed to run a diverse group of companies well. [Union] Carbide's [Robert D.] Kennedy [chief executive officer] dismisses the whole concept: "All that stuff about balancing the cash generators and the cash users sounds great on paper. But it never worked. When corporate management gets into the business of allocating resources between businesses crying out for cash, it makes mistakes." The investment community, he says, is "a better sorter-outer" ["Special Report," 1988, p. 142].

Williamson's dismissal of a key role for technology is consistent with his general focus on cross-sectional analysis of governance structures at a given point in time. This analytical approach contrasts with Chandler's analysis of the evolution of such structures over time. Williamson's transaction-cost approach thus shares with its neoclassical counterparts a static, rather than dynamic, analytical framework. Empirical applications of Williamson's analysis also have been hampered by the lack of measures of either transaction costs or richer taxonomies of organizational structure (one partial exception is Teece, 1981). These weaknesses give much of the work in this tradition an air of post hoc rationalization or tautology. In addition, of course, transaction-cost analysis relies on a characterization of the selection environment and organizational evolution (always efficiency-enhancing) that is assumed rather than demonstrated.

Although Williamson ascribes a secondary role to technology in explaining organizational structure, a recent extension of Williamson's analysis examines the implications of transaction costs for the management and organization of innovative activity. Teece (1986) examines the role of transaction-specific assets (defined as "co-specialized" assets) in firms' strategies for commercialization of new technologies. According to Teece (1986), the limited protection afforded to many types of intellectual property by legal devices, the nature of the relationships among the assets that must be combined to commercialize a new technology (for example, marketing and production skills must be combined with technical expertise), and the availability of such "co-specialized" assets in competitive markets all influence commercialization strategies. Although Teece's (1986) analysis is provocative, it relies largely on anecdotal evidence for empirical support. As in other economic analyses of the relationship between technology and organizations, better measures of the characteristics of the technology and the response of the firm are needed for rigorous empirical work. Currently available data, for example, make it difficult to measure or to predict the strength of "co-specialization" or complementarity among firm-specific assets.

Evolutionary Theories. A recent body of work that is central to any discussion of the interaction between technology and organizational structure is evolutionary theory, developed by Nelson and Winter (1982). Although this body of work devotes little attention to the evolution of organizational structure, its analysis of technological change and its explicit consideration of the consequences of various selection environments are lacking in the other bodies of work discussed in this chapter. In addition to Nelson and Winter's work, the work of David (1985, 1987) and Arthur (1987, 1988) considers the implications of different technological or selection environments for the development of organizations and technologies.

Nelson and Winter (1982) contains a rich and provocative description of organizational and technological change within an economic framework. Building on the work of Schumpeter (1934, 1950) March and Simon (1958), Cyert and March (1963), and other scholars, Nelson and Winter have developed a set of economic models that emphasize dynamics, the processes of adaptation to changes in the economic environment. These scholars describe their framework as evolutionary, analyzing as it does the effect of different selection environments and organizational routines on the development of firms.

The assumptions underlying these models depart from the orthodoxy of neoclassical theory in several respects. In contrast to neoclassical theory, in evolutionary theory firms do not possess complete information on technologies and may be unable to optimize the choice of production techniques and other decision parameters. Nelson and Winter assume instead that bounded rationality, incomplete information, and uncertainty result in the confounding of search behavior and of decisions, preventing the omniscient optimization characteristic of neoclassical theory. In the Nelson and Winter models, firms develop routines—standard operating procedures that adjust slowly and imperfectly to changes in the environment. These routines or decision rules are the behavioral elements that drive the evolutionary model. In addition to developing a model that takes into account the costs and uncertainties of technology transfer and search, Nelson and Winter test the empirical implications of their analysis with simulation analysis. As Scott's review in this volume of the organizational behavior literature notes, Nelson and

Winter's work is closely related to an emerging body of organizational population studies that adopt an evolutionary perspective, emphasizing the persistence of organizational routines and the limited adaptive qualities of organizations.

Its microfoundations and more realistic assumptions about and descriptions of organizational and technological change distinguish this analytical framework from neoclassical theory. The explicitly dynamic focus of the Nelson and Winter analysis also represents an advance over Williamson's theoretical framework. The Nelson and Winter analytical framework, however, has not yielded empirical implications that diverge sharply from those of neoclassical orthodoxy, nor has it been employed to explain phenomena that conflict with the predictions of orthodox theory (as, for example, transaction-cost analysis does for multinational corporate organization). Indeed, one major empirical test in Nelson and Winter (1982) analyzes the ability of a simulation based on evolutionary theory to reproduce the predictions of the Solow growth model, an austerely neoclassical construct. It is also difficult to derive policy implications from the analysis that disagree with those of neoclassical theory. Many of these difficulties reflect the fact that, as in the models already discussed, the data requirements of the Nelson and Winter model for tests at the level of the individual firm (or a cross-section of firms) are extremely demanding. Although the Nelson and Winter analysis contains great potential for empirical work, this potential has not yet been fully realized with the simulation methodology. Nevertheless, the general perspective of Nelson and Winter has inspired and influenced important empirical work by students and colleagues.

Recent studies of individual industries, employing an analytical framework that resembles that of Nelson and Winter, include Cohen's (1981, 1987) analysis of the uranium industry and Malerba's (1985) study of the European semiconductor industry. The effectiveness of these studies suggests that intensive examination of firms' behavior in a single sector over time may provide a more fruitful arena for the application of this analysis than simulation analyses at a higher level of aggregation. As is true of other economic analyses of technology and organizations, the absence of reliable cross-sectional data means that historical research may prove to be one of the most fruitful methodologies for applying the Nelson and Winter framework. Scott's chapter in this volume also singles out longitudinal analysis as a promising avenue for future research on organizational behavior.

Recent work by David (1985, 1987) on the evolution of technical standards is another historical application of an evolutionary model. Although consistent with the approach of Nelson and Winter, David's research also draws on the theoretical models of "path-dependence" developed by Arthur (1987, 1988). David examines the mechanisms through which evolutionary processes, as well as the characteristics of network technologies that exhibit increasing returns to scale, drive choices among technologies and technical standards, standards that (as in the case of the QWERTY typewriter keyboard) may be inefficient. This line of research provides a useful corrective to the optimistic views of the efficiency-enhancing results of natural selection that are implicit to the neoclassical analysis and in the work of Chandler and Williamson. David's work contains little or no analysis of its implications for organizational change, but it focuses attention on the characteristics of the technological environment, another aspect of the relationship between technology and organizations that deserves much more attention.

Conclusions

Thus far, the contributions of economic theory to the analysis of the interaction of technology and organizations have been modest. Neoclassical theory is hamstrung by its assumptions. The alternative theoretical frameworks of Williamson and Nelson and Winter have not yet been fully exploited. None of these frameworks integrates the study of organizational structure and behavior with an analysis of the characteristics of technological change or an intensive consideration of the characteristics of different technologies.

The empirical tradition of economic research has had a certain momentum of its own, however, and has not been overly hampered by rigid obedience to the tenets of any theoretical framework. In a number of areas—including the examination of diffusion and the statistical analysis of the relationships among market structure, firm size, and innovative performance—empirical research in economics has contributed to the analysis of technology and organizations (although, in some cases, as in the research on the so-called Schumpeterian hypotheses, this contribution has been largely negative). Unfortunately, extensions of empirical research in this area of economics, especially in the analysis of innovation, depend critically on the development of better data, but the prospects for improvement in data are extremely dim.

Historical research in economics on the relationship between technology and organizations is less dependent on the availability of cross-sectional data covering diverse industries and firms and has proved to be quite fruitful. Indeed, the work of Chandler and the essentially historical studies in Nelson and Winter (1982) have proved to be influential in economics and policy. Nevertheless, these research methods yield conclusions that rarely can be aggregated or generalized. Their contributions to economic theory, policy analysis, and evaluation have therefore been overshadowed by those of statistical analysis.

In the literature of both economics and organizational behavior, dissatisfaction with cross-sectional empirical analysis and with deterministic theories of the relationship between technology and organizational structure has led to new approaches. In both areas, the most successful empirical approaches often employ historical or longitudinal techniques. Less successful, but encouraging nevertheless, is the emergence within both fields of a strong evolutionary perspective in the theoretical analysis of technology and organizations.

The absence of rigorously derived, widely accepted results and empirical findings on the interaction of technology and organizations is a serious problem. The structure of the R&D system in this economy is undergoing its most profound transformation since 1945, with little evaluation or understanding of the implications of such restructuring for innovative performance. Mounting evidence of the lagging performance of U.S. firms as adopters (rather than developers) of new technologies also suggests the need for improved research on managerial performance and for better education of managers in the development and adoption of new technologies. As policymakers grow more concerned about the innovative performance of U.S. industry and the contributions that publicly supported R&D can make to this performance, they need some basis for program design and evaluation. If their efforts are to be guided by current economic theory and empirical research, it is difficult to be optimistic about the outcome.

References

Arrow, K. J. "Economic Welfare and the Allocation of Resources for Invention." In *The Rate and Direction of Inventive Activity.* Princeton, N.J.: Princeton University, National Bureau Committee for Economic Research, 1962.

Arrow, K. J. "The Organization of Economic Activity: Issues Pertinent to the Choice of Market Versus Nonmarket Allocation." In *The Analysis and Evaluation of Public Expenditure: The PPB System.* Vol. 1. Washington, D.C.: U.S. Government Printing Office, 1969.

Arthur, W. B. *Competing Technologies: An Overview.* Center for Economic Policy Research publication no. 98. Stanford, Calif.: Stanford University, 1987.

Arthur, W. B. "Self-Reinforcing Mechanisms in Economics." In P. W. Anderson and K. J. Arrow (eds.), *The Economy as an Evolving Complex System.* Reading, Mass.: Addison-Wesley, 1988.

Ayres, R. U., and Miller, S. M. *Robotics: Applications and Social Impacts.* Cambridge, Mass.: Ballinger, 1983.

Barker, B. "Decade of Change: EPRI and the Climate for Research." *EPRI Journal,* 1983, *8,* 5-13.

Becker, G. "Irrational Behavior and Economic Theory." *Journal of Political Economy,* 1962, *70,* 1-13.

Caves, R. E. "Industrial Organization, Corporate Strategy, and Structure." *Journal of Economic Literature*, 1980, *18*, 64–92.

Caves, R. E. *Multinational Enterprise and Economic Analysis.* New York: Cambridge University Press, 1982.

Caves, R. E., Fortunato, M., and Ghemawat, P. "The Decline of Dominant Firms, 1905-1929." *Quarterly Journal of Economics*, 1984, *99*, 523–546.

Chandler, A. D., Jr. *Strategy and Structure.* Cambridge, Mass.: MIT Press, 1962.

Chandler, A. D., Jr. *The Visible Hand.* Cambridge, Mass.: Harvard University Press, 1977.

Chandler, A. D., Jr. *Scale and Scope.* Cambridge, Mass.: Harvard University Press, 1989.

Clark, K. B., Chew, W. B., and Fujimoto, T. "Product Development in the World Automobile Market." *Brookings Papers on Economic Activity,* 1987, pp. 719–771.

Coase, R. F. "The Nature of the Firm." *Economica,* 1937, *4,* 386–405.

Cohen, W. M. "Firm Heterogeneity, Investment, and Industry Expansion: A Theoretical Framework and the Case of the Uranium Industry." Unpublished doctoral dissertation, Yale University, 1981.

Cohen, W. M. "Incomplete Markets, Interindustry Firm Heterogeneity, and Investment: The Case of Uranium Exploration." Unpublished manuscript, 1987.

Cohen, W. M., and Levin, R. C. "Empirical Studies of Innovation and Market Structure." In R. Schmalensee and R. Willig (eds.), *The North-Holland Handbook of Industrial Organization.* New York: North-Holland, 1988.

Cohen, W. M., Levin, R. C., and Mowery, D. C. "The Influence of Firm Size on R&D Investment: A Reexamination." *Journal of Industrial Economics,* 1987, *35,* 543–565.

Cohen, W. M., and Levinthal, D. A. "Innovation and Learning: The Two Faces of R&D—Implications for the Analysis of R&D Investment." *Economic Journal,* 1989, *99,* 569–596.

Cohen, W. M., and Mowery, D. C. "R&D Investment and the Correlates of Firm Size." Unpublished manuscript, 1988.

Cyert, R. M., and March, J. G. *A Behavioral Theory of the Firm.* Englewood Cliffs, N.J.: Prentice-Hall, 1963.

Cyert, R. M., and Mowery, D. C. (eds.). *Technology and Employment: Innovation and Growth in the U.S. Economy.* Report of the Panel on Technology and Employment. Washington, D.C.: National Academy Press, 1987.

David, P. A. "Clio and the Economics of QWERTY." *American Economic Review,* 1985, *75,* 332–337.

David, P. A. "The Hero and the Herd in Technological History: Reflections on Thomas Edison and 'The Battle of the Systems.' " Paper presented at conference in honor of David S. Landes, Bellagio, Italy, Aug. 30–Sept. 4, 1987.

Fisher, F. M., and Temin, P. "Returns to Scale in Research and Development: What Does the Schumpeterian Hypothesis Imply?" *Journal of Political Economy,* 1973, *81,* 56–70.

Friedman, M. *Essays in Positive Economics.* Chicago: University of Chicago Press, 1953.

Griliches, Z. "Hybrid Corn: An Exploration in the Economics of Technological Change." *Econometrica,* 1957, *25,* 501–522.

Griliches, Z. "Hybrid Corn and the Economics of Innovation." *Science,* 1960, *132,* 275–280.

Hawley, E. *The New Deal and the Problem of Monopoly.* Princeton, N.J.: Princeton University Press, 1966.

Herriott, S. R., Levinthal, D., and March, J. G. "Learning from Experience in Organizations." *American Economic Review,* 1985, *75,* 298–302.

Hirschhorn, L. "Computers and Jobs: Services and the New Mode of Production." In R. M. Cyert and D. C. Mowery (eds.), *The Impact of Technology on Employment and Economic Growth.* Cambridge, Mass.: Ballinger, 1988.

Kamien, M. I., and Schwartz, N. *Market Structure and Innovation.* Cambridge, England: Cambridge University Press, 1981.

Leibenstein, H. "Allocative Efficiency Versus X-Efficiency." *American Economic Review,* 1966, *56,* 392–415.

Leontief, W., and Duchin, F. *The Future Impact of Automation on Workers.* New York: Oxford University Press, 1985.

Levin, R. C., Cohen, W. M., and Mowery, D. C. "R&D Appropriability, Opportunity, and Market Structure: New Evidence on Some Schumpeterian Hypotheses." *American Economic Review*, 1985, *75*, 20–24.

Levin, R. C., Klevorick, A. K., Nelson, R. R., and Winter, S. G. "Appropriating the Returns from Industrial R&D." *Brookings Papers on Economic Activity*, 1987, pp. 783–820.

Levy, R. A., Bowes, M., and Jondrow, J. M. "Technical Advance and Other Sources of Employment Change in Basic Industry." In E. L. Collins and L. D. Tanner (eds.), *American Jobs and the Changing Industrial Base*. Cambridge, Mass.: Ballinger, 1984.

Lineback, J. R. "It's Time for MCC to Fish or Cut Bait." *Electronics*, June 25,, 1987, pp. 32–33.

Malerba, F. *The Semiconductor Business: The Economics of Rapid Growth and Decline*. Madison: University of Wisconsin Press, 1985.

Mansfield, E. "The Speed of Response of Firms to New Techniques." *Quarterly Journal of Economics*, 1963, *77*, 290–311.

Mansfield, E. "Technological Change: Measurement, Determinants, and Diffusion." In *The Employment Impact of Technological Change*. Vol. 2. Washington, D.C.: U.S. Government Printing Office, 1966.

March, J. G., and Simon, H. A. *Organizations*. New York: Wiley, 1958.

Marschak, J., and Radner, R. *The Theory of Teams*. New Haven: Yale University Press, 1972.

Mowery, D. C. "The Origins and Growth of Industrial Research in U.S. Manufacturing, 1899–1946." Unpublished doctoral dissertation, Stanford University, 1981.

Mowery, D. C. "Economic Theory and Government Technology Policy." *Policy Sciences*, 1983a, *13*, 27–43.

Mowery, D. C. "The Relationship Between Intrafirm and Contractual Forms of Industrial Research in American Manufacturing." *Explorations in Economic History*, 1983b, *20*, 351–374.

Mueller, D. C. "Mergers and Market Share." *Review of Economics and Statistics*, 1985, *67*, 261–266.

National Science Foundation. *An Analysis of the National Sci-*

ence Foundation's University-Industry Cooperative Research Centers Experiment. Washington, D.C.: National Science Foundation, 1979.

Nelson, R. R. "The Simple Economics of Basic Scientific Research." *Journal of Political Economy*, 1959, *67*, 297–306.

Nelson, R. R., and Winter, S. G. *An Evolutionary Theory of Economic Change.* Cambridge, Mass.: Harvard University Press, 1982.

Organization for Economic Cooperation and Development. *Industrial Research Organizations in the United Kingdom.* Paris: Organization for Economic Cooperation and Development, 1968.

Pavitt, K. "On the Nature of Technology." Inaugural lecture, Science Policy Research Unit, University of Sussex, 1987.

Piore, M. J. "The Impact of the Labor Market upon the Design and Selection of Productive Techniques Within the Manufacturing Plant." *Quarterly Journal of Economics*, 1968, *82*, 602–620.

Ravenscraft, D., and Scherer, F. M. *Mergers, Sell-Offs, and Economic Efficiency.* Washington, D.C.: Brookings Institution, 1987.

Roessner, J. D., and others. *The Impact of Office Automation on Clerical Employment, 1985–2000.* Westport, Conn.: Quorum, 1985.

Rosenberg, N. *Inside the Black Box.* Cambridge, England: Cambridge University Press, 1982.

Rosenberg, N., and Birdzell, E. *How the West Grew Rich.* New York: Basic Books, 1986.

Ross, S. "The Economic Theory of Agency: The Principal's Problem." *American Economic Review*, 1973, *63*, 134–139.

Ryan, B., and Gross, N. C. "The Diffusion of Hybrid Seed Corn in Two Iowa Communities." *Rural Sociology*, 1943, *8*, 13–24.

Sah, R. K., and Stiglitz, J. E. "Human Fallibility and Economic Organization." *American Economic Review*, 1985, *75*, 292–297.

Schumpeter, J. *The Theory of Economic Development.* Harvard University Press, 1934.

Schumpeter, J. *Capitalism, Socialism, and Democracy.* (3rd ed.) New York: Harper & Row, 1950.

"Special Report: Learning to Live with Leverage." *Business Week,* Nov. 7, 1988, pp. 138–156.

Spenner, K. I. "Technological Change, Skill Requirements, and Education: The Case for Uncertainty." In R. M. Cyert and D. C. Mowery (eds.), *The Impact of Technology on Employment and Economic Growth.* Cambridge, Mass.: Ballinger, 1988.

Stigler, G. J. "Industrial Organization and Economic Progress." In L. D. White (ed.), *The State of the Social Sciences.* Chicago: University of Chicago Press, 1956.

Teece, D. J. *The Multinational Corporation and the Resource Cost of International Technology Transfer.* Cambridge, Mass.: Ballinger, 1976.

Teece, D. J. "Internal Organization and Economic Performance: An Empirical Analysis of the Profitability of Principal Firms." *Journal of Industrial Economics,* 1981, *30,* 173–200.

Teece, D. J. "Towards an Economic Theory of the Multiproduct Firm." *Journal of Economic Behavior and Organization,* 1982, *3,* 39–63.

Teece, D. J. "Capturing Value from Technological Innovation: Integration, Strategic Partnering, and Licensing Decisions." *Research Policy,* 1986, *15,* 285–305.

Williamson, O. E. *Markets and Hierarchies.* New York: Free Press, 1975.

Williamson, O. E. *The Economic Institutions of Capitalism.* New York: Free Press, 1985.

8

※※

A Technological Perspective on New Forms of Organizations

Raj Reddy

How will emerging technologies influence organizations of the future? This is obviously a challenging and interesting question. This chapter attempts to provide a particular viewpoint in answering this question. We address two basic topics. The first is to map out some important technological trends. The second is to examine how these new technologies will affect the organization. Particular attention is devoted to information management, problem solving, and flexible structure.

Enhancing the quality and timeliness of organizational decision making has long been the object of study of organizational theorists. Methods and procedures in organizations often evolve over several decades. Long after a problem has disappeared, the organizational structure it spawned stays in place, leading to a number of fossils in the decision-making structure. Every so often, a reorganization is attempted in the hope of eliminating perceived inefficiency, with mixed results. The main thesis of this chapter is that effective use of emerging technologies provides the ability for rapid decision making, leading to the improved responsiveness of the entire organization.

Organizations that survive in the future have to be able to respond rapidly and creatively to environmental change. If they insist on sticking to old business practices, they may not be around in another twenty years. An important obstacle to rapid response is organizational overhead, which is often embodied in paperwork and authorization delays. Paperwork comes in many different forms. There are manuals, forms, purchase orders, invoices, requests for quotations, travel-expense sheets, and on and on. Authorization delays may occur by oversight or because people are not at their desks, as well as for more political reasons (contending for scarce resources, or conflict). There is no simple solution to all overhead problems, but I believe that, with a little creative use of technology, we can reduce the time it takes to deal with some of them.

My view of productivity improvement is broader than that in current use in economics. Current measures of productivity are seriously flawed when it comes to measuring improvements resulting from information technology. The current metrics do not account for such intangibles as cost of delays, improvement of quality, increased flexibility, and the resulting increases in sales volume and market share. The current cost-accounting techniques primarily use reduction in labor content as a measure of productivity. More recent research attempts to rectify some of these anomalies. Once we have new models in routine use, we will be able to better estimate the cost benefits of technology insertion.

There have been many speculations about paperless offices. The reality is far from the ideal. Indeed, with the widespread use of word processing and laser printing, paper consumption appears to be increasing. It is reasonable to assume that paper will continue to be used as a medium of communication even a hundred years from now. However, the total quantity of information accessed and communicated will probably increase by one to two orders of magnitude, most of it using electronic media. We may hope that paper will play a different role than it now plays in the organization. Often, paperwork is the symptom of an underlying inefficient organizational structure. I would like to illustrate the delays and costs associated with paper by using two studies we conducted at the Robotics Institute.

The first was an analysis of a large U.S. Navy supply center. This center is estimated to have over $5 billion worth of inventory on a steady-state basis. The interest cost alone would be over $400 million per year. A reduction of even 10 percent in the inventory would save over $40 million per year. One of the main reasons for this large inventory is the lead time associated with procurement within the Department of Defense. It is estimated that each procurement, even of simple items like paper and pencils, takes from eight to eighteen months and involves filling as many as 643 forms of paper. (No wonder we have to pay over $500 for a hammer and $700 for a toilet seat!) The number of approval levels may be as many as fifteen. Given the greater number of forms that have to be filled out and approved, the longer the delay, the greater the cost. One recommendation was to streamline the process and convert it to an all-electronic solution. Forms would be filled in at personal work stations and communicated electronically by local-area and wide-area networks to all members of the organization who needed to know. If someone were on vacation or unable to attend to the approval, the form automatically would go up the chain for resolution. Such a system would have the potential for reducing a three-month decision cycle to a few days or even a few hours.

The second case study involves a large manufacturer of automotive parts. The lead time from concept to production, in this case, varied from fifty to one hundred weeks. Analysis of the situation showed that over 80 percent of delays could be attributed to paperwork. It took over twelve weeks to agree on specifications, over eight weeks to negotiate with raw-materials vendors the costs and schedules of delivery, over six weeks to request quotations from suppliers of injection molds, over twenty weeks before tooling design could begin, and so on. Given that this organization does nothing but produce a few types of parts and engages in similar activities day in and day out, there was a lot of scope for streamlining and automation, with a potential for much faster individual operations.

These two cases illustrate the negative relationship between organizational overhead and organizational responsiveness and the potential impact of new technology on organizational responsiveness. We now turn to identifying some trends in technology that may affect information management, organizational problem solving, and organizational structure.

Technology Trends

In this section, we will examine some relevant technologies and where they are heading. The relevant technologies are computers, communication, artificial intelligence, and automation. Broadly, we may call them *information technologies*. In all of these areas, the cost is coming down, and functionality is going up at an exponential rate. It has been observed that if automotive technology were to change at the same rate, a Rolls-Royce would cost less than ten dollars, give over one hundred thousand miles per gallon, and go at a speed of over one million miles per hour.

Computers. Hardware performance has been improving at a rate of one thousand times in twenty years. That represents about 3 percent compound growth every month. Since 1988, there appears to be an acceleration. Price and performance seem to be improving at a 6 percent compound-growth rate every month, leading to a doubling of performance every year instead of every two years. This appears to be the result of using computer-aided engineering tools in the design of computers themselves.

At this rate, we can expect 100-mips processors and 16-megabyte dynamic random-access memory chips available at commodity prices by 1992. The resulting work stations should cost less than $100 per month, with a five-year amortization and replacement plan. Such systems will significantly influence decision systems involving planning, problem solving, simulation, and scheduling.

Communications. Distributed digital communications will be as important as computers for organizations in the future. The three relevant technologies are fiber optics, satellite communication, and digital radio communications. At present, communication rates over optic fibers are increasing at exponential rates comparable to those for computer technology. This will reduce the cost of video communication and conferencing and access to distributed data bases, and it will permit a five-hundred-page book to be transmitted to any point in the world for less than the price of a cup of coffee.

Satellite and radio communication eliminate the need for costly wiring but suffer from limitations of total available bandwidth. However, for lower data-rate (local) communications, RF spectrum should have adequate bandwidth. Use of local-area networks and wide-area networks for distributed access to information is already widespread and will become increasingly important in the organization of the future.

User Interfaces. For a long time, we have been limited to the use of keyboards for communication with computers. With the advent of the personal computer in the 1980s, graphic interfaces, such as the mouse or touch-sensitive screens, have become routine. The 1990s promise even greater flexibility, permitting voice and vision for human-computer interaction. While these will require significant computing resources, the exponential improvement in computer technology should make it possible for every personal computer and work station to have these capabilities.

In addition, special-purpose data-entry devices (such as bar-code readers, scanners for inputting drawings and handwriting, magnetic-strip readers for credit cards, sound digitizers, image input of x-rays and CAT scans, radio frequency–activated identification tags, and other innovations) promise to provide a plethora of data-acquisition alternatives, making timely access to information easier in future organizations.

Output devices, such as ink-jet printers and laser printers, are already transforming the quality of computer output dramatically. They have spawned an entirely new desktop publishing industry. The 1990s will witness the routine use of color and gray scale in computer-generated output.

Storage. A CD-ROM compact disk used as a storage medium for a computer is able to store about 700 million characters of information. An average book of five hundred pages contains about a million characters, including spaces. Simple compression techniques can reduce the storage requirement by a factor of three. Thus, a single CD-ROM–equivalent storage device can usually hold a personal library of over two thousand books. Even if a book contains pictures and drawings, the storage requirement is not expected to increase by more than 50 percent, on the average. The cost of CD-ROM media is in the range of $2 to $3. The cost of information on the CD-ROM appears to vary according to size and importance of the market.

This raises the prospect that all the information in a typical office (in manuals, file cabinets, bookshelves, and so on) could be stored and accessed much more efficiently in the future, through the use of desktop work stations equipped with optical disk drives. Currently, the cost of such work stations is under $10,000. Much more functionality at a lower cost can be expected to be available by the end of this decade.

Software Technology. This is one area where productivity growth has not kept up with advances in computer hardware. It is estimated that the Department of Defense spends over $30 billion per year on software-related costs, of which over 80 percent is spent on software maintenance. At this point, there are no satisfactory answers to the problem of what is being called "software nightmare."

Research scientists are looking at the following technologies for improving productivity:

- Prepackaged application software, such as Lotus 1-2-3, but for narrower, noncommodity applications
- Creation of a large, reusable software library and extensive training of software engineers in the use of the library
- Systems and languages for rapid prototyping of software systems

- Tools for management of software development (also known as computer-aided software engineering, or CASE).

One of the implications of the high cost of software is that organizations may need to modify procedures so as to conform to standard application packages. Another possibility is to use user-friendly, rule-based application shells, which can be modified by nonprogrammers to adopt a system to the local culture.

Artificial Intelligence. Advances in artificial intelligence (AI) promise to provide organizations with systems (supercomputer work stations on desktop) that can accept voice and vision for man-machine communication, tolerate error and ambiguity in human interaction with machines, provide education and entertainment on a personalized basis, provide expert advice on day-to-day problems, and make vast amounts of information available instantaneously from anywhere around the world.

We cannot do all of these things at present. Research is under way in speech-understanding systems, image processing and vision, natural-language processing, intelligent learning environments, expert systems, and very large knowledge bases. The results of this research are expected to permit a desktop work station to act as a personalized intelligent assistant.

Robotics and Manufacturing. Computer and communication technologies have made possible smaller, cost-effective manufacturing units, permitting decentralized manufacturing systems. Economies of scale are being replaced by economies of scope. By *scope* we mean the range of products that can be manufactured within the facility, without significant retooling and downtime. This in turn leads to the possibility of small-batch production, permitting production on demand. Conceptually, this is equivalent to stockpiling manufacturing capacity instead of stockpiling finished goods in large warehouses. This technology promises the rapid production of custom-made products, such as custom-tailored clothing in one day or customized automobiles in one week.

The implications of the use of intelligent automation resulting from emerging technologies may be profound. With increasing automation, labor content is already less than 10 percent of the total cost of manufacture in several industries. Total quality considerations indicate that labor content will become even lower in the future. Thus, the minimal effect of lower labor costs on total product costs will result in increasing reverse migration of manufacturing facilities back to the United States.

Organizations of the Future

In this section, we will explore the implications of the exponentially decreasing cost of information technology for organizations of the future. We will focus on information management, problem solving, and flexible structures. Although we discuss each separately, they are of course inextricably intertwined. It is the thesis of this chapter that the introduction of information technology will significantly transform the social and organizational fabric of enterprises in the future.

The infrastructure that permits this possibility is an organizationwide computer network with work stations on every desk, the kinds of storage and input-output devices already described, and a network-management system with organizational intelligence (that is, knowledge of the organization with regard to the hierarchy of decision making and monitoring). Once such a system is in place, it promotes a completely different culture. You would not hire somebody today without giving him or her a chair, desk, and telephone. There are overhead costs associated with each of them. A computer work station should fall into the same category. It is an essential tool for creation and communication of information. I think the cost associated with providing a person with a powerful personal work station will be less than $100 per month in the 1990s.

Information Management

Every office in every organization uses paper for creating forms, memos, manuals, proposals, marketing literature, design procedures, manufacturing procedures, procurement procedures, legal agreements, and so on. All of these activities, taken together, represent the sum total of the white-collar workers' portion of the organization, the so-called nontouch labor component. With increasing automation, this component of the cost of products is becoming the dominant cost. It is exactly in this area that effective use of information technology can significantly reduce the time, improve the quality, and increase the flexibility of the product life cycle.

Once a minimal infrastructure of personal computers and networks is in place, one can evolve procedures that are more efficient and incremental, without disrupting day-to-day operations. Thus, a person could either create an electronic form and send it via a local-area network or print it on a laser printer and send it on through conventional interoffice mail. But a fully computerized system can speed decisions through the use of computer and communication technology, simply eliminating the time it takes for paper to move up and down the chain by the use of electronic mail, electronic forms, and electronic documents through local-area networks.

An organization in which each employee has a work station, can access not only local information but also other globally available information through the use of local and distributed networks. This in turn raises a number of problems associated with distributed data bases, such as security, reliability, and access control. Many of these problems already have acceptable solutions. These can be expected to become routinely available on all commercial systems in the future.

Electronic Forms. Currently, many personal computers and work stations have the resolution and graphics capability to simulate physical forms. Further, with information already in the data base, 90 percent of the form can be prefilled in an integrated, intelligent environment. Remaining portions of the document that must be provided dynamically can be stylized, so that the user is prompted for the expected alternatives in a window, with minimal thinking and data-entry time. Once the form is completed, the information can be communicated instantaneously to all members of the organization who need to act on that information. Systems that have an understanding of the organizational hierarchy of the enterprise can ensure that all the affected parties are notified. Use of electronic computer networks reduces the time it takes for intraorganizational communication from days to minutes. Information on the forms will be less erroneous because the system prompts the user with the appropriate alternatives. The time required for filling out forms is reduced, since much of the information can be automatically inferred. The overall impact on the organization should be faster communication and improved productivity.

Electronic Mail. An electronic mail system would permit documents, memos, letters, and forms to be communicated easily, both within and outside an organization. Electronic discussion groups will form among people who could never meet face to face. Data bases of such discussions will form electronic archives of social memory. A number of new standards, such as X.400 and EDI (the electronic data-interchange standard), are emerging to facilitate this communication. Currently, the missing links are nationwide electronic white pages and yellow pages. These are expected to become available within the next few years. The organizational implication of electronic mail is faster and timely communication of relevant information. Broadcasting via electronic bulletin boards will make it possible for the entire corporation to be aware of changes in organizational policy and plans. The cost of letters and memos is currently estimated to be between $3 and $5 per document. With the use of electronic voice mail and other multimedia communication, the cost is expected to be reduced, and functionality will improve.

A negative prospect of electronic communications is the potential for unexpected increases in cost. Every fax communication uses up expensive, chemically coated paper, which has to be paid for by the receiver. Every electronic communication uses up disk space and other computational resources for indexing and filing mail. Therefore, one proposal is to tax the information producers for the cost of resources consumed at the receiving end.

Electronic Assistants. Given the flexibility of electronic communication, a senior manager may indeed receive hundreds of messages every day. Currently, a secretary or administrative assistant filters out the junk mail and decides which documents are important and need the immediate attention of the boss. A large fraction of such activity can be automated through the electronic equivalent of an administrative assistant. With a predefined format, such as the one provided by EDI, it is possible to scan the content of documents and highlight sources, topics, and action items for the decision maker, so that he or she can decide which documents to examine in greater detail. Even with paper communication, information overload is already unbearable. The task of electronic assistants will be to sift through, summarize, and highlight voluminous information that arrives every day, minimizing information overload for busy executives.

Electronic File Cabinets. Storage, retrieval, and indexing of the thousands of documents that arrive at an office consume a significant part of the time of managers and assistants. High-density optical disks capable of holding up to a million pages (approximately 2 gigabytes, which, with some simple compression, will be under 700 megabytes) provide an opportunity to create a low-cost electronic file cabinet. Letters, documents, and drawings arriving in an office can be automatically digitized with scanners and compressed with optical character recognition and image processing. An automatic index of a document can be created with key words, recognized by the system and/or provided interactively by a human assistant. This reduces the time it takes to locate the document and has the secondary benefit of reducing the need for shelf and cabinet space in an office.

Information that is thirty to fifty years old continues to be of extreme importance, in many cases. In Manhattan, drawings of old skyscrapers, for example, are needed for major repairs or reconstructions. In the case of aircraft carriers and submarines, drawings of how to repair electronic subsystems that use vacuum tubes or germanium transistors may be needed from the turn of the century. Information about pipes and electrical wiring, long ago buried under the streets of major cities, is another area.

The Department of Defense (DoD) has recently launched a new program called Computer-Aided Logistics Support (CALS). Every vendor who provides a product to the DoD must also create documentation, so that someone else can make and/or repair the product. Unfortunately, all of it is in English, and we have no way of proving whether the information is adequate. We expect the next generation of CALS to have the information in a form from which computers can interpret and produce the product in an automated machine shop.

Intelligent Documents. Proposals, manuals, requests for quotations, contracts, and specifications are usually created at great cost and expense. Often, a significant part of such a document is the same as one created previously. It is possible to create a customized word-processing system that, using an analogue of a spreadsheet, can fill in the blanks in a canonical document, significantly reducing the time for creation of such documents. This can also have the secondary benefit of highlighting the key attributes that are new in this version of the document. At present, a significant part of the delay and cost in government procurement is due to delays associated with requests for quotations and contractual documents. Many of these delays are aggravated by the fact that the people in charge of such negotiations have inadequate training and have to be excessively cautious. An expert system with knowledge of the rules and regulations can essentially create a completed contractual document, given a few relevant parameters.

Simultaneous Engineering. Sometimes called *concurrent engineering*, simultaneous engineering requires a number of experts from different disciplines to look at a proposed design and critique it from the perspective of manufacturability, testability, reparability, and so on. The design must have not only the structure and dimensions in the form of a drawing but also information about materials, manufacturing processes to be used, cost, and reliability. Often, such information is either missing or unavailable. Thus, an intelligent system must be able to provide automatic defaults ("best guesses") for information missing from the data base.

Design Data Bases. In our project, we tried to accumulate all designs over the past one hundred years. This proved to be a difficult problem because many of the historical data were either forgotten or permanently lost. Our hope was that, given a new design problem, the designer could rapidly examine all the solutions that had been previously employed before making his choice. If by happenstance his choice were similar to one that was already in the data base, then the time for creation of a new design could be significantly reduced by reusing the old design and modifying it with parametric design techniques.

A common problem is that people are reluctant to share data bases that they have created over their lifetimes. Moreover, the so-called data bases are often only in their heads or distributed in the heads of many different people. There is no one place to find out everything one needs to know about a given device. For example, a materials data base has information about every possible material but does not reveal what materials were used by the last five designers. We need to create a market for knowledge, so that product and process knowledge does not have to be constantly reinvented by competing organizations and countries. This would spawn a new knowledge industry, whose commodity would be knowledge, rather than a physical product.

Problem Solving

If activities of an organization are nearly decomposable and independent, then they do not need any coordination. Each group can make its own independent decisions, without affecting other parts of the organization. Occasionally the situation is just the opposite, and activities are highly interdependent. For example, building a dam or a large petrochemical complex in a remote area would create a logistical nightmare. The same problem arises in automotive design when the power train, the fuel system, and many different electronic subsystems all interact with one another, making three-dimensional space allocation under the hood a very complex problem. In such highly interdependent situations, effective use of emerging technologies is likely to provide a competitive edge. The human being, no matter how brilliant, is just not able to analyze a large number of interdependent facts and always arrive at an optimal solution.

Problem solving essentially implies decision making under uncertainty. We need to make a decision even when we do not have all the facts. We know from the theory of bounded rationality that we can utilize only a limited number of facts in formulating a solution. The emerging technologies of supercomputers on desktop and AI provide for the possibility of overcoming the limitations of bounded rationality. The computer can explore thousands of facts under myriad constraints, providing the executive with a list of desirable alternatives.

Personnel Management. In large organizations, personnel management often is nonoptimal because it is difficult to formulate a series of "musical chairs" without having to fire people and hire new people and train them. At Westinghouse recently, one division was laying off ten thousand employees and another division was hiring three thousand new professionals. An information infrastructure would have allowed people in the hiring division to have access to the personnel files in the firing division. A small amount of expertise built into the system would have allowed those files to be searched efficiently, to identify likely candidates for retraining. In this way, a significant number of those people could have been given some training for the new positions, thereby saving the expense of termination and recruitment and eliminating human suffering.

Planning. This is yet another area where we seem to take a very long time before we can introduce the next new product. I was told that it took over seven years of market research and analysis before an automotive company could decide to build the next generation of a sportscar. Not only does this delay cost a lot of money but we also run the risk of losing market share to an aggressive competitor who is able to respond in less time. Information technologies can facilitate developing fail-fast strategies within organizations.

The new technologies that are relevant here are constraint-based reasoning techniques developed within AI. In the past, optimization of a plan needed the use of linear programming, integer programming, or some other optimization technique requiring a mathematical formulation of the cost-benefit function. Unfortunately, not all problems are amenable to mathematical formulation. In AI, informal rules and constraints permit selection of a satisfactory solution by the use of relaxation of constraints when the constraints have no feasible solution.

Design. One emerging strategy for improved productivity is to reduce the design-cycle time or to get the design right the first time. Earlier, we discussed the technique of computer-aided concurrent engineering, whereby experts from each of the subdisciplines are able to provide inputs on a proposed design, eliminating most of the return design errors in the first phase.

The new technologies that are relevant here are schema-based knowledge-representation techniques, which permit a design document to have not only information about shape and dimensions but also information about the manufacturing process (including tools and fixtures needed at various stages and materials to be used), cost information, and testing information associated with the product design.

Processing Monitoring and Improvement. Total quality requires continuous monitoring of large numbers of parameters throughout the entire process of manufacturing. The large amount of information involved makes it impossible for human beings to monitor and control the production process dynamically. Expert systems, which are able to continuously monitor and adapt to the normal conditions of operations, are quickly able to detect any abnormal event and either correct or flag it for human intervention.

The technologies that are relevant here are signal processing and image processing. Using scanners and TV cameras, one can acquire visual data similar to the data used by human operators in inspection. However, the number of data associated with images tends to be very large, ranging from 10 million to 100 million bytes of data per image or drawing. Until recently, computer systems were not powerful enough to deal with such large volumes of data. New low-cost supercomputer work stations are expected to significantly change the use of computer vision and other signal data for process monitoring and improvement.

Diagnosis. The same techniques of process monitoring are also broadly applicable to the diagnosis of malfunctions in such expensive equipment as machine tools, aircraft engines, automotive systems, nuclear power plants, CAT scanners, and electronic switching systems. Diagnostic expert systems can usually be programmed by nonprogrammers who are experts in the specific problem domain. This in turn should make it possible for wider use of computer and communication technologies in manufacturing and service organizations.

The relevant technologies for diagnoses use software shells for knowledge-based reasoning. In cases where a large number of sensors are monitored in real time, the new solutions are able to outperform human capabilities.

Many of these problem-solving situations in organizations tend to be generic in that the same supercomputer work stations on desktop can be used for a multiplicity of purposes if changes are made in the application software. Thus, it is important for organizations to plan for integrated infrastructure of computer communication networks.

Work in AI offers the possibility of capturing expertise within the organization in the form of rule-based expert systems. Such systems can often be used to approve routine (electronic) requests, permitting executives to deal with nonstandard decision-making situations.

Flexible Hierarchies

Currently, organizational structures are slow to change and fairly rigid. This may be due to the fact that an organization's structure is a general-purpose solution. While it is not perfect for doing any one thing in particular, it works over time and is adequate for getting things done, albeit inefficiently. Today we do not understand the process of changing organizational structure. Even when we do it, we do not know how to do it rapidly. It may be possible to combine some of the new technologies with people who are willing to experiment in organizations to develop flexible structures that are at the same time centralized and distributed.

If the problem is to react rapidly to a dynamically changing competitive situation, there can be significant delegation of authority, as is apparently the case at Pepsi. However, if it involves a major policy change, such as the decision to decommission the disaster-management staff at Exxon, it should probably go all the way to the top. Once the entire organization is interconnected with networks and personal computers, one can replace rigid procedures with flexible ones. Certain decisions can be decentralized and yet permit a senior executive to exercise authority and change the direction if necessary. Expert systems that are knowledgeable about organizational policies can act as surrogates for senior executives to approve routine decisions, leaving more time for more complex, uncharted situations.

How will new technologies reshape structural relations within an organization? What happened within the DoD in recent years is illustrative. It is said that, with the introduction of a secure electronic mail network (Milnet), there is a significant horizontal communication bypassing the normal hierarchical structure, often leading to faster resolution of problems.

The use of electronic document interchange (EDI) as a standard means of communication of quotations, purchase orders, invoices, and other transactions is becoming widely accepted among suppliers, purchasing agents, and customers of organizations. The new standard for EDI is almost complete. Research is under way to develop an intelligent EDI capable of accepting free-form and unstructured documents. Occasional human intervention may be needed when a document cannot be automatically interpreted by the intelligent EDI system.

Conclusions

It is clear that information technologies and systems that are on the horizon will significantly change the way we run organizations and make decisions. It will not happen overnight because of the inherent inertia in the social structure of organizations; yet natural evolution should ensure the survival of the fittest, those who are able to utilize technology and tools to reduce delays, shorten delivery times, improve quality, and increase functionality of products. If the United States continues to take four to five years to introduce a new car while Japan can do it in half the time, then obviously Japan will continue to increase its market share.

Organizations that are fast on their feet do not have to be worried about competition because even if they are not first in the market with a new product concept, they can respond rapidly and introduce comparable products before the market wakes up. Those that are too slow, those that insist on doing

business the old way, those that want to take their time to
think about it before making a decision, just will not survive.
The distributed information system presented in this chapter
can help reduce paperwork significantly and, once in place,
can also be used for such other activities as planning, problem
solving, and the use of flexible hierarchies.

Discussion

What follows is a summary of the discussion prompted
by the presentation of this material at the Carnegie-Mellon
workshop.

Q: You've been looking ahead and making projections for
the next twenty years. If you stand at this point and look back
twenty years, are you surprised or do you have any observations about the way in which technologies have been used or
misused?

A: The most interesting example I think of is the telephone
system. It is said that if we still used human operators as we did
forty years ago, 90 percent of the population would be telephone operators connecting the other 10 percent to talk to one
another. But that's an extreme case. Even ten years ago, I
would have been hard pressed to predict the rapid prolifera-
tions of teller machines in banks. You can see where information technology has been very helpful, primarily in banking
and insurance. One place where information technologies
have not yet made inroads is in the U.S. government. Although
the government uses computers, it is not using them in creative
ways. The same is true in many other organizations. It may be
the case that the one person-one computer concept we are promoting at Carnegie-Mellon is equally valid for any other organization. This vision has to be communicated.

Q: Do you practice what you preach? How do you utilize
technology at the Robotics Institute?

A: Indeed, we attempt to do so, though not always with
great success. About seven years ago, we threatened to take

away all typewriters from secretaries' desks. This led to a
lot of unhappiness. It turned out they were partly correct.
Although terminals, networks, and laser printers were adequate for most purposes, we still couldn't type addresses on
envelopes. This led to attempts to use window envelopes,
which for some reason are not as popular as they might be.

Q: What you said was about office automation. What about
research? Your institution has a distinguished record in advanced research. How is research being done differently now
because of technology?

A: I believe it was Herbert Simon who said that the most
creative research requires the use of the most primitive techniques. That is because, when faced with a problem we've
never seen before, there's nothing we can do other than use
some weak method, such as trial and error or heuristic search.
The computer is our laboratory. Every hypothesis and conjec-
ture is validated by attempting to encapsulate it into a computer simulation. Second, like most other scientists, we use
computers to derive structure from large amounts of data.
Finally, we use emerging tools of computer science and AI in
trying to decide what to do next. This is the so-called focus-
of-attention problem.

Q: We often find ourselves in a situation where one part of
an organization does not agree with the other. Is the computer
an adequate medium for people to negotiate?

A: For dissemination of factual information, the computer
turns out to be an excellent medium. For example, a tool
engineer may say, "You forgot to specify what the curvature
of some object is. What is it?" This type of factual information is best provided by electronic means, avoiding telephone
tag. However, if the discussion involves a controversial decision, when there is more than one possible option, unsuper-
vised computer communication turns out to be inadequate
for conflict resolution. Some form of computer-mediated cooperative support system is necessary when there is a person (or
a machine) in charge of the discussion, with the authority to
terminate a line of discussion if it is inappropriate.

Q: So is that a sign that people need to get together?

A: Yes. Either people need to meet or we need to create a
computer-mediated conferencing system. There's a local story
that provides a good example here. I remember when the
computer-room manager decided to rekey the lock to the door
because of lack of security and loss through theft. This one
action caused a great fuss, since not everyone was notified.
The number of messages that went back and forth could have
filled a large sack. The new lock needed to be explained and
a consensus needed to be reached before the action. There's
no way to avoid the time it takes to reach a consensus when
you're trying to do something new or creative, or when there's
a conflict of opinion. In the past, hierarchical structure of the
organization has ensured avoidance of snafus, yet the chain-
of-command structure introduces costs and delays. These can
be reduced or eliminated if computer and networking technology is used creatively, so that everyone who is affected by a
decision is notified of that decision. This would permit rapid
midcourse correction if the decision had some inherent problem. The key issue appears to be formulating new organizational paradigms. In general, the social structure associated
with people and organizations will be very difficult to change.
Thus, an evolutionary rather than revolutionary approach to
change will be more acceptable.

Q: Do you have any opinions about why people at the top
of organizations have been so slow to pick up on technological advances?

A: I think there are several reasons. First is that the current
systems are not reliable enough. Where they are reliable is in
such systems as those used for airline reservations. One would
never think about going back to the old manual systems.
Because the system works and you believe your reservation
is approved via the phone, you can appear at the airport and
be assured of a seat. However, if systems are not reliable
enough or user-friendly, then the chances are that people will
get disaffected and ignore the systems. Social change in the

organizational structure requires many years of routine use for problems and mistakes to be identified and eliminated. Another reason is that many senior personnel have no programming experience, nor are they very informed about the capabilities of computers. Some CEOs are receptive to new ideas and are able to foster experimentation within organizations. Many others are not. I believe a whole new generation of CEOs has to be in place, CEOs who are comfortable with emerging information technologies. Finally, we need to develop more user-friendly interfaces that permit human-computer interaction through voice and vision and are able to provide help on day-to-day problems.

Q: Can organizations really change in fundamental ways, or do you have to just start new organizations? There's a concept from political science that organizational people borrow, called *vested interests*. In your example of the major auto manufacturer, you suggested that the company clean up its act through the use of technology. However, much of the power of midlevel managers in that organization comes from the number of people that they're in charge of and the number of forms that they sign off on. The existing structure is averse to attempts at making things run more efficiently, but it's not going to go away. What was the response of the automotive company when you said, "Clean up your act, and then we'll . . . ?"

A: When competitors are more efficient, effective, and productive because they have incorporated new technology, then sooner or later you must change, too, or perish. Out of those ashes arise new companies that can be more responsive. If you do not adapt, you will not survive. The other possible scenario, which occurs occasionally, is that a company undergoes organizational flattening of structure by reducing the number of its levels. I gather that Westinghouse went from thirteen to six levels. Maybe even six is too many, and they should go to three. You can have a structure where each group is small, self-contained, and responsive.

9

⚜

Technology and Organizations: Integration and Opportunities

Lee S. Sproull
Paul S. Goodman

In this chapter, we present some of the recurrent themes in this book. The themes are building blocks that represent new ways to think about technology and organizations. They represent new areas for research and new ways for conducting research on technology and organizations. For each theme, we will try to identify commonalities as well as divergences among the contributors to the book. The key idea is that there are new opportunities for theorizing and conducting research on organizations.

What Is Technology?

Some may think that this question, coming at the end of a book on technology and organizations, is postmature, yet the eight preceding chapters have offered eight definitions of technology, six domains in which it is found, and at least twenty-five different specific examples of it. We feel obliged (and inspired!) to offer a gentle synthesis across these chapters.

All of the chapter authors include knowledge, machines, and methods in their definitions of technology. Using this minimum set, we define technology as knowledge of cause-and-effect relationships embedded in machines and methods. The knowledge may be certain or probabilistic. It may be codified in formal systems or in folk wisdom. In the preceding chapters, examples of machines include typewriters, CAT scanners, nuclear reactors, and automatic teller machines. Examples of methods include cost-benefit analysis, the measurement of dimensional quality, the vectoring of airplanes, and the controlling of machine tools.

We find helpful Weick's distinction between technology and technical systems. A technical system is a specific combination of machines and methods employed to produce a desired outcome. Examples of technical systems described in the preceding chapters include the Chart Room at DuPont, CAT scanning in the radiology departments of two different hospitals, employment security programs in sixty local government offices, and military command and control during the Grenada invasion. Anticipating our argument on multiway causality in the next section, we want to note that the machines found in a particular technical system are not irreducible givens but rather are themselves shaped by the results of social processes.

The distinction between technology and technical systems orients researchers to particular instances of technology in action. It suggests that empirical work on technology in organizations cannot focus on technology; it focuses on technical systems. Every instance of technology in the real world is one particular combination of machines and methods; no two instances are likely to represent precisely the same combination. Therefore, the effort to aggregate technology effects across settings is likely to produce problematic results. Several authors were dissatisfied with the current standard practice of aggregation in their own disciplines and called for change. Mowery wanted to disaggregate industry-level studies to firm-level ones; Scott wanted to disaggregate firm-level studies to department-level ones; Goodman and Weick wanted to disaggregate individual-level studies to mental models and physical processes. We do not believe that these recommendations represent an infinite regress, ultimately leading economists to study mental models of technology and psychologists to study neuron firings. We do think they sensibly acknowledge the strengths and weaknesses of each discipline's conceptual apparatus for capturing explicable phenomena.

What's New About New Technology?

Weick and Scott represent the extremes of opinion on this question. Weick suggests that stochastic events, continuous events, and mental workload are what is new about new technology. Scott suggests that there is nothing really new about new technology per se that cannot be captured by the old dimensions of complexity, uncertainty, and interdependence.

Some new technologies, like new and improved washing machines, are new only to marketers. They represent only mechanical extensions of functionality or performance. They can indeed be adequately described by the conventional dimensions of complexity, uncertainty, and interdependence. We think, however, that there is a class of technology that is qualitatively different from previous ones and for which new dimensions may be necessary. This is the class of technologies based on programmable machinery.

All technologies prior to computers were based on mechanical models and apparatus. While they might have been quite complex (or uncertain or interdependent), they performed a fixed set of tasks whose instructions could be enumerated. The behavior of programmable technology, by contrast, is more open-ended than any enumeration of its instructions could describe. Thus, new behavior can be produced by new combinations of instructions.

At the cognitive level, understanding and operating programmable technology requires different reasoning skills than does mechanical technology. Sheil (1983) describes these as skills of procedural reasoning. He notes that the heart of procedural reasoning is the ability to separate intentions from general classes of actions. Procedural reasoning underlies all of the dimensions proposed by Weick. New technology is experienced as stochastic because its programmability prevents exhaustive enumeration of its instructions. New technology increases mental workload because procedural reasoning is an entirely new way of thinking. New technology is experienced as continuous because programmable technology can be reconfigured or reprogrammed while it is operating.

At the organizational-design level, programmable technology allows for the possibility of continuous redesign. Reconfiguring mechanical technologies is enormously time-consuming and expensive, and so it happens infrequently. Consider the time it takes to retool an automotive assembly plant to produce a new kind of car. New technology makes possible the nearly continuous production of custom products because of its programmability. It makes possible the nearly continuous production of custom structures, by the same process—that is, new communication technologies can be programmed to connect different sets of people and information for different tasks. Programmability underlies Reddy's proposal for a different structure for every task. Yet despite the vast increase in programmable technology, we do not see continuous redesign or custom structures in organizations.

The distinction between technology and technical systems may help us understand this puzzle and help us reconcile the differences between Scott's view of new technology and Weick's. We have argued that there is an underlying dimension of some technologies that is qualitatively different from that of previous ones: the dimension of programmability. Yet precisely because programmability is new, people and organizations have few methods for managing and understanding it. Therefore, they create technical systems with machines that are programmable and methods that are mechanical. Thus, the technology may be fundamentally new, but the technical systems are not. The technical systems will look familiar to researchers (and to managers and workers). They can be described by the familiar dimensions of complexity, uncertainty, and interdependence.

But these hybrid technical systems must represent an

unstable state. Their performance is often disappointing, if not life-threatening. Presumably, as we have more experience with programmable technology and develop procedural reasoning skills, we will create new methods for combining with programmable machines, in new technical systems. This hope, of course, is subject to all the complications of complexity noted by March and Sproull.

Is Technology a Determinant or Indeterminant Force?

One of the major problems in earlier (and some current) research on technology is the adoption of a technologically deterministic position, which assumes that changes in technology lead to simple traceable changes in social structure. This assumption is implicit in the literatures on technology and deskilling and on technology and job loss, and it partly accounts for the confusion in these literatures.

A dominant theme throughout the chapters is the rejection of the deterministic point of view. Causality is viewed as loosely structured, with reciprocal effects evolving over time. Technology and social actors (individuals, groups) represent the initial causal agents. Changes in technology lead to changes in social structure, as agents in groups or organizations develop constructions of the technology, which in turn change the technology (see Chapter One, p. 21, for a diagram of this process). This reciprocal causation over time leads to evolutions in technology and social structure. This evolution is loosely structured, disorganized, and difficult to predict. In the chapters by Scott, Lynn, and Mowery, there is an important warning about thinking solely of the interaction between technology and the organizational level of analysis. Scott argues that we need to introduce political, ideological, cultural, and institutional factors into the causal arena. In addition, he proposes that moving to the organizational population and organizational community levels of analysis may reorient how we think about the relationship between technology and organizations. The complexity of this causal structure is further complicated by the fact that observed changes can be transient or enduring, predictable or unpredictable.

Our assumptions about causal structure determine to a great extent how we think about technology and organizations. If one adopts the view of indeterminacy articulated in this book, then how one defines problems changes. For example, if causality is characterized as loosely structured, with reciprocal processes, one would not simply examine the effects of a particular technology (say, computer monitoring) on an outcome (say, quality of performance). One would instead examine the intersection between technology and the social meaning assigned to that technology and to the evolution of that technology and social system. The implications of the proposed causal structure bear on research design. The design would have to capture the dynamic relationship between technology and the social construction of that technology.

Moving to longitudinal designs seems almost too obvious. However, a cursory review of the literature shows use of primarily cross-sectional designs. Capturing this dynamic relationship between technology and organizations also poses new challenges for measurement. Throughout all of the chapters, there are proposals to move from some of the traditional organizational research methodology to new emphases on, for example, historical analysis, national character studies, and observational methodologies.

Technology: A Social or Physical Reality?

A major theme of this book is that technology is a socially constructed reality. This means that individuals or groups assign meaning to technology, which in turn provides direction for selecting information, retaining information, and making inferences about the relationship between technology and the environment. This socially constructed model is critical in understanding the use of a new technology, changes in processes or outcomes, and subsequent modification of the technology. The role of technology as a socially constructed reality appears explicitly in the chapters by Weick, Scott, and Goodman and implicitly in the other chapters. Weick pushes the concept of social construction to a strong microperspective, while Scott acknowledges the role of social definitions of technology but argues that there is uniformity (versus individual variability) in these perceptions.

The implications of this view of technology are powerful for conducting research on technology. If one were interested, for example, in how managers use information technology, one key would be to look at the social meaning of this technology. Most accounts in the literature do not consider this concept. While the authors of this book clearly acknowledge the importance of the socially constructed meaning of technology, we do not have a good theoretical understanding of this concept. Current empirical research on the social construction of technology is sparse. There are not only important substantive research questions but also important methodological challenges. For example, how does one measure and represent a socially constructed model of technology over time, in some reliable and valid way?

Technology also exists as a physical reality. We can define technology in terms of size, speed of the work cycle, level of interdependence, and so on. The physical properties of some computer-mediated communications technology permit interactions over time and space that previously were not possible. The switch from synchronous to asynchronous production facilities represents a substantial physical change in the nature of work.

While there appears to be a movement to focus primarily on technology as a socially constructed reality, we feel that some balance is necessary. There are issues that concern technology as a physical reality. These have not been well addressed and have implications for doing work on technology and organizations. In any group or organizational context, for example, one is more likely to find multiple different technologies than one is to find a single homogeneous technology. However, there is a tendency in the literature to conceptualize and measure technology as homogeneous in a given social setting. Many of the measurement strategies for technology tap such dimensions as uncertainty and predictability. Implicit in these measures is an assumption about homogeneity. A number of the chapters question this assumption. Scott, in particular, advocates the department or unit level of analysis for examining the relationship between technology and structure. At this level of analysis, one is likely to find a unitary technology, rather than multiple technologies. Another issue concerns the concept of equifinality. Any given technology can be configured in a variety of ways, to produce the same results. Thus, the implication is that it is not useful to look at aggregate descriptions of technology (for example, teleconferencing); rather, one needs to develop fine-grained descriptions of different configurations of the same technology and examine the differential effects on process and outcomes.

We feel that a fruitful approach would be to increase our understanding of both the social and the physical aspects of technology. The social and physical aspects both represent interesting research arenas. The real contribution, however, will be understanding the intersection between both forms of reality. For example, how do the physical aspects of technology constrain the development and evolution of the socially constructed meaning of technology?

Technology and Different Levels of Analysis

In designing this book, we used level of analysis as a major organizing principle. We focused on the relationships between technology and the individual, technology and groups, technology and culture, and so on, in order to provide the reader with a simple structure to organize his or her thoughts about the relationship between technology and organizations. In addition, our use of level of analysis as a presentation vehicle also parallels how the literature generally is organized.

The problem with this organization is that it may focus the reader's attention on a particular level of analysis or on micro versus macro perspective. That clearly is not our intention. Indeed, another major theme throughout this book is that focusing on the *intersections* between levels of analysis is a key to understanding the relationship between technology and organizations. Different perspectives on this theme pervade the book. In Weick's chapter, there is a movement toward disaggregation to very micro levels of analysis. In Lynn's chapter, which is about a macro topic (culture), there is movement toward incorporating larger units of analysis, called *world systems*. Scott is probably most explicit in arguing for examination of the intersection between different levels of analysis as a way to get new insights into the relationship between technology and social systems. For example, he convincingly shows how institutional and population-ecology perspectives can inform our thinking about technology and organizations.

The key implication for research is that, although we may focus on a particular level of analysis (for example, computer-mediated communications technology and group decision making), it is the *intersection* of this level of analysis with other levels (individual, organizational, institutional) that will provide critical insights.

Technology and Critical Processes

There is a set of processes critical to understanding the relationship between technology and organizations. In every chapter, these processes have been identified, and their role in explicating the relationships between technology and the individual, technology and groups, technology and the organization, and so on, has been delineated. A major theme of this book is that an understanding of the role of technology may be better facilitated by examination of processes versus outcomes. The goal of the authors has been to identify the processes and to provide some conceptual apparatus to improve understanding of the role of technology.

The process by which social constructions of a technology are developed appears throughout this book. Explicit in Weick's discussion of the movement from behavior and output control to premise control is the need to understand the cognitive processes that generate and modify these premises. In Goodman, Griffith, and Fenner's chapter, five processes are presented, which shape schemata in the individual's model of technology. Scott introduces the idea of task conception to provide a more macro perspective on the subjective versus objective views of technology. In almost all of the chapters, the social construction of technology by various social actors is considered theoretically important. Future work needs to extend this process and develop methodologies that will capture the development and change of these social constructions.

Structuration is another process that appears throughout the chapters. This process concerns the interplay among technology, organizations, and action—how technology constrains and configures organizational action, and how action constrains and reconfigures technology. This is a critical process, which is not well developed theoretically and for which there exist few careful descriptions in the technology area. We need to invest resources to better understand this process. It is fundamental to understanding the evolution of technology. Good case histories of this interplay would be a valuable contribution.

The adoption and utilization of new technology is another critical process. This topic is central to the March and Sproull chapter (and appears as well in the other chapters). March and Sproull examine a contemporary case of organizational failure: the failure of senior executives to use modern, computer-based information systems in their jobs. Their analysis examines the assumptions implicit in the design of the information technology and the fit between these assumptions (embedded in the technology) and the actual organizational decision making. They also extend their work to an examination of a more general theory of technological competition, which assumes that technologies that provide technical or institutional advantages will survive. The March and Sproull analysis explains why poor as well as superior technologies will survive. While the general question of how to improve the use of technology has received a good deal of attention in the literature, March and Sproull move from the traditional focus on implementation processes (on the shop floor) to a different process, which generates design assumptions for new technology and which examines the match between these assumptions and organizational functioning.

There is an interesting contrast between Reddy's chapter on new technologies and the March and Sproull chapter. The former enumerates classes of new technologies; the speed and power of these new technologies in search activities, storage, communication, and so on, has a clear objective reality. The March and Sproull chapter, however, acknowledges the objective advantages of current information technology but also acknowledges that this technology is not utilized. As the new technologies specified in Reddy's chapter become available, would we not expect the argument for the lack of use of new technologies still to be viable? A fruitful area of research would be to examine the emergence and utilization of the technologies enumerated in Reddy's chapter. At issue would be the understanding of the emergence and failure of these new technologies.

Conclusions

Scholars and analysts have had an enduring fascination with technology. Technology serves as both mirror and metaphor. People as tool users and tool builders, people as artificers: these are ways we have understood our evolution.

Technology also serves as a force or power to extend human capability. The industrial revolution used technology to extend human physical capability; the computer or information revolution may extend our mental capability. These extensions make technology a potent economic force, and it becomes an arena for questions of control. To what extent is technology controllable? To what extent is it controlling?

Technology also serves as a laboratory. It encourages or forces us to rethink old concepts. For instance, the modern study of cognition has been profoundly affected, both substantively and methodologically, by high-speed computing. Technology also allows us to carry out rapid changes—for instance, through simulation or prototypes—and to assess the results of those changes rapidly.

This is an exciting time for studying technology in organizations—those that produce it and those that use it. Advances in computing technology are profoundly affecting design and manufacturing, transaction processing, information systems, transportation, communication, medical diagnosis, and medical care; few organizations have been untouched by the computer revolution. Few know what to make of it. With conceptualizations like the ones offered in this book, and with the occasions afforded by new technology development, we can anticipate important new research on technology and organizations.

Reference

Sheil, B. A. "Coping with Complexity." *Office: Technology and People*, 1983, *1*, 295-320.

Index

※

A

Abernathy, W., 134, 135, 137
Abstract events, cognitive demands of, 14-15, 28-29, 34, 35
Access to data, 100
Action sequences, interruption of, 23-26
Adaptation to new technologies: competition and, 249; economic models of, 222; population ecologists on, 134
Adler, N. J., 181-182, 194, 196
Adler, P., 11, 13, 40
Adler, P. S., 12, 36, 40, 97, 106
Adoption of new technologies: competence traps and, 162; cultural variables and, 175-177; economic effects, 212; Japanese versus U.S., 175; managers' lack of, 149-156, 157, 161, 263; proponents' strategy, 164; U.S. and, 226. *See also* Diffusion of new technologies
Advanced manufacturing technology (AMT): costs, 106; defined, 93; identity of inputs and outputs in, 103; problem solving and, 105; skills increased by, 97-99;

task interdependence and, 99-100; timely feedback and, 100-101; types of, 91-94; work-group autonomy and, 94-107; work-group boundaries and, 101-102; work-groups and, 87-106
Aguilar, F., 149, 165
Aiken, M., 114, 139, 188, 196
Air traffic control, 11, 16
Ajiferuke, M., 177, 196
Alcoa (Aluminum Company of America), 214
Aldrich, H. E., 115, 118, 133, 137
Allen, M. P., 153, 165
Amber, G. H., 119, 137
Anderson, J. C., 92, 106
Anderson, P., 135, 142
Anderson, R. E., 154, 165
Anxiety, and socialization, 56. *See also* Emotions; Stress
Argote, L., 51, 62, 64, 84, 146, 166
Aronson, S. H., 147, 166
Arousal: effects of, 23-26, 31; interruptions and, 23-26; learning and, 28; performance in relation to, 26-27, 29-32; task conceptions and, 28. *See also* Emotions

Arrow, K. J., 205, 206, 218, 226
Arthur, W. B., 160, 166, 213, 222, 224, 226
Artificial intelligence (AI), 238, 245, 246, 248, 251
Assembly lines, 101
Astley, G. W., 134, 135, 137
Astn studies, 115, 116–117
AT&T, 201, 214
Attention, in relation to emotion, 28
Attewell, P., 46, 84, 130, 137
Automatic teller machines, 255
Automotive assembly plants, vision system in, 65–68
Autonomy, of work groups, 94–97, 103
Ayres, R. U., 212, 226
Azumi, K., 176, 186, 198

B

Bacharach, S. B., 188, 196
Banking, continuous processing in, 11, 12
Bariff, M. L., 164, 166
Barker, B., 210, 226
Barley, S. R., 18, 19, 21, 22, 28, 40, 118, 127, 128, 131, 132, 137
Barnard, C., 152, 166
Barnouw, V., 184, 196
Barrett, W., 90, 107
Bateson, G., 183
Becker, G., 24, 226
Behavior, control of, 34
Belgium, 288
Beliefs in human abilities, 155–156
Bellah, R. N., 178, 179, 196
Benedict, R., 183–184, 195, 196
Berger, P. L., 178, 179, 196
Berkun, N. M., 28, 40
Berniker, E., 1, 3, 4, 7, 8, 14–15, 40
Berscheid, E., 23, 24, 26, 40
Bessant, J., 7, 14, 40
Bhasavanich, D., 180, 197
Bikson, T., 154, 166
Birdzell, E., 201, 230
Bjorn-Andersen, N., 164, 166
Blackwell, M., 154, 166
Blau, P. M., 112, 114, 138

Boddewyn, J., 177, 196
"Book of blueprints, " 204
"Boundary transaction uncertainty," 128
Bowes, M., 211, 229
Braverman, H., 130, 138
Breer, P., 55, 84
Britain, 188, 189, 191, 208, 209
Broadhurst, P. L., 26, 40
Brooks, F., 146, 166
Brown, R. H., 126, 138
Brunsson, N., 156, 166
Buchanan, D. A., 7, 14, 40
Buffers, and just-in-time manufacturing, 103–105
Buitendam, A., 146, 171
Burke, J. G., 8, 40
Burns, J. M., 152, 166

C

CAD. *See* Computer-aided design
CAE. *See* Computer-aided engineering
Calendar system, computer-supported, 152
CAM. *See* Computer-aided manufacturing
Campbell, D. J., 9, 40
Capitalism, 178
CAPP. *See* Computer-aided process planning
Carbon paper, 157
Carlson, E., 149, 171
Carnegie-Mellon, workshop presentation, 250–253
Carroll, G. R., 117–118, 134, 138
Case studies, 77–78, 195
CAT-scanner technologies, introduction of, 19–20, 28, 131, 236, 247, 255
Causation, 13, 50–53, 255, 258, 259; reciprocal, 52, 76, 109
Caves, R. E., 217, 220, 227
CD-ROM, 237
Cellular manufacturing. *See* Manufacturing cells
Chandler, A. D., Jr., 203, 2077, 213, 216, 217–218, 219, 220, 225, 227

Change, technological, 203-204, 265; economic theory of, 211; evolutionary theories of, 221-224; organizational structure and, 216-217; resistance to, 55, 60; response to, 232. *See also* Adoption of new technologies

Chase R. B., 1, 43, 126, 128, 142

Chemical processing plants, 29

Chew, W. B., 200, 227

Child, J., 115, 138, 188, 197

China, 192

Choice, and commitment, 60-61

Chrysanthemum and the Sword, The (Benedict), 183-184, 196

CIM. *See* Computer-integrated manufacturing

Clark, K. B., 98, 100, 105, 107, 135, 137, 200, 227

Coase, R. F., 203, 218, 227

Cognitive demands of new technologies, 14-16, 28-29, 33, 35

Cohen, W., 146, 166

Cohen, W. M., 202, 206, 209, 213, 214, 215, 223, 227, 228

Cole, R. E., 189, 190, 191, 195, 197

Commitment: changing levels of, 60-61; defined, 59; discretionary technology and, 61; functionality of, 60; individual-technology relationship and, 59-61; positive beliefs and, 72; to roboticized machine cell (case study), 72; to vision system (case study), 66-67

Communication, and common language, 79-80

Communication, electronic, 241-242,247; trends in, 235-236

Communities, organizational, 134-135, 136-137

Competence, as trap, 161-162

Competition, 214-215; adaptation to change and, 249; adoption of new technologies and, 194, 253; convergence and, 189; international, 192, 193, 194-195; structural isomorphism and, 134. *See also* Competitive advantage

Competitive advantage: complica-tions in, 156-160; computers as symbol of, 154; diffusion of new technologies and, 157-158; optimality and, 163; social position and, 149; technical capabilities and, 149

Complexity, 126, 256; defined, 113; demands on skills and, 57. *See also* Interactive complexity

Computer-aided design (CAD), 49, 57, 92, 93

Computer-aided engineering (CAE), 92

Computer-Aided Logistics Support (CALS), 243

Computer-aided manufacturing (CAM): information systems and, 93; work group and, 91, 92, 93

Computer-aided process planning (CAPP), 91, 92, 94

Computer-aided software engineering (CASE), 238

Computer conferencing, 252

Computer-integrated manufacturing (CIM), 49, 65; computer literacy and, 57; defined, 93; discretionary/nondiscretionarytechnologies in, 60-61

Computer literacy, 57

Computers, 240, 251; as alien culture, 56; costs of, 239; as symbol of competitiveness, 154; technological trends in, 235, 245

Concurrent engineering, 244

Configurations, taxonomies of, 120-121

Confirmability of research, 77

Consensus. *See* Normative consensus; Value consensus

Constraint-based reasoning techniques, 26

Contingency arguments: loosening of, 121-122; restricting of, 122-123

Contingency theory, 110, 136; limitations of, 118-120; structure-technology relationships and, 110-123; types of arguments in, 111-112

Continuous events. *See* Continuous processes
Continuous processes, 10–14, 126, 256; aptitudes and, 13; failure of, 23; increase in, 11–12; interruptions of, 23; relational information and, 17; reliability and, 11; stochastic events and, 11, 13–14; supervisors and, 12–13
Control, 98; greater worker involvement in, 98; problem solving and, 105. *See also* Monitoring; Numerical control; Premise control; Process control
Convergence hypothesis, 186–189, 190–191
Cooper, W. H., 5, 44
Corwin, R. G., 114, 138
Costs of new technologies, 106, 235, 239
Cowan, R. S., 190, 197
Credibility, 66–67
Crozier, M., 191, 197
Cultural variables: adoption of new technologies and, 175–177; organizational orientations to technology and, 177–185
Culture, defined, 177–178
Culture, national, 194; adoption of new technologies and, 174–193; dimensions of, 179–182, 188–189; organizational culture and, 194–196; technological development and, 185–193
Culture, organizational, 178; national culture and, 194–196
Cyert, R. M., 46, 84, 146, 166, 205, 212, 218, 222, 228

D

Daft, R., 149, 167
Daft, R. L., 5, 44
Dalton, M., 153, 167
Danziger, J., 154, 167
Data, access to, 100–101
Data bases, shared, 244–245
David, P. A., 213, 222, 224, 228
Davis, L. E., 7, 9, 13, 36, 37, 40, 96, 107, 124, 128, 129, 138

Dawkins, R., 163, 167
Dean, J. W., Jr., 55, 85
Decision making, 10, 263; beliefs in human abilities and, 155–156; goal development in, 152, quality of, 232; speed in, 234–235, 243–244, 247–250; timeliness of, 232; U. S. adoption of Japanese mechanisms for, 194; under uncertainty, 245
Decision premises, 35–38; interactive complexity and, 37–38. *See also* premise control
Decision-support technologies, 10, 145–146, 150, 232; assumptions of, 151, 152; commitment and, 61; failure of executives to use, 145, 150–153, 154–156, 158, 159, 263; limitations of, 150–151
Delbecq, A. L., 22, 43
Demski, J., 149, 167
Department of Defense (DoD), U. S., 234, 237, 243, 249
Design, technological trends in, 246–247
Design data bases, 244–245
Deskilling, 46; British versus German view of, 189; images of, 45; managerial control and, 130; problem framing, 72
Deterministic viewpoint, 258–259
Diffusion of new technologies, 149; competitive advantage and, 157–158; defined, 64; economic studies of, 212; interdependencies in, 157–158; lack of (example), 67; rate of, 212–213; social advantage of, 206. *See also* Adoption of new technologies
Digital Equipment Corporation, autonomous work groups at, 103, 104, 106
DiMaggio, P. J., 135, 138, 149, 167
Discretionary technology, 60–61
Distractions, 15–16
Diversity. *See* Complexity
Documents, intelligent, 243–244
Domhoff, G. W, 153, 167
Donaldson, L., 112, 138

Donrblaser, B. M., 152, 167
Dornbusch, L., 125, 126, 138
Dornbusch, S. M., 9, 35, 41
Dove, Grant, 210
Drazin, R., 112, 120, 121, 122, 138
Drucker, P., 177, 186, 197
Duchin, F., 211, 212, 228
Duke, B., 180, 197
Dunlop, J. T., 186, 198
Dunphy, D., 187, 197
DuPont, 145, 201, 214, 255
Dutton, W., 145, 147, 154, 167
Dyer, D., 32, 42
Dynamic control: defined, 98; feedback and, 100

E

Easterbrook, J. A., 31, 41
Economic theories, 200-226; alternatives to neoclassical theory, 201-206, 213-224; on employment effects of new technologies, 211; evolutionary, 221-224; neoclassical, 201-213, 217, 222, 223, 224, 226
Edwards, J. R., 46, 84
Efficiency, technical, 11, 149; 157; cultural differences in achieving, 189-190; information technology and, 149-153; relative superiorities in, 160-161
Egido, C., 147, 167
Egstrom, G. H., 27, 28, 44
Electric Power Research Institute (EPRI), 210
Electronic assistants, 242
Electronic communication. *See* Communication, electronic
Electronic documents, 240
Electronic file cabinets, 242-243
Electronic forms, 240
Electronic mail, 157, 240, 241-242, 249
Ellul, J., 90, 107
El Sawy, O. A., 150, 158, 167
El Sherif, H., 150, 158, 167
Emmett, V., 164, 167
Emotions, 23-29; attention in relation to, 28; defined, 25-26; degree of interactive complexity and, 29-34; interruption of behavior sequences and, 23-26; and performance, 26-29, 31-32; reward allocation and, 61. *See also* Anxiety; Arousal
Empirical research, 202, 255; in economics, 213, 223-224, 225; on innovation, 215; on Nelson and Winter evolutionary theory, 223-224; on research and development, 207-208
Employment contracts, 81-82
Employment effects, economic analyses of, 211
Engineering, expert systems, in 244
Engineers, 99, 100
Enispak, F., 92, 108
Environments: defined, 110; technological, 216, 222, 224
Equifinality, 189-190
Ettlie, J. E., 1, 41, 97, 107
European Group for Organizational Objectives, 109
Evolutionary process, 29, 217-218
Evolutionary theory, 220, 221-224
Exceptions, analyzability of, 5-7
Executives: adoption of new technologies by 164-165; decision making by, 156; diffusion of new technologies and, 157; expert systems and, 248-249; goal development by, 152, 153; information technology and, 145-146, 148; lack of use of new technologies by, 145, 150-153, 154-156, 158, 159, 161, 263; weak-tie systems and, 153
Experimental design, 78
Expert systems, 243-244, 247-248, 248; executives and, 248-249
Exxon, 248
Eysenck, M. W., 27, 41

F

Failures of systems, 1; analyzability of, 5-7. *See also* Normal accidents

Falbe, C. M., 114, 138
Farmer, R., 186, 197
Fax transmission systems, 157, 241–242
Feedback, timely, 100–101
Feigenbaum, A. V., 94–107
Feldman, M., 150, 151, 153, 154, 168
Fenner, D. B., 45, 263
Finholt, T., 153, 168
Finkelman, J. M., 11, 41
Fisher, F. M., 213, 228
Fiske, S., 54, 55, 84
Flexibility, 193, 232
Florman, S. C., 155, 168
Form, W., 130, 138
Fortunato, M., 217, 227
France, 188, 191
Freeman, J., 133, 139
Friedman, M., 204, 228
Frijda, N. F., 27, 34, 41
Fry, L. W., 111, 116, 117, 139
Fujimoto, T., 200, 227

G

Galbraith, J., 113, 129, 131, 139
Galbraith, J. R., 164, 166
Gallie, D., 188, 197
Gangstad, S. W., 26, 40
Garud, R., 136, 143
Gasser, L., 154, 168
General Electric, 201
General Motors, 102, 200–201
Germany, West, 188–189
Gerwin, D., 114, 115, 116, 139
Ghemawat P., 217, 227
Ghiselli, E. E., 187, 197
Giddens, A., 127, 139
Goal development, 152, 153
Goffman, E., 18, 127, 139
Goodman, P. S., 45, 48, 49, 55, 57, 62, 63, 64, 78, 79, 80, 84, 85, 146, 166, 254, 259, 263
Gorer, G., 183
Granovetter, M., 153, 168
Gray, P., 159, 168
Greenwood, R., 128, 141
Griffith, T. L., 45, 63, 78, 79, 85, 263
Griliches, Z., 212, 228

Gross, N. C., 212, 230
Group technology (GT), 93
GT. See Group technology
Gusfield, J., 190, 197
Gutek, B., 154, 166

H

Hage, J., 144, 139
Haire, M., 187, 197
Hanada, M., 117, 119, 120, 140
Hancock, W. M., 5, 41
Hanes, L. F., 8, 15, 16, 23, 44
Hannan, M. T., 133, 139
Hannaway, J., 146, 168
Hansen, R. G., 160, 163, 168
Harbison, F., 186, 187, 198
Hassen, T., 154, 165
Hauschildt, J., 152, 168
Hawley, Z., 214, 228
Hawthorne, N., 156, 168
Hayes, R. H., 98, 100, 105, 107
Henderson, J., 159, 168
Hermann, C. F., 31, 41
Heron, R. P., 114, 140
Herriott, S. R., 162, 168, 203, 228
Heydebrand, W., 114, 139
Hickson, D. J., 22, 41, 111, 112, 114, 115, 139, 140, 141, 146, 168, 176, 186, 198
Hierarchical structure, 252, 253; flexible, 248–249
Hinings, B., 128, 141
Hinings, C. R., 111, 114, 115, 139, 141
Hirsch, P. M., 135, 140
Hirscheim, R. A., 47, 85
Hirschhorn, L., 193, 198, 205, 228
Historical analysis, 213, 225, 245, 259
Hofmeister, K. R., 61, 86
Hostader, D. R., 160, 169
Hofstede, L., 179, 181, 198
Holdaway, E. A., 114, 140
Honda plant, work-group autonomy in, 98
Horvath, D., 176, 186, 198
Hounshell, D. A., 129, 140
Howard, R., 92 108

Huber, G., 148, 149, 169
Hulin, C. L., 3, 41
Human Relations Area Files, 79-80

I

IBM, 101, 102
Idiography, 192
Image processing, 247
Images of technology, changes in, 45
Imai, M., 98, 107
Implementation phase, rewards in, 62-63
Individualism, 179, 181
Individual-technology relationship; 45-84; methodological issues, 77-80; practice issues, 80-84; reciprocity of, 52, 76, 84; schemata and, 50-56; substantive issues, 75-77; theoretical issues, 72-74
Industry, as conceptual category, 135
Information: corrupt use of, 151; new technologies and, 130-131; storage of, 237, 242-243. *See also* Information technology
Information management, 232, 240-245
Information systems (IS), 92-93; defined, 92; on-line data processing and, 100. *See also* Information technology
Information technology, 91-93, 100, 130-131, 233, 264; components of, 144-145; costs, 239; defined, 144; developments in, 145-146; information management and, 240-245; institutional legitimacy and, 153-156; lack of use of, by executives, 145, 148, 150-153, 154-156, 158, 159, 161, 263; managerial needs and, 149-156; negative symbolism of, 155-156, 159; problem solving and, 245-248; productivity improvement and, 233; symbolic significance of, 158; technological trends in, 235-249
Innovation, 213; large firms and,

214; neoclassical theory on, 205-206; Schumpeterian hypotheses, 213-216
Institutional legitimacy: diffusion of new technologies and, 158; information technology and, 153-156; technological innovation and, 149
Insularity, technological, 134
Intelligent documents, 243-244
Interactive complexity, 13, 29-34, 39; ability to cope with, 31-32; decision premises as source of, 37-38 Perrow's concept of, 29-30, 31; personal interpretations and, 33
Interdependence, 256; defined, 113
Interpretations, personal interactive complexity and, 33
Interruptions: of action sequences, 23-26; emotions and, 23-26
Intintoli, M. J., 12, 41
Invention, 63
IS. *See* Information systems

J

Japanese, 98, 249; individualism in, 181; masculinity index and, 181, 182; national character study, 183-184, 185; power distance and, 180; uncertainty avoidance and, 180-181; word-processing equipment of, 192-193; writing system of, 192
Japanese organizations, 106, 118; automobile manufacturing firms, 200-201; import of practices of, 174; versus U. S. manufacturing, 117, 175
Jaques, E., 129, 140
Jelinek, M., 194, 196
JIT. *See* Just-in-time technology
Job loss, images of, 45
Johnson, D. C., 154, 165
Jondrow, J. M., 211, 229
Jones, J. W., 146, 169
Just-in-time (JIT) technology, 93, 174; reduction of lead time and, 104, 106; task interdependence

and, 100; time and inventory buffers and, 103-105; structural changes and, 128; U. S. adoption of, 194; work-group autonomy and, 94, 103-105

K

Kamien, M. I., 202, 228
Kaplan, R. S., 106, 107
Keegan, W. J., 153, 169
Keen, P., 149, 169
Kennedy, Robert D., 220
Kerr, C., 186, 198
Khandwalla, P. N., 18, 41, 115, 119, 140
Kidder, T., 146, 169
Kieser, A., 188, 197
Kiesler, S., 56, 76, 85, 86, 89, 107
Kiesler, S. B., 146, 153, 169, 172
Kirschner, C., 11, 41
Klassen, D. L., 154, 165
Klevorick, A. K., 216, 229
Kling, R., 46, 47, 85, 154, 167
KLM flight 4805, 16
Kluckhohn, C. 183
Koenig, R., 22, 43
Kraemer, K., 145, 154, 167
Kulakowski, D., 26, 40

L

Laboratory studies, 78
Language of technology, need for, 79-80
Law, J., 3, 4, 41
Lawler, E. E., III, 96, 97, 107
Lawrence, P. R., 32, 42, 110, 112, 140
Learning: arousal and, 28; obstruction of, by emotions, 28; stochastic environments and, 10
Lee, G. L., 115, 139
Legitimacy. *See* Institutional legitimacy
Leibenstein, H., 205, 228
Lenat, D. B., 160, 169
Lengel, R. L., 149, 167
Leontief, W., 211, 212, 228

Levels of analysis of technology, 261-262
Levin, R., 146, 166
Levin, R. C., 202, 213, 214, 215, 216, 227, 228, 229
Levinthal, D., 162, 168, 203, 228
Levinthal D. A., 206, 209, 227
Levitt, B., 162, 163, 169
Levy, M., Jr., 183
Levy, R. A., 211, 229
Liebenstein, H., 228
Life cycle, technological, and rewards sources, 62-63
Lin, T., 152, 167
Lincoln, J. R., 210, 229
Lineback, J. R., 210, 229
Local-area networks, 240
Locke, E., 55, 84
Longitudinal studies, 127-128, 137, 224, 225, 259
Lorsch, J. W., 110, 112, 140
Louis, M. R., 56, 85
Lynch, B. P., 5, 42
Lynn, L. H., 146, 169, 175, 180, 181, 198, 258, 262

M

McBride, K., 117, 119, 120, 140
McCorduck, P., 155, 169
McDaniel, R., 149, 169
McGrath, J. E., 26, 42
McGuire, M. A., 34, 42
McGuire, T. W., 89, 107
McKelvey, B., 133, 140
MacKenzie, D., 177, 198
McKeown, T. J., 181, 198
McKinley, W., 114, 138
McCleod, R., Jr., 146, 169
McMillan, C. J., 176, 186, 198
Macro perspective, 39, 125-126
Macy, B. A., 5, 41
Majchrzak, A., 1, 42, 57, 80, 85, 97, 107
Malerba, F., 223, 229
Malone, T., 151, 169
Management, comparative studies of, 186-188
Managers: access to data, 100; as-

sumption of self-fulfilling pro-phecies by, 36-37; autonomous work groups and, 95; charis-matic, 155; conceptual knowl-edge of, 99; controls, 36; decision premises, 35-36; decision technol-ogies and, 149-153; decisions about skills, 97; deskilling and, 130; education of, 226; infor-mation overload and, 242; orga-nizational culture and, 194; performance of, 226;; power of, 253; premise control and, 35-36; psychosocial assumptions of 35; socialization process and, 80-81; technological development and, 37, 190. *See also* Executives
Mandler, G., 23, 24, 42
Mankin, D., 154, 166
Mannari, H., 117, 118, 140
Mansfield, E., 212, 229
Mansfield, E. P., 147, 149, 169
Mansfield, R., 115, 138
Manufacturing: continuous process-ing in, 12; technological trends in, 238-239
Manufacturing cells, 94, 101-102, 103
Manufacturing resource planning (MRP): defined, 91-92; task mea-ningfulness and, 102; work-group autonomy and, 94, 102
March, J., 81, 82, 85
March, J. G., 32, 42, 144, 150, 151, 152, 154, 162, 163, 168, 169, 170, 203, 218, 222, 228, 229, 258, 263, 264
Market failure, 205-206
Markus, M L., 47, 85
Marschak, J., 203, 229
Marsh, R. M., 117, 118, 140
Masculinity norms, 179, 181-182
Massachusetts Institute of Technol-ogy (MIT), 209
Maynard Smith, J., 163, 170
Mead, M., 183
Meaningfulness of tasks, 102-103
Measurement issues, 79-80
Mechanical machines, 193

Melville, H., 156, 170
Mensch, G., 135, 140
Meredith, J. R., 93, 108
Metcalf, J., III, 8, 42
Meyer, J., 122, 126, 135
Meyer, J. W., 140, 142, 149, 170
Meyer, M. W., 114, 141
Microelectronics and Computer Technology Corporation (MCC), 210
Micro-level orientation, 17, 39, 125-126
Microprocessors, and increased flex-ibility, 193
Miles, R. H., 12, 42
Miller, D., 120, 122, 141
Miller, E. J., 129, 141
Miller, J. G., 88, 107
Miller, S. M., 57, 62, 85, 212, 226
Milnet, 249
Mintzberg, H., 10, 42, 120, 141, 146, 170
Mistakes, of operator. *See* Operator error
Mitre Corporation, 209
Mittman, B., 145, 170
Model, mental, 53-56, 73, 76, 255 256; affective components, 54, 70-72; cognitive component of, 54, 69; decoupling from process, 33; development of 55; evaluative orientation, 54; inter-active complexity and, 33; orien-tations, 54; reward allocation and, 61; of roboticized machine cell (case study), 69-72; schemata and, 53, 55; stochastic processes and, 33; structure of, 75; in vision system (case study), 68. *See also* Schemata
Monaco, C., 146, 170
Monitoring, 81, 82; advanced man-ufacturing technology and, 98; electronic, 79; technological trends in, 247; of vision system, 66; by work groups, 91
Moore, J., 145, 159, 162, 170
Morishima, M., 178, 179, 198
Moshowitz, A., 154, 170

Mowery, D., 146, 166
Mowery, D. C., 46, 84, 205, 206, 207, 208, 212, 215, 227, 228, 229, 255, 258
MRP. *See* Manufacturing resource planning
Mueller, D. C., 220, 229
Multidivisional corporations, 218, 219, 220
Multifunction firms, 204-205
Multinational enterprises, 205
Myers, C. A., 186-187, 197, 198

N

Nath, R., 177, 198
National Academy of Sciences, 98, 101, 107
National character studies, 183-185, 259
National Science Foundation, 208, 209, 229-230; University-Industry Cooperative Research Centers Program, 208-209
Negandhi, A. R., 87, 198-199
Neiss, R., 26, 42
Nelson, R. R., 133, 141, 160, 170, 202, 205, 213, 216, 221, 222
Neoclassical economic theory, 201-206, 222, 223; inattention to organizational structure, 204; on innovation process, 205-206; intrafirm issues and, 202; limitations of, 202, 204-205, 224, 226; on survival of firms, 217
New England Energy Development Systems (NEEDS) Center, 209
Newberry, J. F., 114, 140
Nicholas, I., 188-189, 199
Noble, D., 123, 124, 129, 141
Noble, D. F., 190, 199
Nondiscretionary technology, 60-61
Normal accidents, 39
Normative consensus, and diffusion, 64
Norms, cultural, 179
North Carolina State University, 209
Nuclear reactors, 11, 29, 249, 255
Numerical control (NC), 124-125
Nystrom, P., 147, 171

O

O'Brien, J. F., 8, 15, 16, 23, 44
Office automation, 250-251
Ogburn, W. F., 177, 199
Olsen, J. P., 32, 42, 150, 170
Operator error, 14-16, 39
Operators, skills of, 97-98
Optical disks, 242-243
Otpimality, concept of, 163
Organization for Economic Cooperation and Development, 208, 230
Organizational culture, 178, 194-196
Organizational ecology, 133-134
Organziational structure, 252; changes in, 248, 252-253; competition and, 136; economic theory of, 218, 291-221; empirical studies of, 126-127; flattening of, 253; flexible hierarchies, 248-249; hierarchical, 163, 164; information processing and, 113-114; neoclassical theory and, 205-205; as process, 127-128; social systems and, 129-130. *See* Organizational structure-technology relationship; Organizations; Structuration
Organizational structure-technology relationship, 18-23, 109-137, 213, 216-217; alternative economic theories of, 213-221, 224; community level of analysis, 134-136; configurational approaches, 120-121; contingency theory and, 110-123; cross-sectional studies on, 215; empirical studies, 114-117; institutional environment and, 122-123; problem solving and, 245; regularities in, 132; rethinking of, 123, 128-132; size of firm and, 212
Organizational theory, and stochastic events, 8-9
Organizations: as "black box," 204; institutional environments of, 122-123; interrelatedness of, 135-136; longitudinal studies of, 127-128; new forms of, 232-253;

populations studies of, 133-134; structural inertia of, 133-134; survival of, 217-218; work groups and, 94
Ouchi, W. G., 34, 42
Outcomes, positive/negative, 62
Output control, 34-35
Outputs: accountability and, 34-35; identifiability of, 103
Overhead, organizational, 233, 243

P

Paperwork, 233-234
Pattern recognition, 15-16, 23; perceptual narrowing and, 32
Pavitt, K., 206, 230
Pedersen, P. H., 164, 166
Pennings, H. J., 116, 141
Pennings, J., 146, 171
Pepsi, 248
Perceptual narrowing, 31, 32, 37
Performance: in relation to emotions, 26-32; multidivisional corporations and, 219; shifts in technologies and, 162
Perrin, N., 191, 199
Perrow, C., 3, 5, 6, 8, 13, 14, 16, 29, 32, 34, 35, 42, 43, 90, 110, 113, 124, 141, 155, 171
Perrow, C. B., 90, 107
Perry, C. R., 147, 141
Perseverance of schemata, 55
Personnel management, 245-246
Peterson, S., 5, 41
Pettigrew, A., 146, 171
Pfeffer, J., 153, 171
Pheysey, D. C., 111, 112, 115, 139
Photocopiers, 159
Piehler, H. R., 180, 181, 198
Piore, M. J., 205, 230
Planning, technological trends in, 246. *See also* Decision-support technologies
Poole, M. S., 18, 43
Population ecology, 133-134, 202
Populations, organizational, 134-137
Porter, L. W., 187, 197

Portes, A., 190, 199
Powell, W. W., 125, 135, 138, 141, 149, 167
Power, contingency theories of, 22
Power distance, 179-180
Predictability, 49
Premise control, 35-38, 262-263
Preventive control: defined, 98; feedback and, 100; versus reactive control, 98
Problem diagnosis, little activity in, 76
Problem framing, 72-73
Problem solving, 232, 245-248; advanced manufacturing technology and, 98-99s, 100, 105; appropriate time for, 106; under pressure, 23; task meaningfulness and, 102; by work groups, 98-99, 100, 102, 104, 105, 106
Process(es): organizational structure as, 127-128; role of technology and, 262-264
Process control, types of, 98
Process monitoring, trends in, 247
Productivity: information technology and, 233; software technology and, 237-238
Programmable technology, 256, 257
Progressive control: defined, 98; feedback and, 100
Pugh, D. S., 111 112, 115, 139, 141

Q

Quality circles, 174, 181-182; U. S. adoption of, 914
Quality of work life (QWL), 82-83; changes in 82-83; literature on, 74; versus technological changes, 83
QUERTY keyboard, 160, 224

R

Radner, R., 203, 229
Ranney, J. M., 89, 107-108
Ranson, S., 128, 141
Ravenscraft, D., 220, 230

RCA, 201
Reciprocal causation, 52, 76, 84, 109
Recognition, increased (case study), 71
Reddy, R., 232, 257, 264
Redesign. *See* Sensing and redesigning process
Relational information, and continuous processing, 17
Reliability: continuous processing and, 11, 12; assumptions about, 36
Reliability assurance, as craft, 12
Reputation, institutional, 149, 153–154, 158
Research and development, 251; bureaucratization of, 214; changes in system of, 225–226; cooperative programs, 208–209; government-sponsored, 208; in-house, 209; large firms and, 214; socially beneficial, 206; uncertainty associated with, 207. *See also* Research and development investment
Research and development investment, 205–206; empirical research on, 215; market failure and, 206; neoclassical analysis of, 203–204, 205; research on, 215
Research design, 77–78, 259
Research laboratories: in-house, 206–208; independent, 206–208; structural change in 201
Rewards: allocation of, 61–63, 67; manifest versus latent, 62; sources of, 62–63
Rice, A. K., 129, 141
Richman, B. A., 186, 197
Riley, P., 19, 43
Roberts, K., 177, 199
Roberts, K. H., 8, 43
Robey, D., 47, 85
Robotics Institute, 233–234; 250–251
Robots, 49; environmental changes due to, 50–52; schema concerning, 54; surplus meaning, 73; roboticized machine cell (case study), 50–53, 69–72; technological trends in, 238–239

Rockart, J., 159, 168
Roessner, J. D., 211, 230
Roles, and new technologies, 19
Romanelli, E., 135, 142–143
Rosenberg, N., 146, 171, 201, 206, 230
Ross, S., 203, 230
Roszak, T., 155, 171
Rowan, B., 126, 140, 149, 170
Roznowski, M., 3, 41
Rule, J., 46, 84
Ryan, B., 212, 230

S

Sabel, C. F., 129, 141
Sackman, H., 147, 171
Safety, 11
Sah, R. K., 203, 230
Sahal, D., 134, 141
Sakakibara, K., 181, 199
Salancik, G. R., 59, 61, 86
Sampling, methodological issues in, 77
Samuelson, W. F., 160, 163, 168
Scacchi, W., 47, 85, 154, 169
Schein, E. H., 56, 58, 86, 88, 108, 178, 194, 199
Schellenberg, D., 111, 139
Schemata, 53–55, 263; defined, 53; functions of, 54; perseverance of, 55. *See also* Model, mental
Scherer, F. M., 220, 230
Schkade, D., 51, 62, 64, 84, 146, 166
Schneider, L., 92, 108
Schoenherr, R. A., 114, 138
Schonberger, R. J., 93, 108
Schoonhoven, C. B., 119, 142
Schroeder, R. G., 92, 106
Schumpeter, J., 212, 213, 214, 215, 216, 222, 225, 230, 231
Schwartz, N., 202, 228
Scott, W. R., 5, 9, 10, 35, 37, 41, 43, 112, 113, 115, 119, 122, 125, 126, 128, 135, 138, 140, 142, 202, 255, 256, 257, 258, 259, 261, 262
Scott-Morton, M., 149, 169
Scripts, 20
Self-fulfilling prophecies, 36–37

Selznick, P., 152, 171
Sensemaking in new technologies, 1–39, 60
Sensing and redesigning process, 63–64, 67–68
Serendipitous discovery, 150
Sévon, G., 151, 170
Sheil, B. A., 256, 265
Siegel, J., 89, 107, 145, 171
Sifonis, J., 159, 168
Signal processing, 247
Silverman, D., 127, 142
Simon, H., 81, 82, 85, 251
Simon, H. A., 146, 149, 160, 166, 171, 218, 222, 229
Simulation analysis, 222, 223, 251
Simultaneous engineering, 244
Skills: advanced manufacturing technology and, 97–99; of continuous processing supervisors, 12–13; increased (case study), 71; managers and, 130; of operators, 97–98; in stochastic environment, 9–10
Smith, J. E., 27, 28, 44
Social interaction, decreased (case study), 71
Social reality, changes in, 52
Social Security Administration, 160
Socialization process, 56–59; defined, 56; formal/informal, 58–59; managers and, 80–81; positive beliefs and, 72; roboticized machine cell introduction (case study), 69, 72; structured/less structured, 58–59; vision system introduction (case study), 66, 68
Software technology, trends in, 237–238
Solow growth model, 223
Soviet Union, 181, 191
"Special Report: Learning to Live with Leverage," 220, 231
Spenner, K. I., 205, 231
Sprague, R., 149, 171
Sproull, L., 56, 76, 85, 86
Sproull, L. S., 61, 86, 144, 146, 150, 153, 168, 169, 172, 254, 258, 263, 264

Standards: for electronic data-interchange, 241; evolution of, 224
Stigler, G. J., 208, 231
Stiglitz, J. E., 203, 230
Stochastic events, 7–10, 126, 256; continuous processing and, 10, 11, 13–14; emotions and, 23–26; forms of, 9; as interruptions, 23; premise control and, 35
Storage technologies, 237, 242–243
Strauss, A., 127, 142
Stress, 73; degress of complexity and, 29–34; introduction of new technology and, 56; responsibility and (case study), 71; surprises and, 56. *See aslo Emotions*
Strong-tie systems, defined, 153
Structuration, 18–23, 127–128, 263; Barley's analysis of, 19–23; defined, 18, 127; technology and, 18–23
Supercomputers, 245, 247
Supervisors of continuous processing, 12–13
Suresh, N. C., 93, 108
Surprises, 8–10, 60; defined, 59; negative, and values, 62; socialization and, 59; tension and, 56
Surveys, 196; on analyzability of exceptions, 5–6
Survival of organizations, 217–218, 249–250
Susman, G. I., 1, 43, 87, 97, 98, 108, 126, 128, 142
Sweden, 181–182
Swidler, A., 183, 199
Symbols: in Japan, 192; new technologies as, 154–155, 156, 158, 159–160
Systems design, 62–63, 129

T

Tasks: interdependence of, 99–100; meaningfulness of, 102–103
Taylor, J. C., 7, 9, 13, 36, 37, 40, 124, 128, 129, 138
Taylor, S. E., 54, 55, 84
Technical efficiency, and information technology, 149–153

Technical systems, 255, 257–258

Technological change, theory of, 144

Technological environment, 216, 222, 224

Technology(ies): assumptions about, 49–50; change and, 265; components of, 48; critical processes and, 262–264; definitions of, 3–5, 48–49, 89–90, 110–111, 204, 254–256; as force, 264; impact of individuals on, 45–84; as laboratory, 264–265; level of analysis and, 261–262; multiple, 118–119; newer perspectives on, 123–127; range of structures allowed by 129; social assumptions embodied in, 125, 128, 129–130; as social/physical reality, 259–260; social system and, 124; survey items on exceptions, 5–6. *See also* individual-technology relationship; Organization structure-technology relationship; Technology(ies), new

Technology(ies), new: adoption of, 145–148; as cause and consequence of structure, 18–23; classes of, 264; dangerous, 11; diffusion of, 149; empirical studies of, 126–127; as equivoques, 2, 5; failure intervention and, 1; future influence on 232–253; historical development of, 160–161; information created by 130–131; lack of use of, 145, 150–153, 154–156, 159, 263–264; new aspects of, 256–258; perties of, 7–17; trends, 232, 235–249

Teece, D. J., 203, 213, 220, 221, 231

Telephone system, 159, 160–161

Temin, P., 213, 228

Theory: generalizability of 74; levels of, 73–74; problem framing issues, 73–73. *See also* Economin theories

Third World countries, 174

Thompson, J., 100, 108

Thompson, J. D., 8, 43, 110, 113, 125, 142

Three Mile Island, 16, 34

Thurow, L.C., 36, 43

Time: just-in-time manufacturing and, 103–105; legitimation of. for personal activities, 104–105; for problem solving, 106

Timeliness, of decision making, 232

Tolbert, P. S., 149, 158, 172

Total quality controll (TQC), 94

Toyota-General Motors NUMMI joint venture, 200–201

TQC. *See* Total quality control

Tracy, P. K., 114, 138

Transaction-cost analysis, 219–220, 221

Transaction processing, 12

Trends, technological, 232, 235–249

Trist, E. L., 129, 142

Trouble-shooting, and credibility, 66

Trow, D. B., 146, 166

Tuden, A., 8, 43

Turner, C., 111, 115, 141

Turner, J. H., 18, 43

Tushman, M. L., 134–135, 142

Typewriters, 146, 192, 251, 255; carbon paper and, 157

U

Uncertainty(ies), 22, 49, 126, 128, 256; decision making under, 245; defined, 113; handling, 122; of research and development outcomes, 208; stochastic events and, 7–10. *See also* Uncertainty avoidance

Uncertainty avoidance: concept of, 179; cultural differences, 180–181

Union Carbide, 220

Unit production, 12, 13

Unpredictability, 7–10; arouasal and, 32. *See also* Stochastic events; Uncertainty

User-friendly systems, 252, 253

User interfaces, technological trends in, 236

Utilization of technology, 63, 75–76

V

Values: consensus of, 64; cultural, 178–179; positive, emphasis on 61–62
Van de Ven, A. H., 22, 43, 112, 121, 135–136, 138, 143, 152, 167
Van Maanen, J., 56, 58, 86
Vision system (case study), 65–68, 77; credibility problems with, 66–67; defined, 65
Vogel, E. F., 181, 199
Von Hippel, E. A., 149, 172

W

Wachtel, P. L, 28, 43
Wacker, G., 1, 40
Wacker, G. J., 96, 107
Wajcman, J., 177, 198
Wallerstein, I., 178, 199
Walton, R. E., 97, 98, 108, 176, 194, 199
Weak-tie systems, defined, 153
Weber, M., 178, 179, 199
Weick, K. E, 1, 9, 16, 18, 43, 44, 125, 126, 127, 143, 255, 256, 257, 259, 262
Weiner, S., 150, 172
Weisband, S., 148, 172
Weizenbaum, J. 155, 172
Weltman, G., 27, 28, 44
Westeny, D., 181
Westinghouse, 245–246, 253
Westney, D., 199
Wheelwright, S. C., 98 100, 105, 107
Wildavsky, A., 147, 172
Wilensky, H., 149, 172
Williamson, O. E., 202, 203, 213, 216, 218, 219, 220–221, 223, 224, 231
Winner, L., 21, 44
Winter, S. G., 133, 141, 160, 170, 202, 213, 216, 221, 222, 223, 224, 225, 229, 230
Withey, M., 5, 44

Wolf, D., 150, 172
Woods, D. P., 8 15, 16, 23, 44
Woodward, J., 10, 12 44, 110 112, 113, 118, 119, 125, 143
Word-processing systems, technological trends in, 243–244
Work activities, and introduction of robot, 51–52
Work arrangements, defined, 35
Workflow integration, 111
Work groups: advanced manufacturing technology and, 94–107; autonomous, 94–97, 103; clarity of boundaries of, 101–102; functions, 95–96; computer-aided manufacturing and, 91; formal, defined, 87–88; in Honda automobile assembly plant, 98; just-in-time manufacturing and, 103–105; manufacturing resource planning and, 92; nature of, 87–88; new technologies and, 193; problem solving by, 98–99, 100, 102, 104, 105, 106; work shifts as, 102
Workload, mental, 126, 256
Work shifts, 102
Work stations, personal, 239, 240
World systems, 262
Writing systems, and technologies, 191–192, 193

Y

Yates, J., 145, 157, 172
Yerkes-Didson law, 26

Z

Zahray, W. P., 180, 181, 198
Zuboff, S., 1, 44, 75, 86, 99, 100, 105, 108, 130, 131, 143, 164, 173
Zubrow, D., 56, 86
Zucker, L. G., 149, 158, 172
Zwerman, W. L., 115, 143

Lightning Source UK Ltd.
Milton Keynes UK
UKOW041840020513

210123UK00001B/86/P